CW00552632

ENOCH POWELL

ENOCH POWELL

Politics and Ideas in Modern Britain

PAUL CORTHORN

OXFORD
UNIVERSITY PRESS

OXFORD
UNIVERSITY PRESS

Great Clarendon Street, Oxford, OX2 6DP,
United Kingdom

Oxford University Press is a department of the University of Oxford.
It furthers the University's objective of excellence in research, scholarship,
and education by publishing worldwide. Oxford is a registered trade mark of
Oxford University Press in the UK and in certain other countries

© Paul Corthorn 2019

The moral rights of the author have been asserted

First Edition published in 2019

Impression: 1

Published in the United States of America by Oxford University Press
198 Madison Avenue, New York, NY 10016, United States of America

British Library Cataloguing in Publication Data

Data available

Library of Congress Control Number: 2019936330

ISBN 978–0–19–874714–7

Printed and bound in Great Britain by
Clays Ltd, Elcograf S.p.A.

Links to third party websites are provided by Oxford in good faith and
for information only. Oxford disclaims any responsibility for the materials
contained in any third party website referenced in this work.

For Katherine, Daniel, George, and Oliver

Acknowledgements

My interest in Enoch Powell developed after I moved to Northern Ireland to take up a lectureship at Queen's University Belfast. Realizing that Powell's time as an Ulster Unionist MP had been relatively under-explored, and discovering extensive local source material, I initially imagined that I would write a single article about him. My plans changed after I was elected to an Archives By-Fellowship at Churchill College, Cambridge, allowing me to spend Easter Term 2012 working in the Churchill Archives Centre. I began to appreciate just how rich the Enoch Powell papers held in the archive were, and decided to write a book-length thematic study of Powell.

I have received considerable institutional help. The Schools of History and Anthropology, and now History, Anthropology, Philosophy and Politics, at Queen's University Belfast have provided invaluable sabbatical research leave—giving me time for intensive research and focused writing. They have also generously funded extended periods in the archive. The staff at the archives listed in the bibliography have offered expert guidance on their collections. I owe a particular debt to Allen Packwood, Andrew Riley, and the team at the Churchill Archives Centre, who have made my time there particularly productive—not least by delivering material very quickly. I have benefited enormously from Katharine Thomson's exemplary cataloguing of the Powell papers. At Oxford University Press, Matthew Cotton offered enthusiastic support for the book from the outset and much appreciated editorial advice towards the end. The anonymous reviewers—of both the book proposal and the draft manuscript—helped me to frame the project itself and to refine the arguments.

Friends and colleagues have assisted greatly along the way. Peter Gurney and Robert McNamara read the book in its entirety, providing rigorous criticism. Kieran Connell lent me the benefit of his expertise on race and immigration. Stuart Aveyard, Graham Brownlow, and Graham Walker helped me to grapple with Powell and Northern Ireland. I still miss the late Keith

Jeffery, with whom I discussed this book at length in its early stages. Ian Campbell, Marie Coleman, Sean Connolly, John Curran, James Davis, Aglaia De Angeli, Richard English, Elaine Farrell, Peter Gray, Crawford Gribben, David Hayton, Andrew Holmes, Brian Kelly, Danny Kowalsky, Fearghal McGarry, Ashok Malhotra, Chris Marsh, Eric Morier-Genoud, Margaret O'Callaghan, Sean O'Connell, Mary O'Dowd, Sinead O'Sullivan, Olwen Purdue, Emma Reisz, and Alex Titov have helped to make Queen's a congenial place to be a historian. My former colleague Catherine Clinton made me very welcome in Texas when I visited to address a conference on Powell. My friends in the Society for the Study of Labour History, presided over by Keith Laybourn, have taken an interest in my book—even as my fascination with Conservatism took me away from work on the Labour Party. Dave Cochrane and Barry Phipps have provided excellent company during my research stays in Cambridge. Over the years, my work on Powell has benefited from wide-ranging discussions about twentieth-century British History with my PhD students, including Jonathan Best, Morris Brodie, Matt Gerth, Stephen Goss, Paul Lundy, and Conor McFall.

I am fortunate to have had the opportunity to present papers on Powell to audiences at: the Humboldt University of Berlin; the Central European University; Anglia Ruskin University; the People's History Museum, Manchester; the 'Britain and the World' conference in Austin, Texas; the University of Huddersfield; and the University of St Andrews. An invitation to speak on Powell at Sciences Po Lille as my book neared completion gave me the chance to air its main arguments to a specialist audience, including Olivier Esteves and Stéphane Porion.

I am grateful to the Trustees of the J. Enoch Powell Literary Trust for permission to quote from the Powell papers held at both Churchill Archives Centre and the Staffordshire Record Office. Members of the public who corresponded with Powell have not been named. The Conservative Party gave permission to quote from material held in the Conservative Party Archive at the Bodleian Library. The Master and Fellows of Trinity College, Cambridge, allowed me to consult the Sir Dennis Robertson papers. The Trustees of the Liddell Hart Centre for Military Archives did the same for the Sir Basil Liddell Hart papers. I thank Alan Sked for taking the time to share his recollections of Powell and the Anti-Federalist League/United Kingdom Independence Party (UKIP) with me. Parts of Chapter 5 originally appeared in the *Journal of British Studies* (vol. 51, issue 4, 2012).

My family has provided much love and support. My father and late mother enjoyed sharing their own memories of Powell with me. Katherine has been my closest companion for nearly twenty years. Our sons, Daniel, George, and Oliver, have kept my spirits up by making every day great fun.

Belfast
August 2018

Contents

List of Figures   xiii
List of Abbreviations   xv

   Introduction   1

1. International relations   20

2. Economics   48

3. Immigration   75

4. Europe   104

5. Northern Ireland   133

   Conclusion   159

Notes   167
Bibliography   213
Picture Acknowledgements   227
Index   229

List of Figures

1. Enoch Powell speaking at Swinton College, 1949   26
2. Powell filming a BBC programme in Moscow, 1989   45
3. The newly appointed Minister of Health at his desk, 1960   60
4. Powell with Margaret Thatcher at the Conservative
   Party Conference, 1965   62
5. Dock workers demonstrate in support of Powell, 1968   88
6. A demonstration in London against Powell, 1970   93
7. Powell at his desk at home in Belgravia, 1971   111
8. Powell speaking at the 'Get Britain Out' rally, 1974   118
9. The Official Unionist candidate for South Down with Ian Paisley, 1974   139
10. Powell's South Down general-election literature, 1974   140

List of Abbreviations

AFL	Anti-Federalist League
AGM	annual general meeting
BAOR	British Army of the Rhine
BNP	British National Party
CAP	Common Agricultural Policy
CBI	Confederation of British Industry
CEC	Campaign for Equal Citizenship
CIA	Central Intelligence Agency
CIB	Campaign for an Independent Britain
CND	Campaign for Nuclear Disarmament
CPC	Conservative Political Centre
DUP	Democratic Unionist Party
ECSC	European Coal and Steel Community
EEC	European Economic Community
ERM	Exchange Rate Mechanism
EU	European Union
GLC	Greater London Council
IEA	Institute of Economic Affairs
INLA	Irish National Liberation Army
IRA	Irish Republican Army
LCC	Leader's Consultative Committee
NATO	North Atlantic Treaty Organization
NHS	National Health Service
NIO	Northern Ireland Office
NRC	National Referendum Campaign
NUM	National Union of Mineworkers
OUP	Official Unionist Party
PRONI	Public Record Office of Northern Ireland
RUC	Royal Ulster Constabulary
SBC	Safeguard Britain Campaign
SDLP	Social Democratic and Labour Party
SDP	Social Democratic Party
SNP	Scottish National Party
TA	Territorial Army

TGWU   Transport and General Workers' Union
TNA   The National Archives
TUC   Trades Union Congress
UDA   Ulster Defence Association
UDI   Unilateral Declaration of Independence
UKIP   United Kingdom Independence Party
UN   United Nations
UUUC   United Ulster Unionist Council
UVF   Ulster Volunteer Force

Introduction

Enoch Powell

The Conservative, and then Ulster Unionist, politician Enoch Powell revelled in challenging accepted orthodoxies, frequently provoking controversy and helping to establish the future agenda. Powell is best known, of course, for his outspoken opposition to immigration, which dramatically shattered a tacit agreement between the political parties not to inflame popular opinion on the issue. Speaking in 1968, he alluded to the poet Virgil to make a prediction of racial violence: 'Like the Roman, I seem to see "the River Tiber foaming with much blood"'.[1] Powell also adopted distinctive positions on a range of other prominent issues in the post-1945 era. Amid international Cold War tensions, he rejected the twin pillars of British policy— alliance with the United States and an independent nuclear deterrent—and eventually even came to advocate an alliance with the Soviet Union. Despite his deep suspicion of US ambitions, Powell emerged as an early proponent of free-market economics, questioning a degree of party consensus, Conservative as well as Labour, to substantial state intervention and prefiguring some of the policy changes introduced by Margaret Thatcher's governments in the 1980s. As the United Kingdom sought membership of the European Community, Powell strongly opposed the move, emphasizing the threat to British sovereignty—an argument that has resonated in British politics and public life from the 1990s and played a part in present-day debates over Brexit. Yet if Powell's views on Europe have appeared to endure, his stance on Northern Ireland has weathered less well. A fierce opponent of devolution in Scotland and Wales, Powell argued, against a backdrop of the violent Troubles, for the closer integration of Northern Ireland with Great Britain. His view was notably at odds with repeated, and eventually successful, British government attempts to re-establish local legislative control, but this does not detract from the significance of his participation in the still ongoing debate over the new devolved shape of the United Kingdom.

John Enoch Powell, the only child of teachers, was born in Stechford in Birmingham in 1912. He won a scholarship to King Edward's School Birmingham and, from there, a scholarship to study Classics at Trinity College, Cambridge, where he cut a solitary figure but excelled academically, graduating with first-class honours. Already calling himself J. Enoch Powell (to avoid confusion with the classicist J. U. Powell), he secured a fellowship at Trinity before being appointed as Professor of Greek at the University of Sydney at the age of 25. At the same time, Powell had started to write, and publish, poetry. At the start of the Second World War, he returned to England to enlist in the army as a private and rose through the ranks to become a brigadier in military intelligence. Powell voted Labour in 1945—to register his disapproval of appeasement—but, on returning to civilian life in 1946, he worked at Conservative Central Office before winning the seat of Wolverhampton South West in 1950, the Midlands constituency he represented until 1974. Married to Pam from 1952, with whom he had two daughters, Powell first held government office as Parliamentary Secretary at the Ministry of Housing in 1955 and became Financial Secretary to the Treasury in 1957, resigning the following year when calls for cuts to public spending were rejected by the Cabinet. He was subsequently Minister of Health between 1960 and 1963, joining the Cabinet in July 1962 but then, fifteen months later, refusing to serve under new leader Sir Alec Douglas-Home. Powell put his name forward in the Conservative Party leadership contest in 1965 but came third (and last). He was shadow Defence Minister from 1965 but was sacked from the position by party leader Edward Heath after he made his so-called 'Rivers of Blood' speech, in Birmingham in April 1968. From this point on, Powell became one of the best-known politicians in the country, vilified and sanctified at the same time. As his relations with the Conservative leadership worsened, and in opposition to party policy in favour of membership of the European Community, Powell decided not to stand in the February 1974 general election, asking his supporters instead to vote for the Labour Party, which was committed to a referendum on the European issue. Powell subsequently took the unusual step, for a British politician, of contesting a seat in Northern Ireland, South Down, as an Ulster Unionist in the October 1974 general election, which he held until defeated in 1987. Powell died in 1998.[2]

Despite his high profile, commentators have often struggled to find—or to agree on—a unifying theme behind Powell's views on various fronts. This failure has derived both from a disproportionate concentration on immigration and from a deeply polarized, and politicized, historiography. At the hands of his critics, Powell has been portrayed as a populist opportunist and is seen to represent a world view shaped by perceptions of British racial whiteness. On the other hand, Powell's admirers have rightly emphasized the existence of the British nation as the starting point of his analysis but have not fully explored where his political journey took him—or the thinking that lay behind it.

This is a study of Powell in the round. It is not a conventional biography. We already know a considerable amount about the day-to-day detail of Powell's political life, with the longest biography running to over 1,000 pages. Instead, this book adopts a thematic structure—looking, in turn, at Powell's views on international relations, economics, immigration, Europe, and Northern Ireland. With a focus on the debates in which Powell participated, he is set much more fully within the broader historical, as well as historiographical, context than is usual in the traditional biographical format. So far as possible, this account adopts a detached, impartial perspective. It does not seek to enter into discussions about whether Powell was 'wrong' to speak about immigration in the terms that he did or whether, for that matter, he was 'right' stridently to oppose British membership of the European Community. Asking different questions of previously available sources, and drawing on some new ones, this book seeks to understand the development of Powell's ideas and how he chose to deploy them in particular political contexts. With Powell's overall significance deriving not from achievements in either a governmental or party setting but instead from his impact on the overall terms of debate, this endeavour helps us to grasp how, as Prime Minister Margaret Thatcher aptly put it in 1989, he 'commanded influence without power'.[3]

Notwithstanding the twists and turns of Powell's career, the changes over time in his political positions, and the inconsistencies and contradictions in his thought, I suggest in this book that his diverse political campaigns can be understood coherently as part of a long-running and wide-ranging public debate over the 'decline' of the British nation. In this context, Powell, a fervent British patriot advancing solutions to tackle these real and perceived problems, took on opponents from the Right as well as the Left. Decline is, of course, a major theme in modern British history since the late nineteenth century, embracing economic, imperial, international, and national dimensions which rose to particular prominence as a political issue in the years after 1945—as Britain adjusted to its reduced role in the world order, as its economy appeared to flounder, and as the United Kingdom itself looked set to fracture as a result of the pressure of Irish, Scottish, and Welsh nationalism.

Perspectives on Powell

Powell began to generate political interest from 1965—the year in which he contested the Conservative Party leadership and published a volume of his speeches. With many of the speeches expounding free-market economics, Iain Macleod in *The Spectator*, who had known Powell well since the mid-1940s, wrote favourably of the emergence of what was dubbed for the first time 'Powellism'. Yet Macleod also made a point that was to resonate more widely across Powell's career, arguing that his 'thought over the years has not been as remorselessly consistent as it is presented'. Macleod noted that, despite 'his scorn for planners and their plans', Powell as Minister of Health had produced long-term plans for both hospitals and health and welfare.[4]

It was not, however, until after the furore over immigration in 1968 that Powell began to attract considerable public attention and became the subject of two diametrically opposed books by prominent journalists. The *Daily Telegraph* stalwart and political thinker T. E. 'Peter' Utley came swiftly to Powell's defence, praising his approach to both economics and foreign affairs for 'challenging... the Party's fundamental habits of thought'. Utley insisted that Powell was 'emphatically not a racialist in the only intelligible meaning of that expression – one who believes in the natural superiority of some races to others'. Utley further argued that the Birmingham speech was part of a wider pattern where Powell's 'language of political persuasion is always exaggerated'.[5] In response, the radical, left-wing Paul Foot, seeking to 'provide ammunition for a counter-attack', accused Powell of 'inconsistency... and opportunism' in exploiting racist sentiments in society only after coming to appreciate the electoral salience of immigration in the West Midlands.[6] Foot made this point in a context where, as Powell himself regretfully recognized, 'the word "Powellism" ha[d] rather changed its connotations' and become associated with popular responses to his stance on immigration.[7]

In important respects, Utley and Foot set the basic terms of the subsequent debate. Powell now became the subject of dispute between what can broadly be seen as New Left and New Right interpretations. A succession of social scientists, increasingly associated with the Centre for Contemporary Cultural Studies at Birmingham University and the Jamaican-born cultural theorist Stuart Hall, gave credence to charges of racism. They took issue with what they saw as Powell's encoded interpretation of race in absolute terms and his equation of whiteness with Britishness. An early version of this position had been outlined by John Rex, a sociologist from Durham University, on BBC Radio in 1969.[8] In subsequent years, depth was added to this analysis, not least by academics such as Zig Layton-Henry, Paul Gilroy, and Paul Rich. The case was made that the reaction to the 'Rivers of Blood' had demonstrated the depth of the postcolonial crisis facing Britain, with Powell expressing and stimulating fears about the break-up of institutional and social authority.[9] Calling for a more flexible, and constantly evolving, understanding of British identities, this work drew its political inspiration from the New Left tradition that had emerged from dissatisfaction with communism (especially in its Soviet guise) after 1956 but whose younger adherents had been energized by the revolutionary mood of 1968. Politically and academically this body of work informed the cause-driven identity politics of the Left in the 1970s, 1980s, and beyond, seeking to tackle inequalities on the basis of race, as well as gender and sexuality, in order to move away from an earlier emphasis on the class struggle. Increasingly, 'Powell's brand of nationalist racism' was portrayed as 'a powerful resource for Thatcherism'.[10]

This view was countered by the New Right, keen to assert that Powell was not crudely racist and to celebrate his commitment not only to free-market capitalism but also to Parliament as the core component of British 'nationhood'. In itself this was an illustration of the broader point that the New Right contained both economic liberals and advocates of an assertive nationalism, such as those in the Salisbury Group, set up in 1976, who were united in their opposition to what they saw as a 'liberal collectivist consensus'.[11] Powell himself had 'made a resolution against autobiography'.[12] Yet he still sought—in various ways—to exert some influence over the construction of his own reputation.

In 1974, just after he decided not to stand in Wolverhampton South West, Powell engaged in discussion with the politics academic K. W. Watkins from Sheffield University about a biographical study, although Powell did not want Watkins himself to write the book.[13] Watkins moved in distinctly right-wing circles and in 1975 was a founder member, along with business, military, aristocratic, journalistic, and political figures, of the pressure group the National Association for Freedom, which was initially vociferous in its campaigns against trade unions. Utley was initially lined up to write the book but withdrew because of his concern that it would not be 'really different' from his earlier book.[14] The baton briefly passed to the *Daily Telegraph* journalist Michael Harrington, who was, Utley assured Powell, 'fundamentally sympathetic to your views', but the contract with the publisher Thomas Nelson was cancelled in 1975 after Harrington failed to make progress.[15] The proposal for a book now moved forward, with Watkins suggesting Roy Lewis, who was known to Powell as assistant editor of *The Economist* and who had also worked at *The Times*.[16] On Powell's preference, Watkins approached the publisher Cassell & Co., promising not just that Powell would 'set aside as much time as the author requires for a discussion and also will make his papers and files available to the biographer' but that he would 'readily give active assistance to a biographer'.[17] Powell told the publisher that his contribution would be more limited, with the book based on published material, but with a commitment to read it before publication.[18] With Lewis enthusiastic, Cassell & Co. initially wrote Powell into the financial terms of the contract, including royalties.[19] Powell rejected the idea but instead suggested a payment of £1,000 on acceptance of the manuscript, which was duly paid in February 1979.[20] Predictably, the book itself took Powell's line, arguing that nationhood was the 'primary article of faith' that gave Powell's career, including his break with the Conservatives over the European Community, coherence.[21]

A decade later, Patrick Cosgrave emphasized the same theme, telling readers that 'without an understanding of nationhood there can be no real understanding of Enoch Powell'.[22] Employed at the Conservative Research Department in 1970, Cosgrave had produced a memorandum that helped Heath to attack Powell's position on immigration.[23] But, by 1976, working both as a journalist and as an advisor to Thatcher, he publicly adopted a different stance, contending that 'the brutal fact of the matter is that over the whole period of the controversy (which has lasted from 1968) Mr Powell has been more right than the rest of us'.[24] Powell subsequently corresponded with Cosgrave in the early and mid-1980s and encouraged him in his ambition of writing a biography.[25] What emerged was a very favourable study. Cosgrave was now emphatic that 'Powell was right on immigration', adding that while he was 'accused of being a racist, he was merely talking about identity', offending 'the nerves of those who wanted to believe that there were really no differences between peoples'.[26] As Powell read the final version 'for the purpose of correcting errors of fact', Cosgrave implored: 'The biographer suggests that the biographee averts his eyes from the last few pages.'[27] Gushingly, Cosgrave had written: 'Every threat to the nation he has foreseen. When his warnings have been heeded, the nation has benefitted. When they have been ignored, the nation has suffered.'[28]

In the mid-1990s a more critical voice from the centre-right of the Conservative fold emerged. The television journalist and former Research Department employee Robert Shepherd added the qualification that Powell's nationalism, even his attachment to parliamentary institutions, was emotional or romantic in the last resort.[29] This was a powerful point—not least because it echoed earlier assessments from the New Left.[30] Making extensive use of Conservative Party material, Shepherd made it clear that Powell had changed his attitude to membership of the European Community, having—at one point—been supportive of it, despite his awareness that it was a political and military, as well as an economic, grouping. Shepherd insisted that Powell was 'not a racist' but recognized that the 'line between Powell's nationalism and what is generally regarded as racialism at times seems extremely fine' and criticized him for a 'serious lack of judgement' over his Birmingham speech, for which Heath had no choice but to dismiss him.[31] Powell had met Shepherd in 1990 when he was interviewed for the BBC's advance obituary of Thatcher.[32] Yet in 1995, when Shepherd asked to consult 'articles, speeches...and other material' in Powell's possession as well as to interview Powell and for him to read a draft, Powell made it clear that he would not cooperate, citing the fact that 'several persons are already engaged upon this task'.[33] The journalist Simon Heffer was, in fact, at work on Powell's authorized biography, with access to most of Powell's private papers for the first time (before they were catalogued) and abundant interview opportunities.

The pair had met in 1985 when Heffer interviewed Powell for *Medical News* about his (unsuccessful) private member's bill to prevent a human embryo created through in vitro fertilization being used as the subject of experiment.[34] Powell and Heffer established a firm rapport, sharing views on Europe where both sought a 'Europe of Nations'.[35] In late 1994 Powell asked Heffer, then working at the *Daily Telegraph* but soon to move to the *Daily Mail*, to write 'a – or even the – biography' of him.[36] While making

the case that Powell 'was unsuited to be a politician' because of his 'deep
integrity', Heffer's 1998 biography conceded that on immigration there had
been 'destructive effects he had not foreseen'. Heffer insisted, however, that
Powell's position was not 'racial in motive' but instead 'entirely political',
being concerned about identification with the nation. At the same time, the
biography celebrated Powell's 'greatest victory' in the triumph of free-market
economics and, with hostility to membership of the European Union
growing, argued that people had recently 'began to take up his call, using
arguments with which he had provided them'. Incredibly detailed, Heffer's
book was the fullest account of the parliamentary nationhood thesis. It
spoke, however, to the concerns of the late 1990s as New Labour established
devolved government in Scotland and Wales. Heffer, actively involved with
the Campaign for an English Parliament, arguably over-exaggerated the
centrality of England to Powell's conception of Britain, writing that 'the
English at least still cling to the idea of nation' and that in 'his restless, evangelical crusade to tell the English about themselves he was unique among
politicians'.[37]

   In recent years, Powell has continued to excite scholarly interest—in
ways that are still loosely shaped by the rival New Left and New Right
approaches. Bill Schwarz, a former student at the Centre for Contemporary
Cultural Studies, has argued that Powellism, fearing contemporary disorder,
evoked unspoken memories of the racially ordered colonial past.[38]
Camilla Schofield has examined Powell as part of a political generation,
shaped by the experience of the Second World War, whose reference
points—including the danger of invasion in 1940—were reworked to resonate
in a postcolonial context unsettled by the perceived threat from immigration.[39] Meanwhile, the celebratory *Enoch at 100* collection, published in
2012 to mark the centenary of Powell's birth, echoed the parliamentary
nationhood theme.[40]

Conservatism, Unionism, and the British nation

This book is about Powell's articulation of Conservative and Unionist ideas
in specific political contexts. It still remains the case, as E. H. H. Green
argued in 2002, that the presentation of Conservative ideas in general is
under-analysed.[41] This tendency is equally pronounced in the case of
Unionism, despite some significant recent work on its political thought, and

its operation in practice, in both Scotland and Ireland.[42] For both Conservatism and Unionism, Powell's starting premise, as he told a publisher in the mid-1970s about a planned book on 'Britain's Future' that never came to fruition, was 'the central, unifying theme of the nation state'.[43] In 1952, in discussion with his colleague Angus Maude, who had also entered Parliament in 1950, Powell argued that an understanding of Toryism (his preferred self-description and one used, by the twentieth century, to identify Conservatives prioritizing patriotism, maintenance of the nation state, and social order) could be found 'only by descent into its inner, permanent meaning'. He went on:

> The essence must be a view of the state (nation) and of this nation in particular, as an organic entity in time, the life of which is part conscious, part unconscious, like that of the human microcosm. From this view follows a specific attitude to the relationships between individuals comprised in that entity, to sovereignty, class, privilege, liberty. There follows also a specific attitude to change, and to the expansion and contraction of the nation. The natural and the supernatural enter into the composition of the state as they do into that of the individual.[44]

Powell thus defined the nation organically, as a living being—a prevalent trend in Conservative thought.[45] In his correspondence with Maude, Powell also hinted at certain attitudes to both time and change. He further emphasized hierarchy, especially sovereignty, and added that it involved a supernatural or, more properly, spiritual, dimension. Over the course of his career, Powell added substance to these points, consistently attempting to distinguish Toryism from socialism but also changing his view of the geographical boundaries of the British nation as he went along.

As early as 1949 Powell argued that 'the two parties of today were sharply at variance in their attitude to the past'. He continued:

> The Socialist regarded the past as something upon the whole discreditable and regrettable, desired a fundamental change in society brought about in accordance with a theory, and placed his ideals in a Utopia of the future. The Tory, on the other hand, while not whitewashing past errors or wanting to put back the clock, sought inspiration from the history of his country, saw hope for the future only in a national evolution of the nation and saw as his ideal the old England transfigured and transformed. The Tory approach to the past of his party and his nation could be expressed in the words of the commandment: 'honour thy father and mother, that thy days may be long in the land which the Lord thy God giveth thee'.[46]

Powell's commitment to the nation was then instinctive or emotional. Despite his emphasis on England, in 1955 Powell together with Maude, published *Biography of a Nation: A Short History of Britain*, which sought to define 'that self-consciousness which is the essence of nationhood', concluding that:'It [the nation] is that which thinks it is a nation.'[47] As a reviewer noted, the book presented 'the Tory version of history, as opposed to the Whig version ... stressing continuity at the expense of change'.[48] Yet, as the historian A. J. P. Taylor perceptively recognized at the time, there was 'some confusion whether the nation of which they write is confined to this island or includes the whole Commonwealth'.[49] Powell's views were indeed at a point of transition. At the start of the 1950s Powell held that, in the broadest sense, the empire was the nation but, by 1954, he was clear that, with Britain unwilling and unable to defend its remaining empire, collapse was inevitable.[50] As decolonization gathered pace in the late 1950s and early 1960s, Powell grappled with 'a vanished Empire', arguing that 'the nationhood of the mother country remained unaltered through it all'. In this respect, he viewed an acceptance of, and an allegiance to, 'the unlimited supremacy of the Crown in Parliament' characterizing the 'unbroken life of the English nation over a thousand years'.[51] Defining the English nation in terms of the constitutional development of the Crown-in-Parliament had been common practice from the mid- to late nineteenth century through to the 1950s.[52] And, from the late 1940s, Powell himself spent twenty years working—sporadically—on the early history of the House of Lords.[53] Yet, for Powell, this 'dimension of time' not only gave the nation 'the sense of having belonged together in the past' but also 'the expectation of belonging together in the future'.[54]

In 1968, as the Conservatives sought to regain power after four years of Labour government, Powell elaborated further on the difference between Conservatism and Socialism. He argued:

> It is very tempting to treat Conservatism as the same sort of thing as, though opposite to, Socialism. This is a mistake at the outset. Socialism is a system or a theory which can be defined, which would be the same for all branches of the genus *homo sapiens* since, if valid at all, its validity must derive from general characteristics of the human species; and a Socialist party is thus a party, which exists to realise the theory of Socialism, and of which all the members must accept the theory—or a theory—of Socialism. Contrariwise, Conservatism seems to me to be merely an abstraction from observation about the way in which Conservatives live, behave, think, act and, in particular, the way in

which the Conservative party views society and life and acts in politics in the history of this country.

Powell took particular aim at the socialist quest for equality for ignoring the 'variation in experience and in inherent characteristics between one human being and another' and, in turn, applauded the Conservative perspective that acknowledged inequality and sought constructively to work with it.[55] A defence of inequality characterized much Conservative thought.[56] Significantly, Powell further argued that it was possible for 'reform [to be] an admissible concept for a Tory' when 'the benefits of inertia are outweighed by its disadvantages'.[57] This was a revealing comment in light of Powell's embrace of free-market ideas, especially from the late 1950s, that sought to reduce the level of state intervention and to overturn the post-war consensus, a level of agreement between Labour and Conservative over three key elements: first, Keynesian demand management to control the level of unemployment; second, the mixed economy with a substantial public, as well as a private, sector; and third, the welfare state.[58] Powell's commitment to change in certain circumstances pointed not just to an important qualification in his thinking but also arguably towards a paradox within it. Alongside his deep attachment to the nation, Powell engaged extensively with international neo-liberal thought, associated especially with the economist and philosopher Friedrich Hayek, which sought to offer generally applicable principles linking economic and political freedom.[59]

Conflating England and Britain was a common occurrence, especially among the English, but from the mid-1960s onwards Powell spoke more consistently about the British nation defined by the geographical boundaries of the United Kingdom.[60] At the Conservative Party Conference in 1965, as shadow Defence Minister, he asked, 'what do we mean by "the nation"?', and answered, 'I will say what I believe we mean. We mean the United Kingdom.'[61] Three years later, with the rise of Scottish and Welsh nationalism meaning that 'the unity of the realm' could no longer be 'taken for granted', Powell urged 'the Tory Party above all to think and speak about the future of the United Kingdom, because nationhood... is what the Tory Party is ultimately about'. Powell continued developing the position he had outlined in *Biography of a Nation*:

> Nationhood is a baffling thing; for it is wholly subjective. They are a nation who think they are a nation: there is no other definition. You cannot discover nations by poring over atlases; for though geography influences nationhood, it

does not determine it in any specific way...Nations merge with others in the passage of time, while others emerge or re-emerge...language and race are relevant to nationhood, they are not determinants of it...As for the slippery concept of race, all attempts to match it with nationality are foredoomed to failure. The consequence is that the emergence or existence of a nation is only visible when it is there, when it has happened, when the sense of being a nation has been demonstrated to itself and to the outside world in actual fact.

On this basis, Powell was clear that 'if it were ever the settled and preponderant wish of the inhabitants of either Wales or Scotland...no longer to be part of this nation, that wish ought not to be resisted'.[62]

Powell applied the same arguments to Northern Ireland. He had begun to take an interest in Ulster (as he persisted in calling it, a preferred Unionist term but also one widely used in Britain) from the late 1960s.[63] He did this as Northern Ireland became one of the most pressing issues in British politics. These years saw the emergence of the Troubles, as civil-rights protests and marches fed into a long-standing Catholic and Nationalist discontent with the Protestant- and Unionist-dominated government of Northern Ireland. This exacerbated existing sectarian feeling, precipitated considerable street violence, and then developed into a conflict characterized by rival paramilitary violence, with the British Army deployed in August 1969 to maintain the peace but quickly becoming—along with the Northern Ireland police force, the Royal Ulster Constabulary (RUC)—a target for armed Republicans. Powell was, we should note, initially unsure of how to understand the situation. Perhaps influenced by the arrest of two European students in Derry/Londonderry for throwing petrol bombs, and by the significant level of student involvement in the civil-rights movement, he argued that the tensions in Northern Ireland had affinities with the 'purposeless violence and aggression' of the international student revolts the previous year.[64] Yet, by 1971, Powell had clarified his interpretation. By this point, the Republican movement, increasingly dominated by the paramilitary Provisional Irish Republican Army (IRA) and its political wing, Provisional Sinn Féin, was making intensified claims for Irish national unity. Against this backdrop, Powell asked: 'are the people who inhabit the six counties part, or not part, of the nation which inhabits the rest of the United Kingdom, and is this territory which they inhabit part or not part of that nation's national territory?'[65] By the following year, he was explicitly interpreting Unionism in this manner, defining it as 'the assertion...of British nationality, the claim to be part of a whole...the British nation'.[66] Just as in Scotland and Wales,

Powell considered it essential to recognize the wishes of the majority of the inhabitants, but in Northern Ireland this also meant rejecting Provisional Republican arguments that gave primacy to the wishes of the majority in Ireland as a whole, as he told an interviewer from the Irish national broadcaster, Radio Éireann, at his first press conference as an Ulster Unionist parliamentary candidate in September 1974.[67]

Powell was also opposed to the return of devolved government in Northern Ireland, which had been prorogued (suspended) in 1972, and, in his first South Down election campaign, he emphasized loyalty to the Crown-in-Parliament as a central part of his 'Unionist faith'.[68] Powell's position caused friction within Ulster Unionist circles, where the commitment to devolution had become entrenched since the establishment of Northern Ireland in 1921. Indeed, it meant that Powell's outlook was more akin to that of late nineteenth- and early twentieth-century Unionists, most notably the academic jurist A. V. Dicey, who contended that Irish home rule would undermine the fundamental principle of the British constitution: the overriding sovereignty of the Crown-in-Parliament which could do anything except bind its successor.[69] In a wider sense, Powell's overall emphasis on the importance of institutions placed him in a broad conservative tradition dating back to Edmund Burke in the eighteenth century.[70] This strand of Powell's thinking became ever more prominent. In 1976, amid renewed talk of the threat to 'Western' values from the Soviet Union in the ongoing Cold War, and with a debate raging over Scottish and Welsh devolution, Powell told an audience in Scotland forthrightly that: 'There are no such things as national values in the abstract: they exist embodied in institutions, and the exaltation and defence of the values consists in the maintenance of those institutions.'[71] Considering that the 'conviction of human imperfection' lay at the 'heart of conservatism', Powell argued that 'upon this scepticism is grounded its faith in the superior wisdom of institutions over individuals, and of the inherited over the invented'.[72]

Powell's attachment to institutions related not just to Parliament but also to the Church of England. As part of the One Nation Group, a Conservative backbench club formed by MPs who had first been elected in February 1950, Powell argued that 'much of what we think about our country is bound up with what we think about the Church, and...we cannot conceive the future which we hope for the nation unless it can become identical with the Church in a true and lively sense'. Powell's view was that the 'Anglican Church and the Church of Scotland, as established churches, symbolise that essential unity of nation and church...which represents our ideal.'[73] Powell had left the Church of England as a young man, embracing atheism after reading the works of the German philosopher Friedrich Nietzsche, but returned in 1949. Indeed, from the mid-1960s Powell increasingly took up invitations to preach sermons in churches and, in 1994, published a commentary on St Matthew's Gospel (controversially it disputed the Crucifixion, suggesting that Christ had been stoned to death).[74] For Powell, the link between religion and politics grew out of the same instinctive convictions. In a radio interview in 1964, Powell revealingly stated: 'I perceive a distinct connection between the religious forms which are most congenial to me and the political forms which are congenial...what I'd call the Tory view of life – that it can't be entirely secular.' Powell continued:

> I simply mean that congenitally I was Tory in that my characteristic attitudes way back were Tory, were of an instinctive reverence for instance for tradition, for a hierarchy, a dislike of claims of equality, a disposition to see differences more than similarities, a belief that things were better justified by what they were and by their past than by any reasoning....I don't believe that the choice a man makes in politics, any more than he makes in religion, can be founded on reason in the sense of deduction from universally accepted premises.[75]

Yet, for all the light this casts on Powell's overall outlook, the Church only occasionally intruded into the everyday presentation of his political arguments—and did so after he had become an Ulster Unionist MP.[76] Powell's move across the Irish Sea introduced him to a new religious, as well as political, environment, which he found less amenable. He privately lamented the timing of the disestablishment of the Anglican Church in Ireland in 1869, telling a correspondent: 'It was a cruel bit of history's timing that dis-establishment of the Irish part of the United Church of England and Ireland preceded (by some fifty years) the secession of the 26 counties from the union. Otherwise we would presumably (and happily) have today the United Church of England and Northern Ireland.'[77] With Presbyterianism the largest Protestant denomination, Powell made it clear, from the time of his first election campaign in South Down, that he would not be joining the Orange Order, the Protestant fraternal organization, despite its historically close ties to the Unionist Party.[78] Powell had concerns about the practical impact of the association, in terms of inhibiting Catholics from voting Unionist.[79] Nonetheless, the importance that Powell attributed to the

Church of England within the British nation led him to make a couple of provocative statements about Catholicism that were interpreted in the British press as pandering to Ulster Protestant sensibilities.[80] In 1978, amid speculation about the future wife of the Prince of Wales, Powell argued that he should not be allowed to marry a Catholic and still become king. Referring to the entrenchment of the break with Rome in the sixteenth century, Powell contended that, so far as the Church of England was concerned, 'a Roman Catholic Crown would...contradict the essential character of that Church...its derivation of authority from a source both secular and exclusive to the nation'.[81] It was little surprise that Ian Paisley's Democratic Unionist Party (DUP), with its evangelical Protestant strand of anti-Catholicism, signalled its strong agreement.[82] In 1980, amid discussion of a visit to Britain by Pope John Paul II (which took place in May and June 1982), Powell argued that—if this happened—a distinctly 'English nerve' would be touched because the Pope's claim to universal authority stood to undermine the Queen's position as supreme governor of the Church of England.[83]

Sources and approach

This book pays particular attention to the arguments made in Powell's speeches. Many of these are now available online, but some important early speeches—that cast new light on his views—are held among Powell's largely constituency papers in the Staffordshire Record Office, where Powell sent them after leaving his Wolverhampton seat.[84] Powell's notoriety, of course, owes a great deal to one speech in particular. Moreover, in his book on interwar prime minister Stanley Baldwin, the historian Philip Williamson argued for the importance of examining speeches on the basis that, 'in an important sense, politicians are what they speak and publish' because 'politics is a *public* activity and because they need to win support for themselves, their parties, and their causes'. Taking this further, Williamson suggested that 'leaders are normally such because they add something distinctive and persuasive, causing particular importance to be attached to themselves not just by their party and supporters but by opposing parties and other bodies too'.[85] Powell himself was fully aware of the significance of speeches. Seemingly, 'he always ensured that before rising to speak he had kept his bladder full – in order to maintain the tension'.[86] Powell also reproduced some of his speeches in edited collections.[87] At the launch of one of these, entitled *Freedom and Reality* in 1969, he told the audience:

> A practising politician works through speeches and works therefore with the business of the moment, offering judgments and interpretations of changing events and issues. No doubt those judgments and interpretations imply a political philosophy and a self-consistent outlook... The spoken word is the politician's supreme instrument: all ease is ancillary to that. His speeches are, literally, what he has to say.... I do see them as opportunities for deliberate exposition, variation and illustration of a limited number of basic themes. As I look ahead over the engagements of the coming months, certain occasions mark themselves out a long way in advance for particular subjects. Others only fall into their place in the last fortnight or much less, according to current events. Often, though not always, I carry in my mind a sort of shopping list of subjects which I hope to deal with; and it may be many months, if not two or three years, before I get to cover them all.

Powell was also clear that, within each speech, he was attempting to develop an argument:

> My experience is that, contrary to common belief, political audiences welcome a continuous argument, deployed, developed and illustrated and can be easily persuaded to participate with the speaker in working out a train of thought... The beginning and the end of the speech, except on the entirely exceptional or formal occasions, must be between the speaker and his audience. An audience must be won gradually and got to feel they know something of the speaker before they can concentrate on what he has to argue – unlike the newspaper or magazine reader, who must be grabbed and held fast as he rushes by. Then, when they have shared an argument with the speaker, an audience must be given maybe a repetition in a different setting of the proposition of which they are now seized, maybe an extension of it into a larger application on or an embodiment of it into a wider scheme of things; but in the end they must feel that it comes home to themselves and to their life and their actions, if only at the ballot-box next time.[88]

Powell sought to make sure that his speeches quickly reached as wide an audience as possible. Early in his career he had, in line with Conservative Party practice, retrospectively dictated a 100-word summary to Central Office.[89] In October 1963 Ralph Harris, and Arthur Seldon of the free-market think tank the Institute of Economic Affairs (IEA), with which Powell was associated, had suggested that, in advance of his speeches, he should send the press a summary of the 'more outspoken passages'.[90] Powell took some of this on board. The following year he started asking Central Office to pre-distribute copies of the entire speech to newspaper and television sources.[91]

As we attempt to understand exactly what Powell sought to do in his speeches, we face a significant challenge. Powell was clear that 'the politician's business is not with originality of research'.[92] He was, nonetheless, widely read across a range of fields. Yet, as Harris noted with frustration after hearing Powell speak on economics in 1965, he did not readily make 'the lineage' of his ideas apparent.[93] This book seeks to fill in some of the intellectual background but does so against an understanding, as Utley told *Daily Telegraph* readers in 1969, that for Powell these were 'ideas . . . deployed for a political purpose . . . general descriptions of the trend which he wishes to foster in politics'.[94] Also attempting, then, to understand Powell's particular, and evolving, political objectives, this book draws on the extensive Powell private papers held at the Churchill Archives Centre at Churchill College, Cambridge, making use of previously unexploited correspondence. These have been supplemented by the papers of a range of other politicians and public figures and by party and government material—a substantial proportion of which have only become available in recent years.

In a broad sense, of course, we already know that Powell was trying both to influence policy and public debates and to win wider public support. In themselves, these are overlapping undertakings, but in Powell's case there was a greater emphasis on seeking to influence party policy in the years before 1968 and more weight given thereafter to securing wider endorsement for his views. Yet it is important not to draw too neat a distinction: Powell's advocacy of free-market economics in the early and mid-1960s, for example, was aimed mainly at his own party but it was also pitched in terms of giving ordinary people a voice. We should also, at the outset, note the scale—as well as the limitations—of Powell's mobilization of popular opinion. There has been a long-running debate about Powell's precise impact on two closely contested general elections—when he supported the Conservatives in 1970 and then opposed them in February 1974—but there is little doubt that his actions, and speeches, generated great interest at the time, dominating parts of both campaigns.[95] According to the social scientist Douglas Schoen—who later became a prominent US Democratic campaign consultant, most notably for Bill Clinton in the 1990s—Powell constructed a cross-class, and cross-party, alliance of support over immigration between 1968 and 1973, but his working-class backing subsequently became more prominent and, at the same time, his commitment to Ulster Unionism and opposition to the European Community failed to resonate.[96]

Tracing the development of Powell's arguments against that overall awareness of their impact, this book locates them precisely within the specific debates of the time and argues that—taken as a whole—they should be understood as part of a debate about British decline. A number of scholars have tantalizingly noted the potential to understand Powell in this way.[97] Moreover, with a focus on race and immigration, a core argument on the New Left, and those influenced by it, has been that for Powell and Powellism the 'process of national decline is presented as coinciding with the dilution of once homogeneous and continuous national stock by alien strains'.[98] Amy Whipple has recently shown the possibilities of the approach, arguing that letters written to Powell after April 1968—held at the Staffordshire Record Office—revealed 'a profound sense of national decline' that 'integrated the immigration issue into broader critiques of the nation in the late 1960s'.[99] Yet exactly how Powell himself grappled with decline is far from clear. He has been surprisingly peripheral to other discussions of decline, despite the richness of the historiography—especially on the economic front. Economic historians identified actual relative decline as the superior growth rates of Western European continental states, which saw them converge on the higher levels of UK national income immediately after the Second World War.[100] Jim Tomlinson, in particular, has investigated the prevailing and largely unquestioned perceptions of decline, dubbed 'declinism', examining the specific contexts in which these diagnoses have emerged and analysing some of the political uses to which the suggested solutions have been put.[101] There has, moreover, been a recognition that the repercussions of imperial decline intersected with fears of economic malaise that were articulated around the turn of the 1960s.[102] Attention has been given to Thatcher's successful attempt to mould an interpretation of decline in the 1970s, including more than just economics, to suit her own political ends.[103] More recently, wider understandings of decline have examined disputes over Britain's position in the world and arguments about the constitutional integrity of the British state.[104]

Placing Powell fully in this context, we will see him dismissing other interpretations of decline and then, increasingly, advancing his own diagnoses of it. His arguments were part of inter- and intra-party politics, but they also arose from deeper philosophical foundations. In 1966, Powell argued that:

[T]he business of the politician is to look to general principles himself, and to direct the minds of others towards general principles when they seek the causes and the cure of the ills and irritations, man-made or not, by which they are afflicted. It will often then appear that a multitude of individual annoyances and injustices are not in reality separate and individual, but all flow from one and the same source, the breach or neglect of a sound general principle.[105]

Powell did not explicitly unite his arguments around the theme of decline, but he did consider that the nation could best be served by 'a firm, clear appraisal of the real world around us'.[106] At the same time, he recognized that this was difficult because the 'life of nations, no less than that of men, is lived largely in the imagination'.[107] Here there was 'always something "wrong" with men and human societies' because of the need for 'adaptation to its ever-changing internal and external environment' and the 'inability to make any accurate comparison between the present and the past'.[108] Yet Powell still considered that it was the role of politicians to 'try to produce a new mental picture of the personified nation which will be sufficiently in harmony with indefinable facts to be credible and durable'.[109] He relished the presentation of the finely poised public mood that 'might turn either way – to a deepening dejection or to a new and sudden resolve'.[110]

Decline, as a theme, runs through each of this book's chapters. Initially, in terms of international relations and economics, Powell took issue with a 'conviction of national decline' which he saw advanced by Conservatives who clung to the remnants of Empire and by the Labour Party that, erroneously advocating state planning, was especially keen to dwell on Britain's 'subordinate place' in the international economic 'league table'.[111] In Powell's view, allowing the current levels of immigration to continue was 'like watching a nation busily engaged in heaping up its own funeral pyre'.[112] As the 1970s progressed, with events in Northern Ireland and membership of the European Community to the fore, he argued that an assertion of parliamentary sovereignty was needed to demonstrate 'our ability to take a grip upon ourselves as a nation' and to indicate whether the nation possessed 'the fibre or the will to defend itself against other assaults, from within or without'.[113]

I

International relations

Throughout his political career, Powell grappled with what is arguably still the central issue in British foreign policy: the precise nature of the UK's role in the world. In the long aftermath of the 2003 Iraq War, this question—tied to debates about the relationship with the United States—has been fiercely debated. Arguments also raged during the Cold War, although, of course, in the global conflict dominated by the United States and the Soviet Union, which embraced ideological, military, technological, economic, and cultural aspects, they took different forms. We know that Powell was right at the forefront of these discussions. He was a long-standing critic of the alliance with the United States who, amid ongoing decolonization, called for a swifter move away from the Empire and a more tightly defined international role for Britain—one that included, by the 1980s, an alliance with the Soviet Union.

Powell viewed the nation as the core component in international affairs, emphasizing not just the national interest but also the management of a constantly evolving balance of power as guiding principles. This outlook corresponds to what students of international affairs would call a fundamentally 'realist' outlook. Realism is a diverse tradition, tracing its origins to the Athenian general and historian Thucydides, from the fifth century BC, whose work Powell had translated. Gaining prominence in early modern Europe, under the influence of the Italian diplomat and philosopher Niccolò Machiavelli and the English political philosopher Thomas Hobbes, realism held that state policy should primarily or solely focus on maintaining military and economic power, rather than ideals or ethics, in an anarchic international system where no supranational authority exists. After 1945, realism assumed an important place in US-based international relations theory, most notably through the work of Hans Morgenthau.[1] Powell, meanwhile, applied this outlook both to frame his overall perspective on foreign policy and his understanding of international relations and to underpin his response to particular issues—ranging from the Suez Crisis in 1956 to debates over Rhodesia in the mid- and late 1960s. Time and again, he argued that only a proper grasp of the realities of power and geography could prevent the diminution of Britain internationally. This chapter also traces Powell's argument that nuclear weapons—considered essential to the maintenance of Britain's great-power status—were unlikely to be used. As we will see, he made this case, in some detail, privately as early as 1948. He then deployed the argument publicly in the 1960s, seeking to link it with a growing body of government and military opinion. Finally, Powell used this argument to underpin his call for unilateral nuclear disarmament in 1983, amid the wider rise of the largely left-wing peace movement.

American hegemony and the end of the British Empire

In an early journalistic contribution in summer 1949, Powell noted, with some trepidation, the 'formidable position' in which the outcome of the Second World War had left the United States.[2] By this stage, the Cold War Anglo-American relationship had been firmly established. Back in 1946 Winston Churchill, as Leader of the Opposition, had called in his famous 'Iron Curtain' speech for a 'fraternal association' with the United States— involving 'intimate relationships between our military advisers' for 'mutual security'—in order to check Soviet ambitions.[3] Earlier in 1949, the Labour government, with Foreign Secretary Ernest Bevin to the fore and with Conservative backing, had played a prominent part in establishing the North Atlantic Treaty Organization (NATO) as a system of US-led collective defence. Yet Powell was at odds with this type of thinking.

Indeed, Powell had anxiously anticipated the development of American power as early as 1942 when he was based in North Africa. Strikingly, Powell's definition of the national interest was already clear—a concept that Morgenthau later expounded extensively in his *Politics Among Nations* (1949). Powell argued that if 'a foreign state desists from the attempt to interfere with our self-determination, our relations with that state cease to be affected by internal politics'. On this basis, he contended that there was 'no reason to believe that the British constitution will be threatened more by the socialist dictatorship than by the democracy of the United States'. Working on the basis that Britain had to be able to fight a war, if necessary, against the United States, Powell's balance-of-power thinking led him to argue that Britain needed allies to 'counter-balance the material superiority of the United States'. The theory of the balance of power assumed the existence of two or more states of roughly equal strength, the desire of the states to survive and maintain their autonomy, flexibility in making alliances, and the ability to resort to war if necessary. In this respect Powell acknowledged that the total defeat of Germany by the Red Army would create a dangerous 'vacuum in Europe', and suggested that 'a strong and independent Germany is actually in Britain's interests'. Powell had enjoyed a youthful interest in German culture but had increasingly feared war with Nazi Germany from the mid-1930s. Powell's particular concern now was that, with the increase in US naval strength, 'the British Empire would only exist on American sufferance'.[4] Here Powell's definition of the national interest was geographically broad, mirroring his understanding of the British nation at this stage. Reaching across the Pacific as well as the Atlantic, he held that the 'life-principle of Britain's empire is the actual or potential predominance of her navy on all the seas of the world'. Powell was especially concerned about the US aim to eradicate Japanese naval power, because 'the existence of Japan's navy always offers the means to counterbalance America in the Pacific while confronting her in the Atlantic'. At a time when the war was just beginning to turn against Japan but in the same year that had seen the fall of Singapore, until then governed as a Crown Colony within the British Empire, to Japan, Powell suggested that it was in the British interest to preserve its naval strength through means 'not short even of alliance with Japan'.[5]

Within this imperial strategic analysis, India—where Powell was based from summer 1943—assumed a central place. At the end of 1944, he wrote: 'Without the power to deny India to an enemy and to make use of at least its ports and airfields, Britain can neither hold her possessions farther East nor protect the Dominions of Australia and New Zealand nor in the long run maintain even her position in the Middle East.' Powell considered that the Indian population was 'either indifferent or hostile to the British connection', but that it was still essential 'to keep firm and substantial control until the latest possible moment'.[6] Powell took this strategic assumption with him to the Conservative Parliamentary Secretariat, where he worked from 1946 and specialized in defence.[7] By this stage, in the bipolar post-war world, fears of British decline loomed large. Powell argued that the 'only effective answer' to the prospect of 'being crushed economically – which in the end means politically and militarily also – between the two much greater individual powers, Russia and the United States . . . lies in her African and Asiatic dependencies, above all in the Indian Empire'. Aspiring towards autonomous-dominion status for all the Empire, Powell contended that the Indian experience determined the 'hopes of a lasting union between "white" and "coloured" which the conception of common subjectship to the King-Emperor affords'. Powell argued that Britain's 'pride and self-confidence' would be dealt 'a blow' if this proved impossible.[8] In the event, of course, Indian independence was granted by the Labour government in summer 1947. Moreover, much to Powell's regret and contrary to his demand for Britain 'to resume full control', the Conservative Party eventually agreed to it, even though, without agreement between the main Indian parties, it involved the partition of British India into India and Pakistan.[9]

Powell's views were not that distinctive. There was a long-standing link between Conservative (often termed Tory) imperialism and the desire to check decline. And until the early 1950s many Conservatives clung to the idea that the Empire would allow Britain to compete with the United States.[10] Contesting the 1950 general election in Wolverhampton South West, Powell argued—despite the loss of India—for a 'greater imperial unity' with a 'merging and pooling of powers by its autonomous parts in those matters which concern them all', broadly understood to mean economic, defence, and foreign policy.[11] Powell further identified the Empire as a central part of 'the gulf which separates the fundamental beliefs of Tory and Socialist'. Powell argued that socialists saw the Empire as 'imperialistic' greed, operating at the expense of 'workers' with '[n]ational identity and sovereignty . . . only perpetuated by the "ruling classes" in their own interests' and holding the misguided belief that the 'natural state of mankind was universal peace, possibly under some kind of world government'. By contrast, at a relatively early stage in the Cold War when it appeared that large parts of the world were fast becoming increasingly polarized, he argued that:

> It is of the essence of Toryism to view the British nation as something natural and organic . . . From such a Britain the Tory cannot look upon a world merely divided into two, 'democratic' or 'Communist', 'free' or not free, 'Western' or 'Eastern'. He sees instead a wide scene peopled with various individual nations, obeying each the respective laws of their being. Nations, to him, like national sovereignties, so far from being artificial barriers, are the inevitable framework within which mankind lives and associates.

Crucially, Powell viewed the Empire as the nation. He went on:

> The supreme boon which the British Empire confers upon its members, white and coloured alike, is a common sovereignty which spans our world. Our mission towards the colonies is to educate them not to independence but to interdependence, to a more and more conscious and positive unity with the rest. Our mission towards the dominions is to find means whereby, in matters of general concern, our separate identities can still be sunk in common action. In its widest sense, the nation is the Empire.[12]

In one sense, Powell looked backwards. In the late nineteenth century, many advocates of a 'Greater Britain' held hopes of creating—in various ways—a global nation, based on the Empire and possessing a common sovereignty.[13] Yet Powell's wider position was very much a response to contemporary international politics. In a context where China had become communist, and where Franco's fascist regime in Spain appeared increasingly secure, Powell called for a national-interest approach to foreign policy—understood as 'impossible to separate' from imperial policy—that eschewed ideology:

> Guided by its special aims and interests, the British Empire can and must cease to conduct foreign policy on an ideological basis. Jealous of our natural evolution, one must respect that of other countries however different. With the internal politics of Spain, of China...even of Russia herself, we have no business; only our own essential interest gives us the right to range ourselves with or against another power. Britain is uniquely placed to break down that spurious bisection of mankind into two entrenched camps which threatens a third world war.[14]

Yet signs of a change gradually became apparent. Within the One Nation Group in 1951 Powell acknowledged that 'the 19th century Empire was overblown', and he called for a pragmatic assessment of 'what features and parts of it remain essential and what must be done to restore confidence and prestige'.[15] In 1952 Powell expressed his public unease about the emergence of the British Commonwealth, which had been formally constituted three years earlier, amid growing decolonization, as an association of 'free and equal' former members of the Empire, with the British monarch as its symbolic head. Powell took specific aim at what he saw as the nonsense of the Conservative policy of self-government within it, arguing that: 'If a territory is autonomous, then presumably its own government has the power to alter the relation of that country to any other in the world.'[16] In 1953 he dismissed the title of Head of the Commonwealth as 'essentially a sham' in Parliament.[17]

Even so, in 1953 Powell joined the Suez Group of about forty backbench MPs, which sought to maintain military control, amid local political instability, over the Suez Canal in Egypt that was owned by a joint Anglo-French company and was a very important British trading route between the Mediterranean Sea and the Indian Ocean. Like others in the group, Powell's view was that US policy was 'relentlessly directed towards the weakening and destruction of the links which bind the British Empire together'.[18] He was also fearful that Britain 'would have ceased to be a great power' if it proved unable to stand up to Egypt, a 'midget power', and lost control of a 'vital strategic area'.[19] In a wider sense, Powell was concerned that 'no one should imagine that... the rot will stop there', because nothing less than the 'entire British position in Eastern and Central Africa is at stake'.[20] In July 1954 Powell was one of twenty-six Conservative MPs to vote against the government when the Suez Agreement, by which Britain would withdraw from the Canal Zone (with the right to return if it became part of a war zone) was debated in the House of Commons.[21]

Yet Powell's views were publicly about to change. Addressing the summer school of the Conservative Political Centre (CPC), the party's political education body, in 1954, he argued that the 'unstable compromise of Imperial government by the Parliament of Great Britain' had rested on power—on 'Great Britain's ability to give the colonies security and peace unaided'. When this was 'shattered' by the First World War, and with dominions, including Australia, New Zealand, and Canada, increasingly independent, Powell considered that this starkly exposed differences in the 'political institutions of the United Kingdom and the character of its former and present dependencies', making its 'disintegration... inevitable', with the only surprise being that it had taken so long. Powell now saw the process gathering momentum, and becoming increasingly fraught, because of 'the existence within the British dominions of large populations unconnected in origin with the United Kingdom and potentially antipathetic to it by tradition or colour'.[22] Against this backdrop, the formal conclusion of the Suez Agreement in October 1954 proved pivotal; Powell left the Suez Group the following month.[23] He now argued that:

> Britain, and also the Conservative Party, have now to rethink their foreign policy and what used to be their imperial policy on new premises. Territories and positions that had a value as part of a worldwide system may in isolation have no value or less than no value. The Suez agreement showed decisively that Britain was no longer able or willing – there is no real difference – to maintain that world system at one of its vital points, if that meant the exertion of force.[24]

Figure 1. Enoch Powell speaking at Swinton College in Masham, Yorkshire, in 1949. The college was the Conservative Party's residential political education centre.

Despite his stance, Powell, as he later told Labour politician Tony Benn, 'watched with amused detachment the outbreak of hysteria' as Prime Minister Anthony Eden faced Conservative calls for a vigorous response to the nationalization of the canal by the new Egyptian President Gamal Abdel Nasser in summer 1956, defying the terms of the Suez Agreement, under which the Suez Canal Company was not due to return to the Egyptian government until 1968. Considering that any British action 'had come two years too late to be effective', Powell privately did not approve of the Anglo–French invasion of Egypt—ostensibly as peacemakers but later revealed to be in collusion with Israel—that prompted domestic and international out-cry and, with financial pressure from the United States, led to unconditional withdrawal. Frankly, he 'didn't think it was right or could be successful to attempt to invade and get back what we had lost'.[25]

Within the party, Powell now began to push his views. In early 1957, he was invited to join the Policy Study Group that was formed by Home Secretary R. A. 'Rab' Butler as the party regrouped under new leader and prime minister, Harold Macmillan, following Eden's resignation as a result of the Suez crisis. Before the group's first meeting, Powell reflected on what he considered 'the main pieces of mental work before the Party'. In a letter that was circulated to the group, he emphasized 'without hesitation external relations'. He argued the party must 'be cured of the British Empire', consider 'what (if anything) the Commonwealth is', question the working of the United Nations (UN), and 'find its patriotism' in England.[26] In 1951, amid stalemate in the Korean War where the UN had sanctioned US-led action, Powell had argued that it 'exacerbates all disputes without solving any'.[27] Criticism of the UN had long been rife in the Suez Group.[28] It was also the UN that had condemned the Anglo-French invasion. At the group's first meeting, Powell's position elicited little support, with others talking about how to develop Commonwealth institutions.[29] Indeed, Powell's analysis had more in common with Hedley Bull, the Australian-born but British-based realist international relations academic, who viewed decol-onization as an inevitability, considered that nation states would eventually, and naturally, emerge, and viewed the Commonwealth merely as a 'symbol...to prolong the spirit long after life has departed the body'.[30]

Powell also began to advance his views publicly. During the parliamen-tary debate in July 1959 on the Hola Camp, where it emerged that eleven Mau Mau prisoners at a British detention camp in Kenya had died at the hands of the camp authorities and not as a result of drinking 'infected water' as the prison initially claimed, Powell called for 'British stand-ards...where we will still govern'. His speech notably garnered praise from Liberal and Labour circles, where criticism of imperialism had long been more pronounced. Yet Powell's concern was—as Schofield has shown—about Britain: about 'the opinion which is entertained of the way in which this country acts and the ways in which Englishmen act'.[31] Four years later, in 1963, he argued that Britain should 'not...live in the past of a world-wide empire and the dominion of the seas'.[32] Powell was aware of the scale of the challenge, arguing that 'few nations have had, in a single generation, to confront the fact and the effects of such tremendous changes in their world situation as Britain has had to do in the last thirty years'.[33] Yet he was still in the process of working out, and making public, exactly what that meant—as the rest of this chapter will explore.

Nuclear weapons

Powell emerged as a significant critic of the reliance on nuclear weapons. The UK had taken the decision to develop nuclear weapons in January 1947. It was a policy that, from the start, was concerned with maintaining great-power status.[34] As the military historian David French bitingly put it, nuclear weapons enabled politicians to 'retain the illusion that Britain remained a great power for a little longer'.[35] Powell gave considerable thought to nuclear weapons in 1947 and 1948 as he assisted Air Vice-Marshall Edgar Kingston-McCloughry, the Chief of Staff of Fighter Command, with a book entitled *War in Three Dimensions*.[36] Powell gave Kingston-McCloughry his views on chapters as they were written and made his own suggestions about the discussion of nuclear weapons. In August 1949, as the Soviet Union was about to conduct its first nuclear weapons test, which the United States subsequently made public, Powell argued:

> The problem as to whether the atomic weapon will be used arises most acutely when each belligerent knows or believes that the other has the weapon; for here each side will fear the retaliatory use of the weapon by the other...If a country cannot practically guarantee the immunity of its own...population centres then it will not use the atomic bomb for fear of retaliation unless it believes that a single use of the weapon is certain to end the war forthwith...

> There are thus grounds for doubting whether the atomic weapon even in its present form, is by any means certain to be used in a future war... These grounds would be greatly strengthened by any increase in the power of the atomic weapon which may be achieved or supposed to have been achieved.

This led Powell to conclude that 'atomic weapons in their present day form are <u>not</u>, as there is a danger of their coming to be thought, a substitute for other forms of armament'. He considered them 'indispensable, if only to ensure the means of retaliation if required' but viewed them as 'an additional burden which all major powers must in future carry'.[37] And it was indeed only on Kingston-McCloughry's insistence that the book itself emphasized the deterrent value of nuclear weapons. He wrote to Powell frankly that: 'The U.S.A. are convinced of this and I am thinking of sales of [sic] there.'[38]

Powell, meanwhile, publicly related his conclusions to nuclear civil defence. This was an issue on which the government spent a great deal of effort in the late 1940s, but the plans developed soon proved too expensive to implement. This was before the government realization a decade later that a nuclear attack would cripple the country and that civil defence would only minimally reduce casualties.[39] Powell's argument was a prescient one about the overall cost and what he saw as the particular futility of it:

> No doubt, if we made up our minds that nothing mattered but passive defence against atomic attack, we could make a fair job of it. Our cities could be compulsorily dispersed, our junctions and ports put underground or sheathed with material proof against rays and blast, our factories and installations tunnelled into hillsides, and our population drilled in the use of free-issue protective devices. If we did this, then, at the cost of disrupting our whole social and economic life, we would perhaps achieve partial – but only partial – immunity from the consequences of atomic attack. Is it worth it and is it necessary?...the atom bomb in World War III may be like poison gas in World War II – a constant potential menace, but never an actual one. Preparation for passive defence against atomic warfare are therefore against a contingency which is certainly not immediate and which may well not, after all, be a feature of warfare in the future.[40]

As a Conservative MP from 1950, Powell was more muted about nuclear weapons—as British and NATO strategy placed increasing reliance on them, as opposed to conventional forces, to counter the Soviet threat.[41] Yet there were occasional signs of Powell's unease. In 1955 he publicly worried that this had gone too far, with potentially onerous consequences: 'If you are attacked with conventional forces then and haven't got any yourself, you've got to become a nuclear aggressor.'[42] By 1960 he was more outspoken, making clear his opposition to the 1957 Defence White Paper that had been introduced by his own party. He took issue with its premise that 'any future war would be nuclear' and that, as a result, conventional forces could be reduced—the assumption that facilitated the 'electorally popular' end of conscription. Amid rising defence costs, Powell argued that a reconsideration was needed because maintaining 'an up-to-date nuclear deterrent has proved an expensive business, as one weapon after another has been discarded as obsolete after huge sums had been poured into its development'.[43] It was, though Powell did not make this clear, delivery systems that had proved particularly controversial. In 1957 it had been decided to develop a British intermediate-range ballistic missile, Blue Streak, but this was cancelled in 1960 after £65 million was spent on it (soon afterwards the government secured a deal to purchase US Skybolt missiles and, from 1962, Polaris missiles).[44] In this context, Powell argued that Britain should 'abandon the attempt to "keep up with the Joneses" (Russia and America) in maintaining her own so-called nuclear deterrent' but make sure it possessed 'the forces to make it possible to fight a non-nuclear war but major war, if and when it comes'. Powell argued that he did not envisage the return of conscription in peacetime but instead wished to supplement the professional army with the voluntary reserves.[45] The Territorial Force had been established in 1908, and was renamed the Territorial Army (TA) in 1920, but it had been reduced in size from 1960, with TA divisional headquarters merged with regular army districts.[46] On nuclear weapons, Powell still toed the party line. In 1963, arguing that there was a need to preserve 'an influence in the world', Powell suggested this was 'the reason why Britain's possession and retention of an independent nuclear force is so profound a dividing issue between ourselves and our opponents'.[47] This might well have been a sound party political point to make—since the early 1950s unilateral nuclear disarmament had been a significant minority view within the Labour Party—but it was also a clear contradiction of his earlier argument.[48]

As shadow Defence Minister from summer 1965, Powell's radical position became steadily clearer. On his appointment, Powell had considered the TA 'among the first and most important aspects of defence to which I must direct my mind', and he made a case for its expansion in his first party-conference speech in the job.[49] Powell's voice was one among several—as, for example, there had been interest in the TA from the Conservative think tank the Bow Group.[50] There was no doubting how important Powell considered the matter, but he was going against the tide. With the TA's regimental and divisional structure abolished in April 1967, he told the party conference later that year that 'we need to have a true citizen army, not only to provide the means of expansion in war but to keep alive in this country the military spirit and the will to self-defence'.[51] Powell entered more controversial territory as he linked his arguments about nuclear weapons to a wider body of opinion. In 1965 he established contact with the high-profile military theorist Sir Basil Liddell Hart, whose book *Deterrent or Defence* (1960) argued powerfully that the nuclear deterrent did not reduce the need for a conventional defence policy designed to meet a range of threats.[52] Powell described his first visit to Liddell Hart's home as a 'pilgrimage' on which he 'found more support for my conjectures + suspicions than is good for me'.[53] Powell also favourably reviewed *Scientists at War* by Sir Solly Zuckerman, the government's Chief Scientific Advisor, praising Zuckerman for emphasizing that 'non-nuclear war between great and nuclear powers...must...be anticipated and prepared for'.[54] Zuckerman had pedigree on this point. In 1960 he had written: 'In a democracy, one cannot conceive of a Government giving the order to fire first...So why do we have a deterrent at all?'[55] There were also internal military debates to which Powell's arguments related. While the RAF was committed to the nuclear deterrent, the navy was ambivalent, and the army's preference was to favour conventional forces. Within the government, the Treasury was also unconvinced by the arguments for nuclear weapons.[56]

Powell gradually became more outspoken. On 7 March 1967 he told Liddell Hart that in 'the semi-obscurity of the late wind-up of the Army Estimates debate last night I finally sallied forth to war against the nuclear assumption'.[57] Powell forthrightly challenged what he considered to be the government's erroneous premise: that 'there can never again be a war which threatens the safety of the nation, because if such a war were ever to commence, it must speedily be terminated by the inconceivable catastrophe of the nuclear exchange'. Powell argued that nothing less than the 'existence of the nation' was at stake because 'war could nevertheless develop as if they did not exist, except of course that it could be so conducted as to minimise any possibility of misapprehension that use of nuclear weapons was imminent or had begun'. This meant, Powell continued, that it was necessary to have 'an army equal in armament, training and philosophy to any such in

Europe', able 'to play an important and continuing part in continental warfare'.[58] Predictably, Liddell Hart strongly approved of the speech.[59] More significantly, in political terms at least, Labour's Defence Minister, Denis Healey, wrote a public letter to Heath provocatively asking if Powell's views—which he said would necessitate a return to conscription—represented party policy.[60] Heath refuted the point about conscription, but it was more difficult to obscure the appearance of divisions at the top of the Conservative Party over defence.[61]

Within the party the debate subsequently intensified, centring on a pamphlet that Powell had been asked to write for the CPC on 'The Defence of Europe'.[62] In it, he argued that there were 'the strongest grounds, both theoretical and empirical, for regarding the nuclear veto as either wholly incredible or at any rate so far improbable as to make it necessary to be prepared to act on the assumption that it will not apply'. Recent history was central to his case. He suggested that 'during the last 20 years the nations, whether or not they possessed nuclear weapons, cannot be shown to have behaved otherwise than they would have done if the nuclear warhead had not existed'.[63] Powell also made it clear that his overall position was unaffected by changes in NATO policy. These had seen it move away from a commitment to the strategic use of nuclear weapons in the event of a conventional Soviet attack on Western Europe to a graduated, or 'flexible', response—with nuclear weapons introduced only after conventional ones and strategic nuclear weapons only after less powerful tactical nuclear ones.[64] Powell argued:

> The theory that there are nuclear weapons which are not strategic but tactical, and to which the same reasoning therefore does not apply, is ingenious but unsound...This theory states that the losing side in a non-nuclear campaign will at a certain point throw tactical nuclear weapons into the battle on a lesser or greater scale. However, since these weapons are presumed to exist on both sides, then *either* they would be simply a more powerful artillery (in which case there is no reason why the loser should fare better with them than without them), *or* they are so devastating that the object of their use would be to end the war by mutual obliteration (in which case the logic of the strategic nuclear exchange applies).[65]

Influential figures in the party were unconvinced. The shadow Foreign Secretary (and former prime minister and party leader) Sir Alec Douglas-Home accepted that nuclear war was a 'near impossibility' but insisted he could 'visualise it happening' after a process of escalation.[66] In July 1967

Powell was informed by Michael Fraser, the deputy chairman of the party, that the pamphlet would not be published.[67] Powell subsequently pressed the matter with Russell Lewis, the director of the CPC, who had commissioned it, and who now told Powell that the decision had been taken by Heath—provoking Powell's annoyance that he did not 'go direct and tell him so'.[68]

Powell was undeterred. In a paper he prepared for the Leader's Consultative Committee (LCC), the shadow cabinet, in February 1968, he found support for his own arguments in the new US foreign-policy assessment, which considered that there was a rough equality between NATO and Warsaw Pact land forces, NATO superiority in the air, and evidence of an increase in Soviet naval strength. Because this replaced a long-standing belief in Warsaw Pact superiority in ground forces, Powell argued that it made a conventional war more likely. It led him—for the first time—to call for an increase in maritime forces to counter the growing Soviet threat. Douglas-Home was again quick to counter Powell on the likely recourse to nuclear weapons and, in the end, the committee agreed not to comment on the matter publicly at that time.[69] Yet, just the next month, Powell made public his view that the new US assessments implied an increased likelihood of a sea and land war.[70]

Strikingly, however, even after he had ceased to be shadow Defence Minister, Powell did not argue that Britain should relinquish its nuclear weapons. After a talk in September 1968 Powell was explicitly pushed on this point by Alan Clark, who had written works of military history and who was later a junior minister, and a famous diarist, in the Thatcher and Major governments. Powell replied that 'if you dispense with nuclear forces you are, at any rate theoretically, once again in a position to be blackmailed, should your opponent have a nuclear capability and should other nuclear powers not be involved'. Powell instinctively added that this was 'the rational justification, and from my point of view as an Englishman a sufficient justification, for the retention of... nuclear capability'.[71]

The balance of power

A further breach between Powell and the Conservative Party opened up over Powell's desire to restrict geographically Britain's role in the world—an argument that grew out of his views about the end of empire and which he articulated in terms of the operation of the balance of power. Crucially, it also involved Powell offering his opinion on what was fast becoming a major international issue: US military intervention in Vietnam. Amid French withdrawal from Indo-China, the United States had sent military advisers to the area as early as 1950, but their numbers had only increased dramatically from 1961. In 1964 the US Congress authorized military action against North Vietnam, with the first heavy bombing raids beginning the following year. Against this backdrop, Powell argued that 'South-East Asia has posed the post-colonial problem of Europe in Asia and Africa in absolutely classic form':

> The colonial government withdraws or is driven out; the successor government proves too unstable to resist aggression or subversion by Communism; the danger of Communist advance is then felt by the Western powers, and particularly, by America, to outweigh the dangers of involvement yet Western support weakens the successor regime still further, by making it dependent and laying it open to the charge that it is the stooge of imperialism. Thus the West is drawn deeper and deeper into the politics as well as the defence of the country concerned. At last the choice has to be made: one alternative is openly to fight a war against internal and external communism and so initially govern the country in order to do so; the other alternative is to cut one's losses and clear out, leaving events to take their course. This is the choice which now stares America in the face in Viet Nam. If the Americans decided for the latter alternative, a similar choice would probably soon confront Britain in Malaysia.

Powell's stance rested on the argument that:

> The boundary line between communism and non-communism may appear to be fixed by the balance of military force in some one place at some one moment. In reality it will represent a worldwide balance of forces, not military but economic, political and human . . . It could be that in the absence of the Americans the communists would not necessarily prevail in Viet Nam, the resultant regrouping of forces, in South-East Asia and elsewhere, would prove a stronger not a weaker obstacle to the further expansion of communist power.[72]

At a point when he was about to be appointed shadow Defence Minister, Powell's argument went against a degree of cross-party consensus which emphasized the importance of maintaining, and even increasing, Britain's presence east of Suez at the expense of Britain's commitment to Germany, where the Soviet threat was perceived to have lessened. This was the line adopted in the government's February 1965 Defence White Paper and in the Conservative policy document *Putting Britain Right Ahead*, which was published for the party conference in October 1965.[73] At the conference itself, Powell took issue with this perspective. He asserted that Western Europe was central to British defence policy.[74] Recognizing that the 'mutual antagonism' between the Soviet Union and China, the Sino-Soviet split, which had emerged publicly in 1961, undermined the notion of a mono-lithic communist threat, Powell argued that among 'the new independent countries in Asia and Africa, the eventual limits of Russian and Chinese advance...will be fixed by a balance of forces which will itself be Asiatic and African', and whose attainment could be 'delayed rather than hastened by Western military presence'.[75] Powell had prompted debate, but Conservative Party policy remained committed to a presence east of Suez.[76] This con-tinued to be the case even after the Labour government committed in July 1967 to British withdrawal from the Far East, with the Singapore base, by the mid-1970s.[77]

Powell's perspective was underpinned by criticisms of Britain's rela-tionship with the United States. In spring 1966, as part of an attack on the Labour government, he argued that Britain had 'lost the ability to distin-guish between an ally and a satellite, or between a friend and a lackey'.[78] Powerfully, Powell argued that, as US involvement in Vietnam had increased, 'Britain's voice has been that of the obedient commentator', bitingly adding that the 'Soviet Union could hardly have expected more favourable comment from its satrapies in Eastern Europe'. Provocatively, Powell suggested that there could be 'contingency plans for sending at least a token British force to Vietnam'.[79] This was 'denied flatly' by Healey.[80] Wilson was, in fact, continuing the policy adopted by the Conservative government: offering moral support to the United States and providing military training for the South Vietnamese army that was backed by the United States. The Wilson government also clandestinely sold arms to the United States, including napalm. Yet, juggling pressure from within his Cabinet, from the parliamentary party and the rank and file with a commitment to maintaining good Anglo-American relations, Wilson resisted strong US pressure to join the war effort in any form.[81] Meanwhile, Powell also seized on the opportunity created by the French questioning of the structure and organization of NATO, which soon led to France's withdrawal from NATO's military structure, to cast doubt on a core part of the Anglo-American relationship. Since the time of the

Korean War in the early 1950s, NATO had an integrated military command under the direction of the United States. As recently as January 1966 Powell had told his colleagues on the LCC that there was 'no advantage for the Opposition in opening the subject up in public, or at this stage thinking aloud about the future of NATO'.[82] Now, however, he publicly asserted that, in spite of opposition from Washington, there was a need 'to restudy the future of that organisation with minds afresh'.[83]

As he responded to the crisis in Southern Rhodesia, arguing strongly against any further British involvement, the full implications of Powell's position became apparent. Southern Rhodesia had been a self-governing Crown Colony since 1923. In November 1965 Ian Smith's white-dominated government made a Unilateral Declaration of Independence (UDI) as Rhodesia (the name had been adopted the previous year, without British approval, when Northern Rhodesia achieved independence as Zambia), upset that the UK would not move it to independence without majority, i.e. black, rule. In Britain the reaction was formidable and saw calls for sanctions on Southern Rhodesia. Yet Powell argued that it was important to accept 'the extent of our real power today in Central Africa' and 'to recognise that the evolution of events in Southern Rhodesia...is no longer ours to dictate'.[84] While Smith had support from the so-called 'Rhodesia Lobby', most notably the Conservative peer Lord Salisbury and the Conservative MP Patrick Wall, the UK, the Commonwealth, and the UN condemned the UDI as illegal and imposed economic sanctions. Powell was thus pitted against the majority view, but he chose a meeting of the Monday Club, the Conservative pressure group formed in 1961 in opposition to decolonization, to set out his position in the grand terms of abating decline, connecting a 'state of national dejection' to the failure to appreciate the importance of geography and specifically distance. With the Monday Club providing an organizational home for many of those supportive of the Smith regime, Powell directly challenged its core imperialist belief, arguing: 'Our present sense of inferiority...is closely linked with our inability or reluctance to concentrate... in the areas of [our] natural strength – the Atlantic and Western Europe'.[85] By late 1968 he was arguing coldly in favour of 'recognising that Rhodesia is an independent albeit a foreign country, having become so...by successful rebellion'.[86] The following year, as it appeared likely that Rhodesia would declare itself a republic, meaning that it would abandon its professed loyalty to the Crown that it had maintained after the UDI, Powell not only called for an end to economic sanctions but also made a broader argument about why he considered intervention to be untenable:

> There are equal or greater numbers of people around the world who detest and abhor the forms of government which prevail in Russia and the other Communist countries of Eastern Europe...The world will become a mad house if nations which dislike the manner in which others are governed take that as a reason for trying to starve or blockade or bully them into changing to their persecutors' satisfaction.[87]

With a focus on Europe, Powell suggested there was a need to remain vigilant to potential changes in the balance of power there. As early as 1954 Powell had considered it likely that West Germany would 'inevitably seek reunion with Eastern Germany'.[88] By 1967, he saw this explicitly on the agenda, alongside the 'slow loosening of the hold of the Soviet Union over the states of eastern Europe' and the 'rise of a certain sense of community in *Mittel-Europa*'—a contested German term for central Europe, originating in the nineteenth century and often involving some degree of German domination of this area, comprising Czechoslovakia, Yugoslavia, Hungary, and Romania, which were now increasingly determined to distance themselves from the Soviet Union.[89] In summer 1968, amid the Prague Spring, a short period of political liberalization in Czechoslovakia, Powell adopted a geological metaphor to argue that 'after 20 years in which the balance of power in Europe has been frozen – frozen hard – into a simple pattern of East v. West, communist v so-called "free"...now the ice is cracking and breaking, the floes are beginning to move, and new patterns of the balance of power are forming themselves'. Returning to his argument about the rise of Mitteleuropa, Powell speculated that the Soviet Union's 'protective belt of subordinates and therefore expendable allies' was potentially 'dissolving'—a development it 'could no longer forcibly prevent'. Significantly, Powell contended that this would call into question the future of NATO, whose *raison d'être* was the maintenance of a 'tacit but none the less valued symbiosis' with the Warsaw Pact, an institutional expression, for now, of a 'balance of power which gave them equal security'.[90]

In some respects Powell's views were not that far from official thinking. The Foreign Office, for example, expected that the Soviet Union would tolerate increasing autonomy in the satellite states and would certainly not invade Czechoslovakia.[91] Yet Powell's prediction was, of course, wrong. With the Soviet suppression of the Prague Spring in late August 1968, Powell accepted that this 'confirmed that Russia intends the present balance of power in Europe…to continue…and, for the time being, can apparently do so'. Powell now backtracked and said the 'conclusion that NATO is not obsolete is the right one'. Nonetheless, he argued that the events had further significance, reinforcing other conclusions he had already reached about the need for conventional forces. In a context where NATO and Warsaw Pact ground forces were evenly matched, he now argued that 'instead of adding the satellite forces to the Russian forces we must cancel them out against each other and then make a further deduction for what the army used to call "internal security"'. Powell suggested that this meant the 'whole theory of the nuclear deterrent as the basis of the balance of power in Europe falls to pieces' because 'if defence by threat of suicide were a tenable theory at all, you do not contemplate suicide, and no-one will think you do, if confronted by an approximately equally matched opponent'.[92]

'An understanding between Britain and Russia'

Gradually Powell's perspective began to change as he came to see shifts in the global and European balance of power clearing the way for Britain and Russia to become potential allies. Powell's position was based primarily on the premise that Russia did not pose a threat to Western Europe. In the mid-1950s Powell had stated that he did not 'believe that Russia seriously expects to be able to embody a reunited Germany in her own empire: large as is the Russian stomach, it is not big enough to digest Germany'.[93] In 1969 Powell articulated his argument more fully. In part, it was underpinned by a strategic awareness that a 'Soviet offensive against Western Europe would mean war – not nuclear war, but just war – with America and Britain, and Russia would feel no certainty she would win that war, even if she overran the whole of Europe'. More fundamentally, however, Powell suggested that it was a mistake to 'believe that Russia wants Western Europe'—on the basis that 'Russian aims and ambitions in Eastern Europe are no guide to Russian aims and ambitions in Western Europe'. Powell added: 'In East Germany the Russians are already holding a wolf by the ears. The last thing they desire is to quadruple that danger by a conquest which would include in their orbit not a fragment of Germany but the entire German people.'[94]

Powell did not, however, endorse détente, a relaxation of international tension which, as a policy, reached its high point in the early 1970s as it was pursued by the United States, initially under President Richard Nixon and his influential National Security Advisor and subsequently Secretary of State Henry Kissinger. This was the era of the Strategic Arms Limitation Talks, resulting in the SALT I (1972) and II (1979) agreements.[95] Conservative opposition to faith in détente increased from the mid-1970s, with the argument increasingly made, including by Margaret Thatcher as Conservative leader after 1975, that the Soviet Union was actually taking the opportunity to increase its military forces.[96] Powell's argument rested more explicitly on his realist interpretation of international balance-of-power politics. As such, it pitted him against some of the strongest supporters of détente, often found in the Labour Party, who saw it as a means of reforming international relations and of bringing the Cold War to an end.[97] Powell explained:

All states live in a condition of balance which assumes tension. That tension may be excessive or dangerous, but it only becomes dangerous when the balance is disturbed. What we ought to be looking for all the time – what is the business of international statesmanship, in my view as a person who believes there are such things as 'nations' – is to maintain that balance which will prevent tension either breaking or being so relaxed that an entirely new structure is called for at a risk of violence. Clearly, there are circumstances in which naval agreements, military agreements which save both parties money without altering their pursuit of their respective interests, are common sense, and then they'll have 'em. But what I'm complaining of is calling these things 'détente' as though by such arrangements a radical change in the nature of international relations or an elimination of some of the persistent and permanent tensions between states will take place.[98]

Powell also positioned himself against a powerful critique of the Soviet Union, emanating from Liberal and Labour circles, which increasingly emphasized human rights abuses in the communist world, with particular concern for the treatment of political dissidents. Human rights, emphasizing individual freedoms, rose to prominence in the years after 1945 with a commitment to them enshrined in the UN Commission on Human Rights. With the West's rhetorical embrace of them placed against the Soviet bloc's commitment to wider collective rights relating to broader economic and social goals, human rights became a key battleground of the Cold War. From the mid-1970s a concern that human rights were being overlooked amid the quest for détente developed in both the US and the UK and played a part in prompting Jimmy Carter, US President from 1977, to make a search for them an important element of his appeal. At the same time, détente and human rights became formally linked, forming part of the 1975 East–West Helsinki Agreement.[99] Powell's objection to human rights went right to the heart of his views on national sovereignty. He held that a 'human being per se can have no rights, because all rights are the converse of obligations...between human beings in a society'. He considered that there was 'no such thing as society in general; there are only societies in particular'. Powell's view was that 'all international conventions to recognise human rights...involve the cession of sovereignty; that is, they imply the transfer to an external authority of the power to secure enforcement of its decrees inside the respective states'.[100] With the Moscow Helsinki Group set up to monitor Soviet compliance with the agreement, including the commitment to human rights, Powell also made it clear that this undertaking was fundamentally at odds with his view of how states behaved. He considered it 'futile' to attempt 'to bring about a radical alteration of the way in which the Russian state treats its nationals' because, in the final resort, it would always 'act in its own interest'.[101]

In early 1979 Powell argued that 'with an almost geological inevitability...the power balance of the nations of the world' had begun to shift. He saw an important expression of it in the 'rapprochement of the United States with China – and not just China, but a China which appears to be now positively seeking the role of a super-star on the world stage'. This process had begun in the early 1970s under Nixon and Kissinger. Powell argued that this alignment 'could not but release a chain reaction', with the 'Soviets and the Warsaw Pact...out of equipoise with a combination of North America, Western Europe and the new China'. Powell argued:

We may start from the assumption that the antithesis between the USA and the USSR is fundamental – as polar neighbours, as technological competitors on the highest plane, and as mutually uncomprehending ideologies. If Western Europe and China are both to be placed in the American pan of the balance, it must follow that between America and Europe in the Western hemisphere and between America and China in the Eastern hemisphere a counterpoise will be called into existence by sheer necessity. The result of following this reasoning through is to produce a picture which is historically familiar in the West and more novel in the East. Historically the existence of Russia has been the ultimate guarantee of the survival of Britain as an independent nation...in 1812, in 1914, in 1942...Russia has always been for Britain the greatest power out beyond her continental enemy, the only nation possessing the inexhaustible resources of manpower and reserves of space which render her superior to any land army in ability to survive. The fundamental fact of geopolitics has nothing to do with political or any other kind of affinity...When in the last decades of the twentieth century necessity restores an understanding between Britain and Russia, the *entente* will not be *cordiale*; but *entente* it will still be...But what of the Eastern aspect?...The rise of China adumbrates for Japan a relationship with Asiatic Russia not radically different from that of Britain with European Russia.[102]

Powell's argument for an alliance with the Soviet Union was a radical one to make. Hostility to the Soviet Union, and an embrace of the Anglo-American relationship, ran deep in Conservative circles and had recently been energized under Thatcher, who devoted considerable effort to developing stronger relations with the United States and had taken pains to warn of the continuing, and even growing, Soviet threat.[103] Yet, with Thatcher in government after May 1979, Powell made clear his criticism of her foreign policy in practice. Shortly after the Soviet invasion of Afghanistan in late 1979, Powell repeated his argument that Russia did not have any desire to invade Western Europe.[104] He also made clear his opposition to taking any kind of retaliatory action against the Soviet Union, including the proposed boycott of the 1980 Moscow Olympics, which Thatcher followed US President Carter in endorsing but that, in the British case, she was unable to achieve.[105] Powell dismissed the boycott on the basis that the 'judgment of the Russians depends not upon words or upon professions which have only to be examined to be seen to be hollow but upon their estimates of real power and real intentions'. His own view, however, was that Britain 'should not have reacted at all'.[106]

The unfolding of the Falklands War in 1982 brought a significant reconciliation with Thatcher but only intensified Powell's desire to speak against the US alliance. Following the Argentine invasion in April of the British Overseas Territory (formerly a Crown Colony) in the South Atlantic, over which it claimed sovereignty, Powell was invited to discuss the conflict with the Prime Minister on 5 May as the only Privy Counsellor representing a Northern Ireland constituency.[107] Powell praised Thatcher's decision swiftly to dispatch a naval task force and later to launch an amphibious assault. Yet he took issue with the proposition that Britain was now 'obeying the orders of the United Nations', whose Security Council had passed Resolution 502 demanding immediate Argentine withdrawal. He now dismissed the UN as 'an institutionalisation not of law, international or any other, but of the existing constellations of real power'.[108] Powell had been critical of the UN since the early 1950s, but it was only after 1970 that he attacked its 'fundamental contradiction': taking 'as its basis...the sovereign, self-conscious nation' but ignoring the fact that the 'very nature and existence of nation itself are inseparable from force'.[109] Powell argued that 'Britain had acted in her own right and on her own behalf, and had acted because she was a naval power threatened in her own...maritime, element'.[110] As far back as 1969 Powell had identified the strategic importance of the Falkland Islands in enabling Britain 'to give battle and exercise surveillance far out in the Atlantic'.[111] With the Argentine surrender in June, Powell subsequently praised the victory as a 'demonstration of British power and of the will to use it'. He made much of the fact that 'the war was one which the United States obviously did not want it [Britain] to fight'.[112] There was an initial US concern that Argentina would ask the Soviet Union for support, and there was an early attempt to mediate to end the conflict but, as Argentina refused the US peace initiatives, the United States sided with the UK, providing military equipment and prohibiting arms sales to Argentina. For Powell, this ushered in a 'great liberation...when...the scales fell from the eyes of the British public and they beheld the United States not in the fairy-tale disguise sustained so sedulously since 1942 but as that nation really is—divergent from Britain in its interests, attitudes and intentions and neither friend nor foe to this country except as its perception of American advantage and American purpose dictates'.[113]

This realization, according to Powell, provided a wholesale opportunity to debate 'the conventional assumptions of Britain's foreign policy', not just the US alliance and its institutional form, NATO, but also the 'grand theory of nuclear deterrence' under whose auspices US cruise missiles had been stationed in Britain since 1979. With the most vocal opposition to the missiles coming from the Left, Powell now argued that for too long arguments against the nuclear deterrent had been 'monopolised by the pacifists and the weirdy wing of the Labour party'.[114] Powell spoke amid heightened East–West tension, with increased public apprehension about nuclear holocaust that saw growing support for the pressure group, the Campaign for Nuclear Disarmament (CND).[115] He argued, 'I have a premonition that the question of Britain's nuclear armament is not only rising towards peak intensity but is this time approaching the point of decision'. Labour leader Michael Foot was a founder member of CND and continued to advocate unilateral nuclear disarmament, but Powell still called for a challenge to 'an unanalysed consensus...which change of party government did not seriously disturb', with Labour in power as committed to it as the Conservatives. With his position based on the argument that nuclear weapons would not be used, Powell argued that it was possible to conduct the debate 'without recourse to morality or religion'.[116] This was not just an expression of

Powell's determination to avoid the discussion of religion in politics but also a direct response to the long-standing 'moralistic' and Christian tone of much support for unilateral nuclear disarmament.[117] In Methodist circles this stretched beyond purely pacifist sentiment.[118] And Bruce Kent, a Catholic priest, was CND's General Secretary. Powell had, meanwhile, adopted a line of 'patriotic populism'.[119] In the 1983 general election, Powell made the case that there were 'things too important to be left to the experts. There are things too important to be left to the politicians. The nuclear question is one of them. The people at large ought to be enabled to take it in hand.' With the government taking a firm line against CND, and with the Secretary of State for Defence, Michael Heseltine, seeking to link it with communism, Powell warned against considering that those who 'dare to discuss or examine it [the nuclear question] must be evil or unpatriotically disposed'.[120] In his first speech in the new Parliament, Powell went further, making it clear that he favoured unilateral nuclear disarmament. He stated: 'I do not believe that there are rational grounds on which the deformation of our defence preparations in the United Kingdom by our current determination to maintain a current independent nuclear deterrent can be justified', adding that 'I would much sooner that the power to use it was not in the hands of any individual in this country at all'.[121]

A new world order?

In the late 1980s, Powell saw great changes afoot in the balance of power, which led him to argue, once again, for the alignment of Britain and the Soviet Union. Thatcher had played an important role in bringing US President Ronald Reagan and Soviet leader Mikhail Gorbachev together, most notably in a summit at Reykjavik in Iceland in October 1986. Yet, with the two leaders discussing, but not agreeing to, the elimination of all strategic nuclear weapons within ten years, Thatcher now worried that the removal of the US nuclear umbrella from Europe would leave it vulnerable to Soviet conventional military force. Powell, by contrast, delighted in the prospect that the United States would 'no longer be the self-evidently indispensable protector of the nations of Western and Southern Europe'.[122] He was soon talking about nothing less than 'the death and burial of the American Empire'.[123] As Gorbachev met Thatcher at the end of 1987, Powell argued that this represented a 'profound rearrangement' in international relations. As 'Central Europe (Mitteleuropa) is beginning to be discerned', Powell argued that 'Britain and Russia are starting to rediscover and explore the mutual interest of those on either side of Middle Europe in a counter-balance'.[124] He considered that this would be especially important if Germany—which had been 'frozen' into the 'most unnatural division of all'—was reunited.[125] Tellingly, Thatcher's own view in October 1986 had been that 'Gorbachev clearly was trying to divide Europe from America'.[126]

By 1989 Powell's stance towards Russia was increasingly favourable. As he had first prematurely speculated in 1968, he now argued that Russia 'no longer contemplates maintaining the alignment between itself and the Warsaw Pact countries of Eastern Europe by military intervention'.[127] In April 1989 Solidarity, which had led the protest movement against Soviet control in Poland since 1980, was legalized, and partly free elections were called for June. In May, Hungary dismantled its border fence with Austria, allowing an outflow of people from East Germany. Powell's views received wide airing as he was asked to present a BBC *Byline* programme, stepping in for the *Daily Telegraph* journalist John Keegan at the last moment and undertaking two visits to Russia in May and June.[128] With the programme entitled 'Embracing the Bear', Powell argued that 'what the Russians are looking for...looks remarkably like sovereignty – a continuing but non-political focus of the obedience and loyalty of a whole nation'.[129] This was important because Powell considered that 'Britain has a deep interest in Russia's ability, for the first time in its history, to find its own solution to the problem of combining the durability and authority of the state with the accountability of the state's servants to the governed and with the consent of the citizenry to the policies and behaviour of its government'.[130] By November, as the Berlin Wall fell, Powell argued that developments 'taking place on the other side of the Channel have resurrected, as never before since the mid 19th century, the question of nation', with 'a will to self-determination' and 'self-government' 'crashing through all existing political barriers', meaning that 'nationality stands revealed as a natural force.'[131]

The end of Soviet control over Eastern Europe had seemingly vindicated Powell's fundamental outlook on international affairs, but the events that followed—the collapse of the Soviet Union by the end of 1991 and the corresponding emergence of the United States into a position of unparalleled dominance in world affairs—soon troubled Powell. In the first instance, he expounded arguments about the national interest as a guiding principle in

Figure 2. Powell filming the BBC programme 'Embracing the Bear' in Moscow, May 1989.

foreign policy more fully than ever before. With the Iraqi invasion of Kuwait in summer 1990, Powell argued that national security, 'the only reason for which British Servicemen ought to be ordered into action', was not threatened, adding that 'Saddam Hussein has a long way to go yet before his troops come storming up the beaches of Kent or Sussex'. Acknowledging

that the 'world is full of evil men engaged in doing evil things', Powell
frankly argued that, 'We as a nation have no interest in the existence or non-
existence of Kuwait.' Repeating the argument he had made about South
East Asia in the 1960s, Powell argued that every 'advance in power or territory by a Middle East state produces a shift in the regional balance of power
and adds to the forces, physical and political, arrayed against further advance',
adding that if 'the balance of power in the Middle East ever mattered, it was
to a British Empire which exists no more'. With the UN Security Council
condemning the invasion and calling for unconditional withdrawal, Powell
argued that if 'we are bound by the votes of a body representing countries
no more concerned than we are with what Iraq is or Iraq does, we have
given up responsibility for our own actions' [132]

As British military intervention looked likely, Powell took on the 'false-
hood' about the UN that he had earlier described as 'the theory of the
indivisibility of peace, the proposition that war in one part of the world
necessarily exposes nations in other parts of the world to an increased risk
of war'.[133] Arguing that it was an overall and regional balance of power that
preserved peace, Powell dismissed the argument that there would be 'no war
if everybody else forcibly opposes a potential belligerent or punishes an
actual one', because it wrongly assumed that 'states whose interests are not
involved can adjudicate impartially upon the causes of conflict and ought to
risk their own blood and treasure where they themselves are not endan-
gered'.[134] With the US-led assault on Kuwait and Iraq taking place from
mid-January 1991, Powell lashed out at the United States, arguing that the
'equilibrium has now been radically disturbed through the impact of non-
regional military power, through the United States reaching out from a
totally separate geographical context and drawing into the orbit of its intervention other non-Middle Eastern powers like France and Britain'. Yet
Powell argued that Britain's 'oceanic perspective' alongside Russia's 'Asiatic
perspective' meant that they 'ought therefore to be mutually comprehend-
ing and mutually supportive in the construction in Europe and in the
Middle East of a regional balance of power'.[135]

Later in 1991, the developing situation in Yugoslavia, which was bitterly
fracturing along ethnic and nationalist lines, even though it involved
civil war, led Powell to assert the same point about the imperative of
non-intervention:

> The state called Yugoslavia has ceased to comprise inhabitants who are willing
> to be governed as such. What will be the consequences of that, who are we

to decide?... War, called civil war is one way of ascertaining, perhaps the only available way. If we say that there shall not be civil war - and even more, if we take upon ourselves to try to prevent civil war - we usurp the decision who shall govern whom and how and where and within what boundaries. Who gave us that right? Who said it was any business of ours?... It would be our business if one outcome or another were to be dangerous to our own security, though, if so, the danger would need to be distinct and palpable, with no question of any interest beyond security, such, for instance, as some contingent economic advantage or disadvantage.[136]

Powell was even more outspoken, as there were increased calls for humanitarian intervention. With the balance of power in mind, Powell argued that 'by delaying the attainment of that equilibrium, the so-called "humanitarian" endeavours of the interventionists are prolonging the suffering of those whom they purport to be attempting to help: by intervening in what is no concern of ours, we are doing evil, not good'.[137] Powell put the case very coldly, but he was taking the same line as many others in the Conservative Party, including the Foreign Secretary, Douglas Hurd, who, explicitly concerned with the national interest, argued that no national interests were at stake. This issue was becoming an increasingly contested one, with, for example, the Conservative MP Patrick Cormack arguing that it was in British interests to act in defence of both NATO and the UN, the argument being that the national interest was tied to the institutions of which the UK was part.[138]

By the middle of 1992, Powell had developed his position into a full-blown critique of the 'new world order', a term that had gained increasing usage to describe the hegemonic position of the United States. He argued that this had originated in the United States at the time of the Gulf War and 'did immense damage', as the 'United States, wearing the mask of the United Nations, persuaded us to repel the invasion of Kuwait, an independent state, by Iraq, another independent state'. He argued that a further development had taken place as the UN made a 'flagrant and unjustifiable attempt to intervene in the internal affairs of Yugoslavia' and had thus become a 'self-contradiction'.[139] Powell once again explicitly linked Britain's relationship with the United States to decline. Despite his hopes about US demise, he was now as pessimistic as during the Cold War and, with pressure on the UK to adopt a 'peacekeeping' role, he argued that much 'of our present malaise arises from the abject subordination to America and American purposes'.[140]

2

Economics

Speaking in 1988, Powell readily admitted that, in economic terms, what 'used to be called Powellite... has recently been re-designated Thatcherite'.[1] With much of the biographical writing about Powell produced after this point, we have a clear long-term sense of how this happened. In the 1950s and 1960s, working in a very different context—one where free-market ideas were relatively marginalized—Powell had adumbrated a large part of what became the economic agenda of the Thatcher governments in the 1980s: a general opposition to state control and planning; a concern to prioritize control of the monetary source of inflation; the privatization of previously nationalized industries; and cuts to direct (income) tax. Recent research has, moreover, sought to delineate the specific influence of Powell on the Conservative policymakers surrounding Thatcher, placing his contribution alongside broader trends in economic opinion—both domestically and internationally.[2]

Powell put his own particular twist on the intellectual framework that underpinned his position, which in today's terminology would be called a 'neo-liberal' one. Neo-liberalism is an overused, and often crudely applied, term in twenty-first-century public life.[3] Not least through the work of Ben Jackson, we are, however, beginning to understand the phenomenon more precisely.[4] There is little doubt that Powell embraced the core tenets of the perspective. In 1970, Milton Friedman, the pre-eminent neo-liberal economist based at the University of Chicago, told a correspondent that Powell had 'a clearer conception of the relation between economic and personal freedom, than any other major political figure I have ever met'.[5] Indeed, Powell used this connection both to support his strategic call for the Conservatives to emphasize choice in contrast to Labour control and to sustain dramatic arguments that in government first Labour, and then the Conservatives under Edward Heath, were totalitarian and 'fascist'. Powell also engaged closely, from an early stage, with the neo-liberal Institute of

Economic Affairs (IEA) think tank, and it was through his association with the IEA that he developed his assault—at the turn of the 1960s—on the prevalent left-wing call for further state planning to reverse British economic decline. Yet, as this chapter shows, there were issues on which Powell took a different stance to the bulk of neo-liberal opinion—with his commitment to the National Health Service (NHS) being a case in point. Eventually on board with Thatcher's attempt to link economic change with national revival, Powell also savaged what he saw as her misguided attempt to connect education policy to economic growth in a bid to prevent international economic eclipse.

Towards the 'freer economy'

Powell fought his first campaign in the Normanton by-election in early 1947 in a context where the Labour government was still talking about the creation of a 'planned socialist economy' (despite its increasing reliance in practice on Keynesian techniques) and was in the process of undertaking a substantial programme of nationalization—including coal and energy—that eventually amounted to about 20 per cent of the economy.[6] Powell made a case for the detrimental economic impact of 'state socialism' where 'centralisation' led to 'bureaucratic slowness and rigidity'.[7] Along with many other Conservatives, he cited housing under Aneurin Bevan, where the government had not met its promised quotas of houses built, as 'a fine example of the disastrous consequences which come from applying Socialist principles to the life of Britain'.[8] In the aftermath of the Second World War, there was an acute housing shortage in Britain. Bevan arguably prioritized quality over quantity in council houses and had only reluctantly agreed to a target. Nevertheless, the failure to achieve it was readily exploited by the Opposition, which was, with deputy leader Anthony Eden playing a prominent role, committed to the extension of the 'property-owning democracy'.[9] Powell echoed this note too, stating that 'Conservatives believed that the institution of private property . . . corresponded to a deep urge of human nature', unlike 'Socialism, which strove to whittle away the incentives to enterprise, to self-help and to thrift'.[10]

Powell took his arguments further to suggest that 'State planning . . . must inevitably lead to the destruction of . . . constitutional liberties'.[11] With a considerable extension of state control over the economy, Powell contended that some people were now 'reluctant to disclose their political views for fear of jeopardising employment or livelihood under the State or a public authority'. Even more provocatively, Powell argued that the 'Gestapo, as yet in a mild form and under the reassuring title of "inspectors" or "Enforcement Officers", pry into our private affairs to see if we are breaking any of the multitudinous orders and regulations by which our lives and actions are restricted'.[12] Powell's remarks mirrored Winston Churchill's famous comment during the 1945 general election that 'No Socialist Government conducting the entire life and industry of the country could afford to allow free, sharp, or violently-worded expressions of public discontent. They would have to fall back on some form of *Gestapo*, no doubt very humanely directed in the first instance.' As historian Richard Toye has emphasized, there was a wider context here in which insults of this kind were exchanged between the Conservative and Labour parties, with the latter arguing that Conservatism was a 'kind of cryptofascism'. It has also been suggested that Churchill was influenced by Friedrich Hayek's argument in *The Road to Serfdom* (1944) that political and personal freedom depended on economic freedom and that state planning led to totalitarianism.[13] This position certainly became part of Powell's overall framework, but it is necessary, right from the start, to draw some distinctions between Powell and those closest to Hayek.

In 1947 Hayek had formed the Mont Pelerin Society, a discussion group on economic liberalism, whose members soon developed a 'distinctly neo-liberal ideology' that involved a powerful critique of the 'Keynesian welfare state'.[14] Powell was, however, more in tune with earlier traditions of neo-liberalism, such as that articulated by Walter Lippman in the mid-1930s—the point when the term neo-liberal itself began to be used—that also opposed socialist central planning but accepted parts of the welfare state.[15] Even in Normanton, a mining constituency where his Labour opponent was a miner, Powell made clear his opposition to nationalization, alongside a brief reference to the 'limitations' of Keynesian methods.[16] Powell was adamant that 'each in his own sphere, usually knows best how to conduct his business and meet emergencies' and 'knows what are his own desires and how to fulfil them', but he added an important qualification:

> Conservatism has always believed that the Government has the duty of watching carefully and studying deeply, the pattern of the community's life, so that where the state, on behalf of its citizens as a whole, has to intervene to render indispensable aid, or to prevent social evil, the intervention may take place in the right form, at the right time and place, and cause the minimum interference with the life of the community and the freedom of the subject.[17]

Powell expressed a particular commitment to the NHS and—at this stage—to the universal social security provision of national insurance.[18] It is worth remembering, however, that Powell's views here did not set him apart from his Conservative colleagues. A commitment to these schemes had been accepted, in some form, by the Conservative Party in the wartime coalition government. And, with legislation to establish them passing Parliament in 1946, there was also a growing recognition in Conservative circles of their public popularity.

Powell reflected further on economic and social policy as one of the original members of the One Nation Group. The group's inaugural publication, *One Nation* (1950), sought—in Powell's words—to articulate a 'true Tory social policy' which operated on a 'fundamentally different' premise to the Socialist one. Powell argued:

> The Socialist aims at equality (sometimes disguised as equality of opportunity) and sets no limit to the sphere of government. He therefore uses the social services as a deliberate means of equalisation and fearlessly entrusts to the State the responsibility for fulfilling all the individual's needs. The Tory believes that inequality is not only natural and inevitable, but within the framework of a sound society is of infinite value. He sets definite limits to the sphere of government and the responsibilities of the State, and would preserve and strengthen those of the individual and the family.[19]

This outlook underpinned what Robert Walsha has described as the 'principal contribution of *One Nation* to Conservative thinking... its rejection of socialism's universalizing welfare tendencies in favour of the considered prioritizing of social provision'.[20] Powell's 1952 book *The Social Services: Means and Needs*, co-authored with Iain Macleod, pushed in the same direction, asking whether social-service provision should rest on a means test—something that had proved controversial amid high unemployment in interwar Britain but which chimed with a developing Conservative rank-and-file opinion in favour of a more selective approach.[21]

Powell left the One Nation Group in 1956, having been appointed Parliamentary Secretary at the Ministry of Housing at the end of the previous year, but he continued to engage with the same themes.[22] In 1957, as a member of the party's Policy Study Group, he suggested 'the whole machinery of social security has to be overhauled'.[23] Powell held that 'the insurance principle had broken down'.[24] In suggesting a solution, Powell followed neo-liberals, including Hayek, who advocated a national minimum through collective provision.[25] Powell's particular concern was old-age pensions, where, seeking to reduce overall cost, he argued that 'the only solution is to move over on to the basis of need: to guarantee to all in retirement a minimum income which could and should be substantially above the present National Assistance scales'. In a comment that made clear both his commitment to the welfare state but also his demand for reform, Powell argued:

> The reality is that the State owes everybody a livelihood in retirement (or mis-fortune, for that matter)...We are today paying vast numbers and amounts of insurance benefits to recipients who do not actually need them (and inciden-tally in all cases have not actuarially earned them either), while paying others less than they need and so sending them on to the National Assistance Board.[26]

So far as the wider economy was concerned, Powell's thinking was initially hampered by his lingering commitment to the Empire. In his first election campaign in Wolverhampton South West, he spoke of his commitment to 'competitive enterprise working in a framework of Empire unity'.[27] Viewing 'profits and rewards' as 'the most powerful stimuli', Powell subsequently argued in One Nation circles that the 'freer economy' offered a way for Britain to 'regain much of its former pre-eminence and be able to act as a proper partner and when needs be competitor of the present greatest economic power in the world, the United States'. Yet, alongside his call for 'much greater freedom of trade throughout the world', he argued:

> We are welcomed much more warmly in the Dominions and the Countries of the British Empire, and so Britain should always first try in these territories to find and develop the raw materials which are needed. Imperial Preference and other tariffs are essential tactical weapons for developing industry and trade though they are not ends of policy.[28]

As Powell began to argue that the Empire's collapse was unavoidable, these commitments were quietly dropped as other aspects of his thinking were developed more fully. In 1954 the One Nation publication *Change is our Ally*, which Powell jointly edited, argued that the 'efficient co-ordination' of indus-try could only come about under a system that prioritized 'the exercise of consumer choice' and economic competition.[29] Three years later, on the Policy Study Group, Powell called for 'another wave of denationalisation, to be carried out in the next Parliament', arguing forcefully that 'the idea of a free economy was irreconcilable with this great block of capital investment which was unrelated to the general economic situation except by arbitrary decision'.[30] Significantly, broader trends were moving in Powell's direction. By the middle of the 1950s there was growing Conservative rank-and-file discontent with 'inefficient' public ownership, with the newly formed

Middle Class Alliance and the People's League for the Defence of Freedom particularly animated on the issue.[31]

As Financial Secretary to the Treasury from 1957, Powell also began to articulate broadly monetarist arguments, an increasingly important aspect of neo-liberal politics, which viewed inflation as a monetary phenomenon generated largely by public spending and sought to control it as a priority over unemployment.[32] In November 1957, Powell had publicly expressed his concern about the 'supply of money' and argued that 'until inflation is definitely halted, every proposal that means higher expenditure in the Budget ought instantly to be met by critical questioning and if need be by protest and contradiction'.[33] In January 1958, Powell, together with the Chancellor of the Exchequer, Peter Thorneycroft, and the Economic Secretary to the Treasury, Nigel Birch, resigned from the government after having their call for larger cuts in estimated government expenditure rejected. Powell was later adamant that this was 'essentially a monetarist protest'.[34] Taken as a whole, some qualifications are necessary. The lines of the dispute were blurred and in practice were about the size of cuts rather than the cuts per se. Thorneycroft, moreover, despite his anxieties about inflation, was also concerned about maintaining a low level of unemployment.[35] Yet, for Powell himself, the incident showed that he had absorbed some monetarist thinking—influenced by his discussions with the Cambridge economist Sir Dennis Robertson.[36] Indeed, Powell's debt was clear when, in 1960, he told Robertson that he hoped to 'continue to sit at your feet'.[37]

The free society and a 'new kind of patriotism'

From 1959, Powell took a new direction as he began to collaborate outside party circles. He started to work closely with the IEA, which had been formed by Antony Fisher in 1955 to advance free-market politics and was now led by the economists Ralph Harris and Arthur Seldon. The IEA was part of an international neo-liberal network spanning out from the Mont Pelerin Society and had been set up on Hayek's prompting.[38] It was not exclusively Conservative. Hayek was emphatic that he was not a Conservative because the term implied opposition to change and an inability to offer an alternative direction, and he described himself—with misgivings—as a liberal.[39] Seldon was a supporter of the British Liberal Party, where forms of neo-liberalism had first been articulated in the 1950s.[40] Powell's involvement grew after Harris invited him to write a book for the IEA entitled *Saving in a Free Society*—in which he expressed his view that the 'terms "free economy" and "free society" are to me interchangeable'.[41] Powell was soon discussing 'the educational work of the Institute and...how this might be put to the best use in the next year or two' with Harris, Seldon, Fisher, and others.[42] After Powell was appointed Minister of Health at the end of July 1960, he pledged 'to continue exchanges of ideas – sub rosa', i.e. confidentially.[43] This whole approach was in keeping with IEA strategy, shaped by Hayek, to concentrate on influencing elites rather than public opinion and, thereby, to disseminate ideas in policy debates.[44]

As early as 1960, Powell related free-market economics to his concern to tackle the 'fear of falling behind in the economic race'.[45] This was a reference to the growing tendency to compare British economic performance unfavourably with that of West Germany, France, and Italy. From a broadly left-wing perspective, urging more economic planning, this was the line taken in both Andrew Shonfield's *British Economic Policy Since the War* (1958) and, a little later, in Michael Shanks's *The Stagnant Society* (1961)—both 'Penguin Specials'.[46] These comparisons were possible because, by the late 1950s, new types of economic calculations and statistics—most notably concerning national income, industrial production, productivity, and shares of world trade—saw UK performance increasingly placed in an international context.[47] In an IEA publication, Powell made clear his objections: the international comparisons were 'notoriously insecure'; the continental economies were simply catching up after both a later start to industrialization and substantial war damage; and progress had been made 'not merely unforeseen and unprovided for by the organs of state direction, but often in spite of them'.[48] Powell was particularly riled by the publication of the renowned anti-communist Arthur Koestler's edited collection of essays entitled 'Suicide of a Nation' in the left-of-centre literary magazine *Encounter* in July 1963 which, as the title suggested, saw the situation in dire terms and called for much greater state direction of the economy.[49] Encouraged by the Conservative Minister without Portfolio and later editor of the *Daily Telegraph*, Bill Deedes, Powell had attempted to publish a reply in *Encounter*, but this was (politely) rejected by its co-editor, the poet and writer Stephen Spender.[50] Powell did, however, get the chance to air his response the following year in the IEA's rejoinder to Koestler, *Rebirth of Britain*. Here Powell likened the frequent recourse to statistics to 'the habit of a hypochondriac taking his pulse and temperature every five minutes and going into a tizzy over every rise or fall', and he spoke of the enormous task of 'overcoming prejudices which have been allowed to harden against the market economy'.[51]

The debate reached into party politics too. With Harold Wilson as a key influence, Labour had seized the opportunity to argue that more planning would boost performance, making this case forcefully in the 1961 policy document *Signpost for the Sixties*, which put British performance in an explicitly comparative context.[52] In response, Powell lamented that 'the socialist opposition, ready as always to decry their own nation, have compiled "league tables" designed to show that we do worse than anyone else'.[53] In 1963, he developed this into a more positive point. With much of the 'declinist' literature discussing the harmful effects, economic and psychological, of Britain's lingering imperial commitments and suggesting more broadly that there was something 'wrong' with British society, Powell argued:

> Every nation, to live healthily and to live happily, needs a patriotism. Britain to-day, after all the changes of the last decades, needs a new kind of patriotism and is feeling its way towards it. Whatever may have been the past, the basis of that pride and that hope for Britain to-day is overwhelmingly economic . . . The policy which matches such a patriotism [is] not a policy which would like to concentrate all the economic decisions that really matter in a little group of planners at the centre. It is a policy which wants to meet change half way, which tries to widen the field for enterprise and competition, which is not afraid to leave important decisions to be taken by people for themselves, which rewards and encourages success instead of penalising it, which is not ashamed that the nation and its members should seek the best return from their efforts and their resources.[54]

Explicitly talking about the need to replace 'the old, imperial patriotism of the past', Powell envisaged a coming battle that would pit 'the free society versus the Socialist state', with consequences that extended 'far beyond economics'.[55] In 1960 the IEA had given Powell a copy of Hayek's *Constitution of Liberty*, with Powell subsequently telling Harris that 'I do not remember when I read a book with so much enthusiasm'.[56] Later that year, the IEA introduced Powell to Hayek himself.[57] Against the backdrop of the ongoing Cold War, Powell now echoed Hayek:

> It is no accident that wherever the state has taken economic decision away from the citizen, it has deprived him of his other liberties as well. It is not that there was some peculiarity in the character of the Russians or the other Communist nations which predisposed them to servitude. It is that state socialism is incompatible with individual liberty of thought, speech and action.[58]

Powell sought to give these points a wider resonance. He memorably described the choice as that between the 'market or the machine gun'.[59] Developing an argument that mid-nineteenth-century economic liberals had outlined—in embryonic form—amid the rise of consumerism, Powell further contended that the 'free enterprise economy' was 'the true counterpart of democracy . . . the only system which gives everyone a say'. He went on: 'Everyone who goes into a shop and chooses one article over another is casting a vote in the economic ballot box . . . nobody, not even, the poorest, is disenfranchised.'[60]

Powell's engagement with arguments about economic decline was unusual for a Conservative politician at this stage. In government since 1951, the Conservatives usually found themselves held responsible for any supposed failings.[61] Yet Powell's position was not just an attack on Labour but also on his own party. Enid Russell-Smith, a senior civil servant who worked closely with Powell at the Ministry of Health, described how he sought to challenge 'a certain malaise in the Conservative Party'.[62] First and foremost, he called on the Conservatives to present themselves unashamedly as a 'capitalist party' and 'to tell itself and others, loud and clear, what it stands for . . . and what kind of future it wishes for the nation'.[63] With the Conservatives defeated in the 1964 general election, Powell intensified his free-market advocacy within the party. Speaking at Swinton Conservative College, the political education centre, he considered it significant that a period in opposition offered the party the opportunity 'to find a new position' that combatted 'the aching feeling that other nations know where they are going, and that somehow we do not'.[64] Tellingly, at a point when he was publicly criticizing British subservience to the United States in international affairs, he told an audience from the American Chamber of Commerce that while the United States had 'much to teach us about the principles of capitalism and free enterprise', it was ultimately 'not the free economy that stands to be judged by the United States, but the United States by the free economy'.[65]

The role of the state

At the same time, Powell engaged in a parallel debate over the role of the state, which brought him into conflict not just with the Conservative Party but also the IEA. His overall view was that it was possible to 'reconcile free enterprise and planning in building the future of Britain, provided that the state doesn't try to plan those things which free enterprise can do better'.[66] Powell was clear that the state had responsibility for national security, the 'outer frame or condition precedent of the nation's life'. He also considered that 'the maintenance of law and the prevention of crime, are essentially, at all times and in all places, the business of the state'.[67] This was, to a large extent, uncontroversial. However, so far as the economy was concerned, Powell entered more contested waters.

Powell made a sweeping attack on the 'group of policies known collectively as aid to "underdeveloped" or "developing" countries' on the basis that they were 'both futile and harmful to those countries themselves'. Powell considered that the money spent on aid programmes 'would produce greater value if invested elsewhere, or if invested in the same countries but in different directions' and so was 'contrary to the interest of both parties to the transaction'. He added that 'the fact that they are supplied to and through governments eliminates at the outset the market forces which might at least have selected the most profitable applications, and gives the maximum play to political factors, with their built-in bias towards prestige projects and works of national, partisan or even personal glorification and self-advertisement'. As such, he considered that aid programmes would likely produce more 'disenchantment and recrimination than gratitude and a common front against the alternative philosophy of communism', one of the underlying motivations at this time, especially from the United States, which sought a larger multilateral effort.[68] Powell's position related to his rejection of the Commonwealth (between 1958 and 1971 at least 80 per cent of British aid went to Commonwealth countries). It was also part of his challenge to consensus because there was broad agreement between Conservative and Labour on the need for a substantial aid programme.[69]

In domestic terms, Powell made it clear that he did not support the use of prices and incomes policies, controls that sought to restrain inflation.[70] He had, as Minister of Health, awkwardly endorsed them.[71] Now, with Labour in government, he published an article in The Times, which argued that they could not be effective because a 'substantial proportion of incomes are not determined collectively at all' and that 'supply and demand will continue to determine a great mass of remuneration at levels which bear no relation to any national decisions designed to achieve a given overall rate of increase'.[72] As the government established the National Board for Prices and Incomes, Powell was at odds with the view of the Conservative leadership that 'we should wait and see how things worked out with the government's incomes policy'.[73]

Powell was also opposed to regional planning policy, through which both Conservative and Labour governments sought to play an active role in maintaining industry, and therefore employment, across the UK. Speaking in Scotland in April 1964, and addressing the fact that unemployment there was twice the national average, Powell derided the response of the current Conservative government 'inducing or cajoling particular firms and industries to establish themselves in places which they would not otherwise have chosen' through, for example, government loans and tax concessions. Powell argued that this distorted market processes, adding that if 'labour were perfectly mobile...the level of unemployment would be precisely the same everywhere' and suggesting that 'many Scots have grumbled and grizzled and moped themselves into a state of immobility'.[74] Powell's position—and his rhetoric—was, of course, provocative. It was, therefore, unsurprising that it met a powerful response from Quintin Hogg, the Secretary of State for Education and Science (who had renounced his peerage as Viscount Hailsham in a bid to become party leader in 1963). Hogg argued that 'the justification of the continued use of the term "Unionist" in our title [the Conservative and Unionist Party] is the belief in the fundamental unity of interest of the inhabitants of this island'.[75]

Powell found himself at odds with the IEA over his support for the NHS. Powell had continued to be held in high regard in the IEA, being the 'chosen guest of honour' at a lunch for sympathizers in the City in November 1964.[76] In January 1965 Harris reported to Powell Hayek's view that 'all our hopes for England rest now on Enoch Powell'.[77] Having been an IEA guest at the Mont Pelerin Society's conference the previous year, Powell accepted an invitation to join the society in September 1965, with his subscription paid by the IEA.[78] And it was John Wood from the IEA who edited the volume of Powell's speeches that had been recently published as *A Nation Not Afraid*. Yet there was already an incipient fault line. The IEA had devoted considerable time and effort to delineating its opposition to the welfare state. Using public choice theory, it related the welfare state's weaknesses to the failings of public-sector monopolies as a whole.[79] The firm IEA view was that universal welfare was incompatible with individual choice and independence.[80] Powell saw it differently. While he was Minister of Health, he acknowledged that 'a comprehensive State service has its dangers', with its centralized nature making it 'cumbrous and unresponsive...to the world around it'. He went on:

> These disadvantages apply anywhere; but in the field of health and medical care they could be specially dangerous, for here is a field in which it is the individual mind, the local experiment, even the chance observation, which bring about the great advances.... Not only the methods of medical care, but

the nature of the need for it are constantly changing. All sorts of alterations are going on in the nation—economic, social, demographic, changes in the structure or the population, psychological.

Nevertheless, Powell argued that:

> Those who framed and hammered out the National Health Service were not unconscious of these dangers, and they deliberately built into its structure elements of' independence, both lay and professional to be a counterpoise. The contractual status of the general practitioners, dentists and opticians, the separate representation of the doctors and other professions in the structure of the Hospital and Executive Council services, the power and authority of the professional colleges and professional associations.

Furthermore, Powell added: 'For the Service's own sake, I attach the highest value to the fact that medical service and care is also available outside it and that completely independent organisations exist in the field to support and conduct research.' He was clear that the NHS was 'intended to be comprehensive . . . not, in my view, intended to be exclusive'. With these important qualifications established, and at a time when his criticism of economic planning was intensifying, Powell saw a clear place for a plan in the NHS, allowing the state to 'combine great power and force with singleness of purpose'.[81] At the Ministry of Health, Powell drafted a White Paper for a ten-year hospital-building programme which Enid Russell-Smith considered to be 'something no other country has ever done'.[82] Powell also worked on a long-term plan for care in the community—though it did not, in the end, come to fruition. Nevertheless, George Godber, the Chief Medical Officer in England between 1960 and 1973, later told Powell that, with his two plans, 'I have no doubt that your years at the M/H did more for the Service than any other period.'[83]

Powell was indeed passionate in his commitment to the NHS. He disassociated himself from long-established right-wing defences of government health provision. He said he 'would scorn to justify it – even if the assertion were true – on the basis that somehow it promoted economic and productive efficiency'. Instead, Powell argued that it was 'completely triumphantly, justified on the simple ground that a civilized compassionate nation can do no other. It, and all the other social services, is the corporate recognition by the community of its common obligation to its individual members.'[84] In *A New Look at Medicine and Politics* (1966), Powell wrote of the 'general public interest in seeing that medical care is provided for the members of society in a wide range of situations'.[85] The IEA was alarmed. After reading a

Figure 3. The newly appointed Minister of Health at his desk in the Ministry, 28 July 1960.

pre-publication copy, Harris told Powell that he feared 'lasting damage'.[86] Harris's wider concern was that taking 'medicine out of the competitive market' was 'most damaging to the general thesis you would advance for the supply and demand of (almost) all goods and services'. Harris was particularly disappointed that Powell had dismissed an idea advanced in IEA circles: vouchers for people to spend as they wished on government-approved provision that would increase 'fruitful competition between a state provision and private insurance by reducing the "high barriers" of differential cost between the "free" service and a full cost private alternative'.[87] Powell had written that:

> The service in its present form is in effect a universal scheme of mutual insurance. Unless therefore massive numbers opt for vouchers and insure themselves, a premium equal to the cost per head of the service will be insufficient to insure any but the 'best risks' against the whole range of medical contingencies; and

the same logic applies, *mutatis mutandis*, to a voucher scheme for certain specified types of medical care only. Thus a voucher scheme resolves itself merely into a method of increasing state expenditure upon medical care.[88]

Geoffrey Howe, who was increasingly active in the IEA—and later Thatcher's first Chancellor of the Exchequer—but who had just lost his seat after less than a year and a half in Parliament, also privately pressed Powell. Howe took up the standard IEA line that 'a nationalised health service reproduces all the deficiencies with which we are familiar in the industrial field' and urged Powell to remember that 'many of your supporters . . . believe that we can and should begin eroding, outflanking, reforming or overturning the NHS monolith' as part of the quest for the 'free society'.[89] Seldon, meanwhile, took issue with Powell's comment that the 'growth of private medical insurance . . . does not appear to have been accompanied by an appreciable net increase in the volume of medical care rendered outside the National Health Service'.[90] Citing the examples of the United States, Canada, Australia, New Zealand, and the Republic of Ireland, Seldon suggested that the 'potential demand for private medical care was very large indeed'.[91] Powell's curt response was that the 'experience in other countries where there is no free "comprehensive" state service is hardly relevant'.[92] After the book was published, Seldon made his criticisms public.[93] The book had indeed been damaging to the IEA cause. In his review, Richard Titmuss, the Labour-supporting Professor of Social Administration at the London School of Economics, who had done much to define the characteristics of the universal welfare state, chose to emphasize Powell's argument that vouchers would increase public expenditure on health, damningly contending that 'these so-called reforms are simply devices for providing bigger and better Welfare States for the rich at the expense of the poor'.[94] This prompted Harris to write to Powell in anguished terms: 'See how you have comforted the common enemy.'[95]

Conservative choice and Labour control

By 1966 Powell had certainly established a reputation as the Conservative Party's 'most outspoken ideologue'.[96] Yet he also had an increasingly clear sense of how these ideas could be packaged in political terms: he began to argue that 'choice' should become the Conservative rallying cry, with attention paid to 'the economic sphere . . . because there the characteristic difference between Socialism and Conservatism lies'. Powell had a particular awareness how to do this while the Conservatives were out of power:

> As a fighting party in opposition, we must concentrate on the areas of politics which are live, which are automatically news, and where the antithesis between ourselves and our opponents is at its maximum. If we do that, we shall find that a very simple and plain theme runs through it all. The secret of political success is to present a single, simple, coherent theme that everyone can interpret in their own terms. That was the secret of the rise of Socialism. State control was given as the answer to everything. We can present the same simplicity and consistency.[97]

A commitment to 'individual choice' as the 'central message of the Conservative Party' led Powell into a debate over advertising.[98] Taking his cue from the IEA, he had long considered that 'a man's attitude to advertising is the acid test of whether he really believes in the free economy, the sovereignty of the consumer and all the rest'.[99] Speaking in 1967, at a point when Douglas Jay, the President of the Board of Trade, was instituting an inquiry into the industry, Powell argued that advertising was 'the basic means of bringing to the customer's notice the range of choice that is available to him' and the process that 'enthrones the customer as King'.[100]

Figure 4. Powell with Margaret Thatcher at the Conservative Party Conference in Brighton, 16 October 1965.

Meanwhile, Powell criticized Labour control. With the formal launch of the National Plan, to be implemented by the new Department for Economic Affairs, he argued that the government, in order 'to control the economy in the sense of bringing about a certain pattern of economic activity', intended 'a massive transfer of decision from the citizen to the government' which would undermine 'the liberty and independence of the individual'. Echoing a point he had made in the late 1940s, he now warned about the 'totalitarian implication of socialism'.[101] As the government sought to work with the trade unions and business to maintain incomes policies and to implement the National Plan, Powell developed his argument further:

> We are today in imminent danger of slipping unawares into that form of state socialism which is known as fascism, whereby the control of the state over individuals is exercised largely through corporations which purport to represent the various elements of society, and particularly the employers and the employees. There is an ominous ring of the corporate state about the present relations between the Government, the T.U.C. [Trades Union Congress] and the C.B.I. [Confederation of British Industry].[102]

Increasingly, Powell's criticisms were directed against a fixed exchange rate. As long ago as 1949 Powell had said that giving Sterling 'its free market value in the trade of the world' was an important part of 'our battle for economic freedom'.[103] Now Powell linked his arguments to what he saw as a misguided contemporary concern about the balance-of-payments deficit as a sign of wider economic decline. On taking office in 1964, Labour had argued that the problem was one of efficiency and competitiveness, which the government sought to tackle through its National Plan. A recent historical assessment has concluded that the balance-of-payments 'problem' was not, in the main, about efficiency but was instead about 'overstretch' in international policy and accordingly eased by the early 1970s.[104] In some respects, this perspective would have chimed with Powell's views on Britain's world role, but he did not make that connection. Instead, Powell's position was that with the introduction of floating rates the artificial problem would disappear—the argument being that a fixed system would always see some states in deficit while others were in surplus. Even while he was in the shadow cabinet, which remained committed to fixed rates, Powell made the direction of his thinking clear. In 1967, with the government forced to devalue the pound sterling, but remaining committed to a lower fixed rate ($2.40 instead of $2.80), Powell described this series of events as 'a positive orgy of self-abasement'.[105] Increasingly emphasizing that governments were responsible

for inflation through their control of the money supply, Powell rejected
arguments that sought to establish a relationship between inflation and the
exchange rate.[106] Meanwhile, Powell advocated floating rates within the
One Nation Group with some success, and he had published an IEA
pamphlet on the proposal.[107] Once outside the shadow cabinet after April
1968, he made his argument absolutely clear. Referring to the balance of
payments deficit, he argued:

> This is nothing to do with their inflation and our inflation, their growth rate
> and our growth rate, their competitiveness and our competitiveness. It isn't, and
> it can't be. It is because their money has been undervalued while our money
> has been overvalued. At the expense of our national pride and self-confidence,
> as well as indebtedness to other countries and repeated violent interference with
> the course of our own economy, we have been forced to maintain our money
> at a price, in terms of other money, at which our payments do not balance.[108]

At the Mont Pelerin conference in September 1968, Powell asserted that the
fixed rate had 'become a powerful engine for the extension of government
control over the individual'. His particular target was the UK travel allowance,
introduced in late 1966, which—with the aim of saving foreign exchange—
had imposed a basic limit of £50 per person on the amount of currency
that could be taken out of the country. Seeing a fixed exchange rate as 'the
supreme "commanding height" of a controlled economy', Powell argued
that: 'Every interference with a price – as here with a particularly important
price, the exchange rate of a national currency – leads inexorably to interference with other prices and thus to the substitution of state control for
market forces.' Referring to the Bretton Woods system, established in 1944,
which had committed each of its members (the United States, Canada,
states in Western Europe, Australia, and Japan) to the maintenance of a fixed
exchange rate by providing rules for the commercial and financial relations
between them, Powell then added a further—but familiar—dimension to
his argument: criticism of the United States. He argued that the 'fixed
international parities of the post-war world were an American design',
which played a 'psychological role in maintaining American hegemony' by
ingraining the presumption 'that world trade somehow depended not on
the maintenance merely of fixed parities but of these fixed parities' (i.e. with
£1 pegged at $2.80).[109]

Powell also related his argument about choice and control to education.
So far as secondary education was concerned, he saw Labour's expressed
desire to eradicate the public schools and to introduce the comprehensive

model across the state sector, at the same time as removing the autonomy of direct-grant schools, as an overall 'policy intended to deny choice in the public system and the choice of the individual to obtain or offer services outside the public system'.[110] Powell had, at the time of the publication of the Robbins Report in 1963, which called for an immediate expansion of universities and of student numbers, spoken favourably about it as 'the self-expression, of a national will for progress in education' and urged that 'the nation as a whole should note it and take pride in it'.[111] Powell was, at this stage, seemingly in line with the spirit of the report, which was not just framed in meritocratic language but also, as Peter Mandler has shown, made in a democratic context which assumed that the numbers of those qualified to attend university and the numbers of those who wanted to do so 'would and should increase consistently for the foreseeable future'.[112] By 1968, however, it was apparent that Powell saw things differently. He had already taken issue with Labour's growth targets as a means of exerting government control over patterns of production, leisure, consumption, and saving.[113] Now he adapted this argument to higher education—in a speech to the annual conference of the Conservative National Advisory Committee on Education. In the first place, he rejected the government's contention that an increased number of higher-education students led to increased growth. Powell's view was that 'the volume of education, being one of the "good things" of life, is likely (though not certain) to increase with economic growth', meaning that if there was 'a relationship of cause and effect at all, it is the other way round'. Powell considered that adherence to a mistaken premise was used to justify increased public spending and warned that 'as the proportion of state money in total higher education expenditure rose, the institutions and their staffs would lose economic freedom... which ultimately depends on control over the funds'. Amid rising student discontent, Powell further argued that viewing students as 'performing an indispensable function' by 'furnishing the means of future economic growth' had led them collectively to demand greater control over their education, threatening university independence from another angle.[114]

In place of government control, Powell called for much more choice, with the market prescribing the directions in which higher education developed. Powell explained: 'If a lecturer is incompetent, then his lecture theatre will be empty; if a course is futile, it will have few enrolments; if a qualification is irrelevant or excessive, it will not be sought – or so it should be.' Instead, Powell argued that increased state involvement had 'largely eliminated these forces, so that the whole process becomes arbitrary'.[115] Powell did not explicitly mention subject choice but this was, at least in part, his target—with good reason. In the late 1950s and early 1960s left-wing calls for more state planning had lamented what they saw as an old-fashioned bias towards arts subjects that inhibited economic growth, with C. P. Snow's *The Two Cultures and the Scientific Revolution* (1959) being a prominent example of this approach. More recently, under the Labour government, especially with Anthony Crosland as Secretary of State for Education and Science, there had been moves to push university expansion in directions that favoured science and technology at the expense of the humanities.[116] Powell pointed to a solution. In summer 1968 he had said he wanted to see 'a large and growing proportion of further and university education which by its nature and content could be self-financed and self-determined'.[117] At the beginning of the following year, Powell chose a meeting hosted by the Oxford University Conservative Association to announce his support for an important IEA initiative: the creation of what became the University College at Buckingham in 1973 (and the University of Buckingham a decade later), the UK's first private university, financed through student fees, service income, and gifts and endowments.[118] In the event, the private university sector in the UK has remained small, with Regent's University London becoming only the second private university in 2013. Yet Powell hoped that Buckingham would be the start of a great initiative:

> We can envisage whole areas of higher education tending to move across into the voluntary sector from the state sector, while conversely the state sector, as often happens elsewhere, would learn and acquire from the voluntary sector. Men, methods and even institutions would move both ways; but the total result would be a system of higher education which in form, volume and content reflected the demands and needs of the community in a way impossible if public provision were automatically to be multiplied by rule-of-thumb.[119]

The battle with the Conservative Party

At the 1970 general election, the Conservative leadership, from which Powell was estranged, appeared to be travelling in his direction—with manifesto pledges 'to reject the philosophy of compulsory wage control' and 'to stop further nationalisation, and create a climate for free enterprise to expand'.[120] This change of tack had seemingly emerged from the shadow cabinet pre-election planning conference held at the Selsdon Park Hotel in Surrey. In reality, the changes to the party's perspective were limited, with only minimal discussion having taken place among the shadow cabinet on the principles of economic policy. Yet, with the press and the Labour Party portraying the conference as evidence of a new market-orientated Conservative leaning, this gave an appearance of coherence to the party platform that Heath took pains not to repudiate.[121] Indeed, it was notable that the IEA greeted the Conservative election victory with some optimism.[122]

By the end of 1970, however, divisions began to emerge between Powell and the new Conservative government as he asked it to demonstrate its willingness 'to make serious inroads into nationalised industry'.[123] From summer 1968 Powell had publicly called for a full-frontal attack on the nationalized industries, with gas, electricity, and the Post Office as early candidates for denationalization.[124] Powell had reason to be optimistic. He had spoken as Nicholas Ridley, who embraced free-market economics and who had managed Powell's party-leadership campaign in 1965, undertook a party review of nationalized industries—which can be seen as the early stages of the process by which the Conservatives became committed to denationalization from the mid-1970s and undertook substantial privatization in the 1980s, notably including British Telecom and British Gas. Powell did not use the term privatization, which came into political usage in Britain in 1970.[125] But it is clear that he envisaged the same basic process: he sought the conversion 'of the physical assets from public debt into equity shares, thus transferring responsibility for the future management, replacement and renewal of the assets from the public and its political and administrative servants to the equity owners and their agents'.[126] Yet, under the Heath government, Powell's hopes were thwarted as policy appeared to move in the opposite direction.

In 1971, as the government nationalized the aeronautical division of Rolls-Royce, the luxury car and aero-engine manufacturer that had financially collapsed, Powell offered fierce criticism. He argued that the government had 'cast doubt and discredit generally upon that belief in the principles of capitalism and private enterprise for which the Conservative Party stands'.[127] Calling for 'the unfettered play of the market' in order to 'heal our injured pride and regain our ancient confidence', he argued that there was absolutely 'no case for a system of capitalism and private enterprise where the government intervenes spasmodically here and there to prevent results which the system would otherwise produce'.[128] Powell was also increasingly at odds with the government over trade unions. Powell had previously expressed his disapproval of trade unions from a free-market perspective, criticizing them for attempting to fix the price of labour through picketing.[129] Yet, as Heath suggested that union pay claims needed to be restrained to help reduce inflation, Powell disagreed. He took the same position as Milton Friedman who, holding that inflation was caused by the government's expansion of the money supply, considered that union wage-bargaining did not affect the overall price level. This was why, according to Powell, in 'the matter of inflation, the unions and their members are sinned against, not sinning'.[130] Indeed, Friedman wrote to The Times in defence of Powell's position in 1973—prompting Powell to express his delight that 'the Master himself should come to my defence'.[131] Yet it is worth remembering that an increasing number of neo-liberals saw it differently. Harris, for example, followed Hayek in arguing that trade unions played an important role in shaping a political context in which the government, pushed to maintain full employment, followed expansionary policies that increased the money supply.[132] Powell's views also went against an inevitably cruder, popular view that trade unions had some role in causing inflation.[133] As Heath introduced a statutory prices and incomes policy in November 1972, beginning with a ninety-day freeze, Powell savaged Heath for acting 'in direct opposition to the principles' on which he was elected and for having 'taken leave of his senses'.[134] Powell also attacked the Conservative government, using language he had previously deployed against Labour. With the government working closely with the TUC, Powell argued that its actions were those of 'a particular kind of totalitarian regime', dominated by corporations and thus 'fascist'.[135] The following year, in less overblown language, Powell argued that 'the conflict today between the two front benches...has ceased to be between socialism and a free society, but is between two managed states – a managed socialist state and a managed capitalist state'.[136] By late 1973, with Heath confronting the National Union of Mineworkers (NUM), insisting that they had to accept pay restraint, Powell further argued that the government's incomes policy was socially divisive, creating 'antagonism...between the state on one side and the various classes and interests in the community on the other side'.[137] As Powell's divergence from the Conservative leadership became greater, he was able to call on wider support from neo-liberal circles. In September 1973, Harris told Powell about a private lunch with John Wood and Arthur Seldon at which he had been 'named on the first count as Prime Minister-elect, to replace one who is leading the Conservative Party to destruction!'[138]

The build-up to Powell's decision not to contest his seat in 1974 was, as we will see, to a large extent about Europe, but economic considerations were also important in both the short and long term—amid an atmosphere of crisis. In November 1973 the NUM had introduced an overtime ban in order to restrict coal production, which had, in turn, been met by the government introduction of the three-day week for industry, together with restrictions for domestic consumers, to conserve supplies. Oil prices had soared after the 1973 Arab–Israeli War, but Powell emphasized the domestic dimensions of the issue—and the government's responsibility. With a full-blown strike looking likely, Powell argued that 'inflationary financing has put the unions into a position where their powers, both real and imaginary, are maximised'. In this context, Powell was, as he told the Conservative MP and prominent Monday Club figure Patrick Wall, deeply opposed to the prospect of a general election that would lead to a headlong 'rush into electioneering as an alternative to governing'—a pithy comment in light of the subsequent Conservative campaign slogan, 'Who Governs Britain?'.[139] Informing George Wilkes, the chairman of the Wolverhampton South West Conservative Association, that he would not be contesting his seat once an election had been called, Powell emphasized that throughout its term the government had introduced policies which were 'directly opposite to those we all stood for in 1970'.[140] Indeed, Powell would have been reassured when Friedman swiftly wrote to him saying that, so far as prices and incomes policies were concerned, he was 'surely doing the right and proper thing by refusing to go along with a policy so utterly misguided and so utterly disastrous in its long-term consequences'.[141]

In summer 1974, as politics remained volatile with a minority Labour government in power, a grouping led by Harris—but also including his IEA colleagues Seldon, Fisher, and Wood as well as Friedman, John Jewkes, the Oxford professor and author of the anti-planning classic *Ordeal by Planning* (1946), and Lord Coleraine (formerly Richard Law), the Conservative peer who was an early exponent of free-market ideas—wrote to Powell as a possible 'leader who can best be trusted to rid the nation of this threat to the life of our economy and society'. They were at one with Powell in identifying the monetary source of inflation, in calling for further cuts in public expenditure, and in seeking cuts to subsidies to private industry. There was, however, a sticking point—and it was a familiar one:

Your emphasis on the incomparable superiority of the market mechanism over collective decision-taking cannot consistently be applied to the economy in general while excluding the welfare sector. A programme to stop inflation could thus usher in a new era of widening consumer choice and satisfaction with public services.[142]

Yet Powell's reaction to developments within the Conservative Party diminished this support. After the February 1974 general-election defeat, Keith Joseph and Margaret Thatcher, respectively Secretary of State for Social Services and Secretary of State for Education and Science in Heath's government, moved towards a public endorsement of free-market economics, setting up the Centre for Policy Studies think tank. Joseph had become particularly interested in monetarism and urged its application in a speech in Preston in early September, when he said that inflation was 'threatening to destroy our society'. Powell now cuttingly said he had 'heard of death-bed repentance ... but perhaps it was more appropriate to refer to post-mortem repentance'.[143] In response, Harris warned Powell that 'repeated personal attacks' on Joseph were 'likely to prejudice your standing in the eyes of others we respect and, therefore, to weaken the role you may be able to play in rescuing the country from the perils that lie ahead'. Instead, Harris considered that 'a public pronouncement of a major change of kind by a politician took a good deal of courage and merited praise'.[144] He feared that Powell would be seen as 'pursuing a vendetta'.[145] This may indeed also have been the impression given during the 1975 Conservative Party leadership contest, which saw Thatcher emerge as the standard-bearer for the free market. Bitingly, Powell told a meeting of the Selsdon Group, formed in protest at Heath's movement away from the principles established at the Selsdon Park conference, that:

If the Conservative Party is seeking a successor to Mr Heath who will re-establish the principles which were trampled upon in office, I will tell them where not to look. It is no use looking amongst the members of the Cabinet which, without a single resignation or word of public dissent, not merely swallowed but advocated every single reversal of election pledge or Party principle.[146]

Grappling with Thatcher

Powell continued to adopt a critical stance towards the Conservative Party— even as it embraced, with Thatcher as leader, free-market economics. Indeed, Powell appeared almost as critical of his old party as he was of Labour. In 1978, with a general election anticipated, Powell told the Westminster Chamber of Commerce that this was not 'a decision between two sets of fairly clearly formulated and sharply differentiated alternatives'.[147] So far as the trade unions were concerned, Powell argued that both main parties were misleading the public by 'building up and protecting the myth of increasing and overweening trade union power' for their own ends:

> The Conservatives think that if they can frighten sufficient of the electors with the bogey of dominant trade unions, manipulated by sinister left-wing or Marxist operators, that will enable them to win the next election, without either explaining what exactly they would propose to do about it...The Labour Party, on the other hand, believe that exaggerating the power of the unions and frightening the electorate with what might happen if the unions got the bit between their teeth can sell themselves as the only party capable of keeping on terms with the unions.[148]

Meanwhile, a breach opened with Hayek and Friedman, which occurred as Thatcher increasingly identified with them, embracing Hayek's *Constitution of Liberty* and being briefed by Friedman at 10 Downing Street in February 1980.[149] Famously, a *Daily Telegraph* magazine interview with Hayek in September 1975 made public his disagreement with Powell that had occurred at the 1972 Mont Pelerin meeting at Montreux in Switzerland. When a silence was proposed in memory of the eleven Israeli athletes who had recently been killed by Palestinian terrorists at the Munich Olympics, Powell had objected on the basis that it was 'no part of the group's function to make a judgment about such an event'. Hayek considered that Powell 'may have been literally correct' but that his stance hinted at an 'emotional instability about him'.[150] Hayek swiftly wrote to Powell about his 'appalling indiscretion'.[151] But Powell indignantly took issue with the fact that 'you should associate "emotion" with my protest, whether justified or not, against the Mont Pelerin Society presuming to single out for commemoration a particular group amongst all those done to death by violence throughout the world in a particular period of time'.[152] Not all those present disagreed with Powell—but for different reasons. Wyndham Davies, a medical doctor who was a Conservative MP between 1964 and 1966, considered that Friedman—who proposed the silence—was 'at fault' for 'trying to introduce Zionist politics into a private economic gathering'.[153] Karl Popper, the philosopher of science, thought likewise and held that Powell had 'protested rightly against a pro-Israeli bias'.[154] For his part, Harris privately agreed with Powell but thought he had 'caused unnecessary offence'.[155]

The public spat deepened. Powell was churlishly dismissive of Friedman's award of the Nobel Memorial Prize in Economic Sciences in 1976 for his work, including that on monetary theory, arguing that 'it ought to have been divided in the ratio of two to one between Lord Thorneycroft and myself, because we got there a long time before he did'.[156] This was, of course, a reference to their resignations from the government in 1958 but, even though Powell had placed an emphasis on the monetary source of inflation at that stage, it was undoubtedly Friedman who had later provided the fine-grained economic explanation and demonstrated its applicability as policy, with his presidential address to the American Economic Association in 1968 being a particular milestone.[157] Powell decided not to renew his member-ship of the Mont Pelerin Society in 1980, ostensibly on the grounds that he had 'so little opportunity, owing to my other commitments, of participating in any of its activities'.[158] He let Harris know his real reasoning: 'uneasiness on my part in the presence of the Society is increased by what seems a ten-dency to resolve itself into a Hayek Adulation Society, with a minor niche for Friedman'. With Hayek having made a number of interventions into British politics in the last few years, including a letter to *The Times* in which he suggested that a 'limited democracy might indeed be the best protector of individual liberty' but warned of the dangers, in that regard, of 'unlimited democracy', Powell told Harris:

> As you know, I admired and valued much of Hayek's work, but I dislike his teutonic habit of telling the English, whom he does not in the least under-stand, how to set about governing themselves. After all, Hayek, Friedman and Co. have not put to the practical political test the principles of free market economics. I am content that their academic labours should bring them laurels; but it is perhaps understandable if those who have reaped thorns in the same cause in real life are disinclined to add their contributions to those laurels.[159]

At the same time, Powell's criticism of Thatcher continued. In September 1980, with the Conservative government in power for more than a year, Powell argued that they 'had not got their ideas sufficiently organised before they came into office'. In particular, he criticized the government for sim-ultaneously attempting to reduce direct taxation, public expenditure, and the growth of the money supply.[160] These were, in Powell's view, all desirable undertakings in their own right. He had, for example, called for nothing less than the halving of income tax in 1968.[161] But he objected to the pursuit of all these objectives at the same time. Powell had a point. Economic historian Jim Tomlinson has recently argued that, despite the government's professed commitment to a coherent monetarist programme, 'the policies implemented in this period were poorly thought out, incoherent and pursued...with little serious analysis of what might follow for the level of economic activity and unemployment'.[162]

Yet Powell's stance slowly changed. With Thatcher under increasing scrutiny as unemployment rose in 1981, Powell weighed in behind her. He had been told by Anthony Courtney, a prominent figure in the Monday Club, that an 'encouraging gesture...would help her a lot at a very difficult time'.[163] Speaking in the House of Commons immediately after Thatcher on 28 October, Powell now argued that she was absolutely right to resist the reflation of the economy for which the Labour Party called.[164] With Powell's respect for Thatcher increased by her handling of the Falklands crisis, Powell also took the government's side over the miners' strike of 1984–5, which had been called in a bid to resist colliery closures in the loss-making coal industry. In a high-profile intervention, Powell challenged the Archbishop of York's open letter to the Durham miners, in which he had written that 'I believe we owe it to future generations not to close pits before they are properly worked out, just as we owe it to the present generation not to destroy jobs until there is an overwhelming case for doing so'.[165] Fully supporting the notion that the market should shape the future balance of the economy, Powell retorted that the 'immorality is to attempt – by ecclesiastical authority on His Grace's part, by physical coercion on the miners' part – to compel our fellow men to waste their brains and labour so that we may continue undisturbed to waste our own'.[166] Powell saw the strike as representative of a 'general predicament of a society caught up in a rapid and continuing economic revolution' in which 'the whole nation, and not only the mining industry, has to surmount a high and daunting threshold'.[167] In this sense, Powell was at one with the Thatcherite narrative that linked economic changes with national revitalization. Yet, at the same time, Powell objected to some key policies, and their underlying rationales, undertaken by the Thatcher government.

Education was a prime example. With a renewed emphasis on the vocational dimensions of education amid high youth unemployment, Powell objected to 'the heresy that education is useful, with the corollary that education produces economic wellbeing'. Powell considered that this view was used 'to justify not only the expenditure of public money upon the provision of education but a bias in spending that money towards branches of education which they are pleased to regard as signally useful and economically advantageous'. In this sense, Powell took aim at 'the praise bestowed on "science"'—an issue he had broached in the late 1960s. His view was that the 'state which

tries to use its power to exalt one kind of learning to the disadvantage of the
other is an inhuman and a barbarous state'. He continued:

> Education is a Good Thing (capitals) because man has an insatiable appetite
> to learn and to understand... It not only needs no secondary justification. It
> actually shrivels at the touch of secondary justification. To claim that we pro-
> vide public money for teaching and learning in order that our factories and
> our enterprises may be more profitable, productive and (accursed word) com-
> petitive is as sinful as to claim that we pay for doctors and hospitals in order to
> have stronger and healthier soldiers, busier bureaucrats and more productive
> factory workers.[168]

Powell took the same attitude to higher education. With the government's
1985 Green (discussion) Paper emphasizing, in the words of Keith Joseph,
the Secretary of State for Education and Science, that it was 'vital for our
higher education to contribute more effectively to the improvement of the
performance of the economy', Powell lashed back. He argued that it was
'barbarism to attempt to evaluate the contents of higher education in terms
of economic performance'.[169] In the same vein, the announcement, three
years later, that publicly funded student maintenance grants were to be partly
replaced by loans prompted Powell's damning verdict that this 'necessarily
carries the false implication that such an education is (and ought to be) calculated to furnish earning power after graduation'.[170]

In 1987 Powell dismissed government education policy more strongly
than ever as a misplaced effort to combat decline. As Kenneth Baker, now
Education Secretary, stated that there was to be a statutory national curricu-
lum for schools in England and Wales, Powell took issue. Calling instead for
curricula to be set by the universities—which sat at the top of the education
hierarchy—Powell argued:

> The state, it is declared, must prescribe and police the content of education
> because only so can that education which meets the purposes of the state be
> secured. It is the old Bismarckian logic in modern dress. Britain, so it is declared,
> is uncompetitive and is being overtaken by other nations, by Western Europe,
> by Japan, by America. The supposed failure, which no one seems to have the
> courage to deny, is laid at the door of education.[171]

3

Immigration

Immigration was, without a doubt, the area where Powell had—and continues to have—the greatest public impact. While he certainly sparked debate, most would consider that the overall effect was entirely negative: legitimizing the expression of racial hostility in both the short and long term and contributing to the development of a racial aspect to British national identity after 1945.[1] As with foreign policy and economics, Powell's stance went against a degree of cross-party consensus. Yet, while he became a public critic of the Anglo-American alliance and an advocate of free-market economics at an early stage in the respective debates on those issues, on immigration Powell initially held back. As a result, an accusation of political opportunism has understandably dogged Powell since the late 1960s: a charge that he took up the issue only when he thought it would have public resonance. With access to archives, the biographies by Robert Shepherd and Simon Heffer have enabled us to appreciate that Powell privately expressed unease about the impact of immigration as early as 1955, even if this only became part of his public argument after 1964. Alongside an awareness of the shocking rhetoric that Powell deployed, often invoking a sense of great danger to the nation and its future, we now also have a clear sense of how Powell consistently called for a tight definition of UK citizenship, distinct from that of the Commonwealth.

The development of Powell's arguments in opposition to immigration can be understood as populist in a classic sense—suggesting that the people were being misrepresented, even misled, by government and party elites.[2] Despite being propelled right to the forefront of the public stage after April 1968, Powell struggled to control the political agenda, even as he attempted to link immigration to a wider argument about social disorder. On the contrary, his stance on immigration played a significant part in shaping how Powell came to be seen, especially from the mid-1970s, as being on the extremes of British politics. This chapter also suggests that we need to modify our understanding of a further aspect of Powell's position. He did come to contend that the erosion of a homogeneous electorate, especially in terms of colour, stood to undermine the operation of democracy, a certain type of 'decline', but he did so very slowly, giving the argument its fullest exposition only in the 1980s and 1990s—more than a decade after he had first gained public notoriety over immigration.

Citizenship, democracy, and discrimination

After 1945, immigration from the Commonwealth occurred at a rapid, and initially accelerating, pace. With the growth concentrated in certain towns and cities, the estimated size of the non-white population of Great Britain (i.e. excluding Northern Ireland) was: 30,000 in 1951; 400,000 in 1961; 1.4 million in 1971; 2.1 million in 1981; and 3 million by 1991.[3] Powell's initial position on the issue was shaped by his support for the Empire, and endorsement of economic protection within it. Speaking in 1949, as the prospective Conservative candidate in Wolverhampton South West, he argued that 'we must reduce or remove the barriers to free movement within the Empire of goods, of money, and above all, of human beings'.[4] Having come to see the end of Empire as inevitable by the end of 1954, Powell privately joined the debate on Commonwealth immigration the following year. By this stage, migration from India and Pakistan was increasing—a trend that was to continue—but West Indians from the Caribbean remained the largest group. Powell was prompted to intervene by the publication of a statement by the Bishops of Lichfield and Birmingham (A. Stretton Reeve and J. Leonard Wilson) in the *Express & Star*, the main local Wolverhampton newspaper, about a bus strike by West Bromwich Corporation transport workers, in defiance of the Transport and General Workers' Union (TGWU), over the employment of an Indian immigrant as a trainee bus conductor. The bishops had argued that a colour bar 'was not reconcilable with Christianity'.[5] Powell now grappled—for the first time—with the question of 'the influx of British subjects not of European race into the United Kingdom'. Refuting the bishops' argument, Powell made it clear that he considered this another area in which religion should not intrude into political debate:

> This wider issue of coloured immigration is one which I find it difficult to
> decide on religious grounds. It is most certain that Christ died for all men
> whatever their colour, and that for this reason and many others black and

white are equal in the sight of God. But so are Englishmen and Frenchmen; yet we do not allow Frenchmen to obtain employment on the West Bromwich buses, nor do we condemn the Durham miners as irreligious when they strike against the employment of Italians. It may be said that the French and Italians are not British subjects, whereas the Indians and Jamaicans are. In saying this, however, we have quit the ground of religion and entered upon that of law. Christianity can know nothing of the British Nationality Act 1948.

Powell made an argument he was to repeat time and again. He called for an amendment to the Act, which had created a common UK and Commonwealth citizenship that 'would put the Jamaicans in the same cat-egory as the French and the Italians or at any rate would distinguish them from citizens of this country'. Fearing, even at this stage, 'perhaps insoluble and certainly intractable political problems', Powell stated—but did not explain—the further argument that large-scale 'coloured' immigration was incompatible with democracy:

> It appears to me that in any democratic country, (by which I mean a country where counting heads has practical importance), any readily visible differences between human beings inevitably result in political frictions. Where such dif-ferences are very slight or where the sector of the population so distinguishable is very small, no harm results; but where any considerable part of a population has distinctive characteristics, I believe that the working of institutions such as ours cannot fail to be endangered. However wrong-headedly and gropingly, I believe the strikers in West Bromwich to have apprehended the dangers for this country of any appreciable coloured population becoming domiciled here.[6]

This important document played a part in prompting the historian Peter Brooke to argue that Powell's opposition to immigration, as notably articulated in the 'Rivers of Blood' speech, was about a commitment to national homogeneity as a prerequisite for democracy.[7] This chapter will show that Powell did indeed attempt to substantiate this case—but not until well after 1968.

In the meantime, Powell was involved in Conservative Party discussions about immigration in the late 1950s, but he did not publicly speak about it when the issue was raised in Parliament and in the press, most notably by Conservative backbencher Cyril Osborne.[8] We should recognize, however, that before 1960 strong opposition to immigration was limited among Conservative MPs.[9] In 1961, as the Conservative government considered restrictions amid rising Commonwealth immigration, Powell, on the min-isterial committee on immigration control, took the same position he had in 1955: he called for the creation of a new citizenship of the United

Kingdom in order to restrict 'coloured' immigration. Powell's argument was, however, rejected by the committee on the basis that it would weaken Commonwealth ties.[10] In the event, the 1962 Commonwealth Immigrants Act sought to reduce numbers through a system of limited employment vouchers—a very different approach to the one advocated by Powell.

From 1964, Powell said more about immigration. He did so at first anonymously, arguing as 'A Conservative' in *The Times* that the Commonwealth was a 'farce' and 'the cause of the massive coloured immigration in the last decade which has inflicted social and political damage that will take decades to obliterate'.[11] Here Powell was making a point that resonated as the decade went on and the public became increasingly disillusioned with the Commonwealth, especially because it was the source of 'coloured' immigration.[12] The 1964 General Election was a turning point for Powell amid the controversy caused by Peter Griffiths's campaign in Smethwick—a nearby constituency to Wolverhampton South West—where, against the prominent sitting Labour MP Patrick Gordon Walker, who had been shadow Foreign Secretary, he fought a campaign that exploited crudely racist unofficial slogans, most notably, 'If you want a nigger for a neighbour, vote Labour'.[13] *The Observer* on 4 October reported that Griffiths had cancelled an invitation for Powell to speak on his behalf because 'Mr Powell, who is extremely hostile to bringing race into politics, was thought an embarrassment'.[14] There was a counterclaim that Powell had refused to speak.[15] In any case, Powell now published an article in the *Express & Star*. He had already stated that he sought 'a homogeneous community, local and national'.[16] Now, accepting that 'immigrants will often wish to retain for a long time some of their distinctive customs and beliefs', Powell argued that 'the idea of them as an unassimilated element in our society, living apart in certain districts and following certain occupations, is unsupportable'. Considering that integration would take 'generations', Powell argued that it would be 'altogether impossible . . . except upon one condition: that the problem, already so formidable, is not increased further'.[17] In itself, Powell's definition of integration set him apart from the increasingly influential interpretation of it given by Roy Jenkins, the Labour politician who was shortly to become Home Secretary, in 1965: 'not . . . a flattening process of assimilation but . . . equal opportunity, accompanied by cultural diversity, in an atmosphere of mutual tolerance'.[18]

Griffiths's subsequent triumph at Smethwick, together with the strong performance of the Conservatives across the Black Country as a whole, had further impact on Powell. He discussed the matter with the psephologist David Butler.[19] Powell was particularly struck by his first-hand observation from canvassing that 'support of the Conservative cause was at least as much in evidence in so-called "working class" areas and occupations as on middle-class, owner-occupied suburban roads'. As his party entered opposition and he became more critical of other aspects of its policy, he warned that the 'public silently but firmly despise those who decline to acknowledge uncomfortable facts on their own doorsteps' which was 'seen over immigration'. He dismissed the Labour response of 'self-righteous unction' over Gordon Walker's defeat at Smethwick but also suggested that 'Conservatives will have only themselves to blame if they acquiesce in a taboo being placed on issues which are live and real to millions.' Powell was now clear that: 'Immigration was, and is, an issue. In my constituency it has for years been question number one, into which discussion of every other political topic—housing, health, benefits, employment—promptly turned.'[20] Until recently, Powell had himself, of course, not given immigration prominence in his publications or prepared speeches. That said, he insisted to Paul Foot in 1969 that:

> I am sure that in reply to questions at public meetings at the 1959 general election, and probably earlier, I stated (what had been my opinion since about 1955) that such a change in the law of citizenship was right and necessary; but I have not been able to trace a newspaper report of such a reply.[21]

Powell now pushed his arguments within the party, exerting particular influence on the leader Douglas-Home, as the new Labour government, which had attacked previous Conservative legislation as contravening Labour's commitment to free movement within the Commonwealth and to equality, sought to extend restrictions along the same lines at the same time while also introducing legislation to combat racial discrimination.[22] Urging Douglas-Home to seize the momentum in January 1965, Powell made his first call for the government to assume power to assist 'voluntary repatriation', alongside the compulsory repatriation of illegal immigrants and the introduction of 'some limitation' to the right of entry given to dependants (spouses and children under 16).[23] Douglas-Home expressed agreement and, in a speech at the beginning of February, echoed the call for a voluntary repatriation scheme.[24] Yet opinion in the shadow cabinet was divided.[25] There was, moreover, an awareness of just how delicate the issue was. In March, Thorneycroft, who became shadow Home Secretary later in the year, warned that 'there was a risk of the Conservative Party being seriously

split on this issue, with much of the Party being in favour of tighter control
and the rest insisting on better treatment for immigrants'. With a desire 'not
[to] have so tough a policy on immigration that we offend the middle vote',
the Leader's Consultative Committee (LCC) considered that 'it was essential to talk about integration at the same time as talking about control'. With
the decision not to oppose Labour's discrimination bill, which made discrimination illegal in public places and extended the 1936 Public Order Act,
making it illegal to incite racial hatred through peaceful means in addition
to some kind of 'breach of the peace', the LCC concluded that it 'was most
important for members of the Leader's Committee to make balanced and
reasonable statements on the subject'.[26] Despite Powell's position, and differences of opinion within the Conservative Party, what was, in effect, a
bipartisan approach to immigration had, therefore, emerged.[27]

In this context, Powell became a more outspoken public critic of immigration. At a time when he was making the case strongly for the free
economy, Powell had already privately sought to debate the assumption
'that Commonwealth immigration results in an increase of the average
incomes of the "original" inhabitants' with the retired academic economist Allan G. B. Fisher.[28] This was a powerfully entrenched opinion, especially because it was the demand for labour that, during the buoyant 1950s,
had brought many immigrants to Britain in a seemingly self-perpetuating
pattern. Yet, amid widespread debate over British economic performance
that had gathered momentum in the past few years, Powell argued publicly that immigration was actually hindering productivity, a key economic
measurement:

> It is a mistake to think that because immigrants are willing to be hewers of
> wood and drawers of water, they are increasing productivity by setting other
> workers free to do more productive tasks. The actual effect is probably that
> some mechanisation, re-organisation, capital investment, which would other-
> wise take place, does not happen, and consequently our productivity all round
> is lower than it would have been. Britain is not an underdeveloped colonial
> country with untapped natural resources which only wait to be exploited by
> immigration, nor is it an economy, like that of Switzerland, with a superabun-
> dance of capital and cheap power that can be turned to advantage with a
> selected and imported workforce.[29]

Powell also began to use statistics in an attempt to sensationalize his argument. He began simply by drawing attention to official figures. In May 1965,

at a point when he claimed to seek 'negative immigration . . . a net outflow of immigrants' through assisted voluntary repatriation, Powell emphasized that there had been 75,000 immigrants in the past year.[30] In November 1965 he noted that 33,000 had arrived in the first half of that year.[31] Calling immigration a 'visible menace'—an indication that colour was the issue—in 1966 Powell introduced predictions about the level of future immigration.[32] During the general election he argued that, at the current rate, there would be a further two and a half million immigrants by 2000, which Powell called 'an appalling prospect, which would render the social and human problem that we have already well-nigh insoluble'.[33] In an article for the *Sunday Express* in July 1967, Powell drew attention to a recent government estimate that by 1985 there would be three and a half million 'coloured' Britons and again emphasized voluntary repatriation as a means of preventing 'a major racial problem'.[34] The response of Heath, as party leader, revealed the difference between them. He told Powell that 'the psychological effect of stressing immigration control and repatriation while saying nothing about the need to improve race relations here would encourage the racial intolerance which undoubtedly lies below the surface in many parts of the country'.[35] Powell strongly refuted this in terms that set the scene for subsequent events. In a context where Roy Jenkins as Labour Home Secretary was drafting a stronger Race Relations Bill that sought to extend anti-discrimination law into private employment, housing, credit, and insurance, Powell told Heath that:

> I find in my constituency in the last few weeks an ominous deterioration, which is taking the form not of discrimination by white against coloured but of insolence by coloured towards white and corresponding fearfulness on the part of white. It is this which will be exacerbated by the projected legislation on discrimination and which we shall have to take into account in making up our minds on our attitude.[36]

Powell had maintained that immigration 'was an accident' which had come about through nationality legislation that was 'one of the last relics of empire'.[37] Now, in late 1967, he made a particular claim about the process amid the entry of Kenyan Asians into Britain. Suffering discrimination from the Kenyan government, 4,000 of them arrived in Britain in August and September with British passports issued by the High Commission in Nairobi. They were entitled to these because when, on Kenyan independence in 1963, a citizen of Kenya had ceased to be a UK and Colonies citizen, this had excluded the minorities of Asian, as well as European, Kenyans. Powell argued that this was 'an unforeseen loophole in legislation' and called for it to be closed.[38] He took the same line here as Duncan Sandys, the Secretary of State for the Colonies at the time of Kenyan independence, but stood opposed to Iain Macleod, his close associate who had held the Colonial brief between 1959 and 1961, who argued that the government had made a specific pledge to the Kenyan Asians. In February 1968 the Labour government ended the unrestricted right to enter, but the historian Randall Hansen has shown that Powell's interpretation was not accurate. In events that unfolded just after Powell left the Cabinet in October 1963, there had been a general awareness that Asians would be exempt from the citizenship restrictions.[39]

Powell soon took his position further. Arguably, events in the United States affected him. As early as 1964 he had been concerned that 'any substantial addition to the immigrant population would...entail upon Britain the evils of a deeply divided nation and society, which we witness, for example, in the United States'.[40] Powell had visited the United States for the first time in late 1967 and was further unsettled by the racial tensions that had underpinned riots in Detroit and Chicago earlier in the year.[41] Speaking at Walsall in February 1968, he now dramatically presented the white population in certain areas as the embattled, and neglected, minority. He spoke of the 'hopelessness and helplessness which comes over persons who are trapped or imprisoned, when all their efforts to attract attention bring no response' and said that this was 'the kind of feeling which you in Walsall and we in Wolverhampton are experiencing in the face of the continued flow of immigration into our towns'. Powell went on:

> We are of course in a minority...Out of over 600 Parliamentary constituencies perhaps less than 60 are affected in any way like ourselves. The rest know little or nothing and, we might be tempted to feel, care little or nothing. Only this week a colleague of mine in the House of Commons was dumbfounded when I told him of a constituent whose little daughter was now the only white child in her class at school.

Powell further argued that the government's Race Relations Bill was likely to pander to communalism, often taken to mean allegiance to a particular ethnic group rather than to wider society, which had been the 'curse of India'. Powell drew attention to the dispute in the Wolverhampton Transport Department over the right of Sikhs to wear untrimmed beards and turbans. Powell's view was that the Sikhs were being 'made the material for communal agitation', had 'the same right as anyone else to decide which, if any, of the rules of their sect they will keep', and were merely being asked to follow 'the same rules as their fellow employees'. Powerfully, Powell added: 'It will be the opposite to the equal treatment of all persons within the realm if employers are placed in the position of adjudicating upon the requirements of their employees' religion. The issue in this instance . . . is not racial or religious discrimination: it is communalism.'[42]

The River Tiber

When he gave his infamous speech to the annual general meeting of the West Midlands Area Conservative Political Centre at the Midland Hotel in Birmingham on 20 April 1968, Powell repeated many of the points he had already outlined: the white population in certain areas as the threatened minority; statistical estimates; and opposition to the Race Relations Bill. He did so in a deeply provocative manner, especially through his use of examples, accompanied by direct quotations.[43] This was a tactic adopted against a backdrop where it appeared, as the political scientist Richard Rose wrote in *The Times*, that '[p]ublic confidence in the ability of the leaders of the two major parties to deal with the nation's problems had reached a post-war low'.[44] Powell argued that he was saying what 'thousands and hundreds of thousands are saying and thinking . . . not throughout Great Britain, perhaps, but in the areas that are already undergoing the total transformation to which there is no parallel in a thousand years of English history'. In a famous passage, he used, as Bill Schwarz has shown, 'overseas' to imply a white dominion.[45] Powell stated:

> A week or two ago I fell into conversation with a constituent, a middle-aged, quite ordinary working man employed in one of our nationalised industries. After a sentence or two about the weather, he suddenly said: 'If I had the money to go, I wouldn't stay in this country'. I made some deprecatory reply, to the effect that even this government wouldn't last for ever; but he took no notice, and continued 'I have three children, all of them been through grammar school and two of them married now, with family. I shan't be satisfied till I have seen them all settled overseas. In this country in fifteen or twenty years' time the black man will have the whip hand over the white man'.

Powell estimated—in the absence of any official statistics for that far in the future—that by 2000 the immigrant population would be 'in the region of

5–7 million, approximately one-tenth of the whole population', concentrated
in such a way that 'towns and parts of towns across England will be
occupied, largely or wholly, by different sections of the immigrant and
immigrant-descended population'. In advocating 'the encouragement of
re-emigration...with generous grants and assistance', Powell was in line
with the official party position, but he was stepping outside the party's deli-
cately poised compromise on the Race Relations Bill. When the LCC met
on 10 April there had been a frank discussion on the party's tactics ahead of
the debate in the House of Commons on the 23rd. Quintin Hogg, the
shadow Home Secretary, subsequently recalled that 'Enoch, with a face like
a sphinx, remained silent throughout the debate.'[46] Indeed, on the official
minute, Powell was not specifically recorded as expressing any particular
view, but hostility to the bill was noted on the grounds that 'any legislation
in this field might be harmful and exacerbate rather than improve race relations'. In the end, however, the committee decided to move a reasoned
amendment which, welcoming the bill's intention, argued that in practice it
would be ineffectual and even counterproductive. Adopting a partially
binding two-line whip, the LCC also instructed its MPs to vote to decline
a second reading to the government bill.[47] There was, to be sure, a recognized degree of ambiguity about the Conservative position.[48] Yet, alongside
the libertarian argument which took objection that 'any citizen should
be denied his right to discriminate in the management of his own affairs
between one fellow-citizen and another', Powell told the audience at the
Midland Hotel that the bill would mean that immigrants were 'elevated into
a privileged or special class'. Repeating the point he had made privately to
Heath in summer 1967, Powell contended:

> The discrimination and the deprivation, the sense of alarm and of resentment,
> lie not with the immigrant population but with those among whom they have
> come and are still coming. This is why to enact legislation of the kind before
> Parliament at this moment is to risk throwing a match onto gunpowder.

Citing the strain on the provision of health and school education, pressures
created by a process on which they were 'not consulted', Powell then read
from a letter sent to him after his Walsall speech to emphasize the 'sense of
being a persecuted minority which is growing among ordinary English people
in the areas of the country which are affected'. Adopting the image of the
defenceless white female, his words have become notorious.[49] He went on:

> I am going to allow just one of those hundreds of people to speak for me. She
> did give her name and address, which I have detached from the letter which

I am about to read. She was writing from Northumberland about something which is happening at this moment in my own constituency: 'Eight years ago in a respectable street in Wolverhampton a house was sold to a negro. Now only one white (a woman old-age pensioner) lives there. This is her story. She lost her husband and both her sons in the war. So she turned her seven-roomed house, her only asset, into a boarding house. She worked hard and did well, paid off her mortgage and began to put something by for her old age. Then the immigrants moved in. With growing fear, she saw one house after another taken over. The quiet street became a place of noise and confusion. Regretfully, her white tenants moved out. The day after the last one left, she was awakened at 7 a.m. by two negroes who wanted to use her phone to contact their employer. When she refused, as she would have refused any stranger at such an hour, she was abused and feared she would have been attacked but for the chain on her door. Immigrant families have tried to rent rooms in her house, but she always refused. Her little store of money went, and after paying her rates, she has less than £2 per week. She went to apply for a rate reduction and was seen by a young girl, who on hearing she had a seven-roomed house, suggested she should let part of it. When she said the only people she could get were negroes, the girl said "racial prejudice won't get you anywhere in this country". So she went home. The telephone is her lifeline. Her family pay the bill, and help her out as best they can. Immigrants have offered to buy her house - at a price which the prospective landlord would be able to recover from his tenants in weeks, or at most a few months. She is becoming afraid to go out. Windows are broken. She finds excreta pushed through her letterbox. When she goes to the shops, she is followed by children, charming, wide-grinning piccaninnies. They cannot speak English, but one word they know. "Racialist", they chant. When the new Race Relations Bill is passed, this woman is convinced she will go to prison.'

Powell had publicly warned about the difficulty of achieving integration since 1964. Now he went further. He explicitly argued that integration into a population meant 'to become for all practical purposes indistinguishable from its other members' and identified 'marked physical differences, especially of colour' as a principal hindrance. While he recognized that there were some immigrants 'whose wish and purpose is to be integrated', he argued that 'to imagine that such a thing enters the heads of a great and growing majority of immigrants and their descendants is a ludicrous misconception, and a dangerous one to boot'. Returning to the theme of communalism and the example of the Sikhs at the Wolverhampton Transport Department, Powell presented an apocalyptic vision of the future with aggressive immigrant groups seeking control:

Now we are seeing the growth of positive forces acting against integration, of vested interests in the preservation and sharpening of racial and religious differences, with a view to the exercise of actual domination, first over fellow-immigrants and then over the rest of the population. The cloud no bigger than a man's hand, that can so rapidly over-cast the sky, has been visible recently in Wolverhampton and has shown signs of spreading quickly... For these dangerous and divisive elements the legislation proposed in the Race Relations Bill is the very pabulum they know to flourish on. Here is their means of showing that the immigrant communities can organise to consolidate their members, to agitate and campaign against their fellow citizens, and to overawe and dominate the rest with the legal weapons which the ignorant and the ill-informed have provided. As I look ahead, I am filled with foreboding. Like the Roman, I seem to see 'the River Tiber foaming with much blood'.

Racialism and opportunism

A Gallup opinion poll, taken days after the speech, found that 96 per cent of people had 'heard about or read about' it.[50] Its immediate effect was to set in motion parallel debates about racialism and opportunism which, linked to Powell's lack of constructive proposals, saw him consistently on the defensive for the next two years. With support from key members of the LCC, including Hogg and Macleod, the Shadow Chancellor, Heath promptly dismissed Powell from his post as shadow Defence Minister because his speech had been 'racialist in tone and liable to exacerbate racial tensions'.[51] Powell responded that Heath must have known 'it was nothing of the kind' and went on to accuse Heath of 'playing down and even unsaying policies and views which you hold and believe to be right, for fear of clamour from some sector of the press or public'.[52] A little later, Powell spelled out his position in the *Birmingham Post*: 'What I would take racialist to mean is a person who believes in the inherent superiority of one race of mankind to another, and who acts and speaks in that belief. So the answer to the question of whether I am a racialist is "No".'[53] Yet the charge was widespread. *The Times* called the speech 'racialist... calculated to inflame hatred between the races', prompting Powell to withdraw from a lunch with its senior editorial staff that had been arranged the previous month.[54] *The Times* also reported the comparison made by the former Conservative MP Humphry Berkeley between the ethnic prejudice of Powell and the anti-Semitism of the one-time leader of the British Union of Fascists, Sir Oswald Mosley, a suggestion for which Berkeley later apologized after writing a favourable biography of Powell.[55]

At the same time, there was also substantial public, as well as political, support for Powell—with some of it explicitly rejecting charges of racialism. Only two national newspapers supported Powell—the *Daily Express* and the *News of the World*—but they had a combined circulation of over ten million.[56] Famously, a group of immigration officers at Heathrow Airport, as private individuals, 'heartily endorse[d]' Powell's position.[57] On 23 April between 800 and 2,300 dockers—depending on estimates—marched to Parliament to demonstrate their support for Powell.[58] A Gallup poll in early May found that 74 per cent of those questioned agreed with the speech, with 15 per cent disagreeing and 11 per cent giving no opinion.[59] Within a fortnight, Powell had received about 100,000 letters from members of the public—of which only 800 were critical of him. Powell allowed Diana Spearman, who had worked at the Conservative Research Department, to look at these letters, and she went on to make an important intervention in the debate. Selecting a sample of 3,537, she argued that only 71 of them were racialist. Yet Spearman had adopted a very narrow definition of the term. This covered 'general accusations against the immigrants, the use of words generally considered offensive to them, such as nigger and coon' and even then added the qualification 'unless they occur in letters in which a specific complaint is made'.[60] Douglas-Home argued that Powell's 'language may have been ill-chosen and extravagant but he is not and never has been a racialist'.[61] Gilbert Longden, the Conservative MP who had collaborated with Powell in the One Nation Group, issued a statement in support of him, saying that his 'fears for the future of this Country if the immigration of other races is allowed to continue are fully justified'.[62] The Monday Club, whose membership was growing rapidly at this point, expressed overall support for Powell on immigration.[63] The government itself had swiftly decided that Powell would not be prosecuted for incitement to racial hatred under the terms of the 1965 Race Relations Act—not least because intention was so difficult to prove—but the manner in which it merely offered a 'bald announcement of the decision', without going into detail, indicated an awareness of the need to tread carefully amid a heated debate.[64]

The charge of opportunism emerged as the scale of popular support for Powell became clear. Richard Crossman, Lord President of the Council and Leader of the House of Commons, captured a sense of this in his diary, where he recorded his impression that Powell was 'appealing to mass opinion right over Parliament and his party leadership'.[65] In the House of Commons on 23 April, as the Race Relations Bill was debated, Hogg accused

Figure 5. Dock workers demonstrate in support of Powell, on their march through London to Parliament, 23 April 1968.

Powell of not consulting his colleagues, alerting two television networks and 'by-passing the Conservative Office' in distributing the speech to the press.[66] Powell, in turn, denied calling the television networks and said he had issued the speech through the West Midlands area of the Conservative Party, a common practice, he suggested, when speaking in his own area.[67] Significantly, the *Express & Star*, which had supported Powell's Walsall speech but criticized the 'overstatement' in Birmingham, now suggested that Powell had a tendency to be evasive, with its journalists 'consistently rebuffed' when they approached Powell for comment on immigration.[68] The editor, J. Clement Jones, who knew Powell and his family well, maintained his line despite Powell's objection.[69] In further correspondence, Jones left Powell in no doubt about his personal view: 'I deplore and still do, the inflammatory nature of parts of your Birmingham speech, and regard its timing as a political manoeuvre rather than as being motivated by long felt deep concern for the problems of the people resident in this area.'[70] Notably, the attack on Powell also came from those who agreed with him. The Conservative MP Jasper More, who considered that the Race Relations Bill stood to make 'our immigrant population...a privileged class', told his constituents of his 'personal regret' that Powell 'should not have made such speeches ten or twelve years ago'.[71] Powell publicly replied that he had called for immigration controls in government and party circles since the mid-1950s.[72] Powell had indeed done this, but there was also no doubt that his public record on the issue did not go back as far as certain other anti-immigration campaigners.

The accusation of opportunism on Powell's part was linked to the claims about the widow. Powell had, in fact, quoted directly from a letter sent to him from the north-east of England, which had opened: 'I am writing to you on behalf of the poor and inarticulate white people whose whole lives have been disrupted by the flood of immigrants let into England by successive Governments, and especially by this one.'[73] Powell had further correspondence with the author, assuring them about his commitment to concealing their identity.[74] Writing to The Times, a community liaison officer from Oxford stated that a 'large number of racialist anecdotes of this kind is in circulation'. Indeed, she had recently heard one from someone who claimed it was 'about an old lady in London (not Wolverhampton) whom a friend of hers knew' but with '[a]lmost every circumstantial detail...the same'.[75] The Express & Star, with its local knowledge, was unable to identify the widow.[76] Powell was asked for further information. In a letter sent to the press, the Labour MP David Winnick argued that 'if I as an MP received such information I would wish to know the main particulars to see what help could be given to the person'.[77] Powell's reply was emphatic: 'I never disclose except at their request particulars likely to assist in the identification of constituents – or indeed other individuals – whose cases I may use to illustrate circumstances or problems.'[78] Yet there is no indication that Powell had verified the identity of the woman about whom the correspondent had written.[79]

By this point, one part of the speech was causing Powell anguish—as he told his fellow Conservative MP John Biffen, who had seconded him in the 1965 leadership election. Powell realized that, in his quotation from Virgil's *Aeneid*, he had misquoted: it was the Sybil, not the Roman, who saw the Tiber 'foaming with much blood'.[80] In any case, the debate continued with suggestions of opportunism featuring in both favourable and critical assessments of Powell. The Conservative historian John Vincent argued that Powell was 'basically pursuing a perfectly respectable end – personal ambition – by using a perfectly respectable means: the desire of the great bulk of British opinion'. Revisiting the claim of Powell 'allegedly refusing to speak at Smethwick', Vincent considered it unproblematic that 'before 1964, when the country was supposedly unconcerned, he was as quiet on this point as any other politician' and thereafter made an 'adjustment to the racialist victory at Smethwick'.[81] Yet Powell was quick to write to Vincent, insisting that the explanation was a 'double booking'.[82] As he researched his book on Powell and immigration, Paul Foot was particularly keen to test how far Powell had been 'consistent and courageous' in his views on the issue.[83] Concluding that he had not, Foot had probed Powell—who had offered to cooperate—rigorously.[84] Foot had also sought the views of Harold Gurden, a prominent opponent of Commonwealth immigration in the late 1950s.[85] Indeed, it was indicative of Powell's perceived vulnerability on this issue that he asked Gurden, who had consulted him, to collaborate to 'verify our recollections'.[86] In the event, Gurden did not reply to Foot.[87]

Powell's consistency was also challenged from another direction by a swathe of neo-liberal opinion. After Powell's speech at Walsall in February 1968, Harris had told Powell that the 'throwing up of barriers' was inconsistent with his free-market perspective. Powell replied that it 'had not occurred to me that you, or anyone, could think this'. Instead Powell argued that it was 'right and necessary that any country should have the legal discretion whether or not to admit within its boundaries those who wish to settle there, and, for this purpose, to distinguish between "its own people" and the rest of the inhabitants of the world'.[88] The publication of Powell's *Freedom and Reality* in April 1969 brought this issue right to the fore. Reportedly, Friedman had asked: 'What has happened to Enoch Powell? His position on labour migration is quite inconsistent with free market principles.' Samuel Brittan, the economic commentator at the *Financial Times* and a significant free-market voice, spelled out Powell's divergence, seeing Powell's 'economic liberalism . . . allied uneasily with an attachment to the nation state as the absolute political value' while most 'economic liberals' considered 'the national interest as a function of the interests of the individuals who compose it' and were 'highly suspicious of supposedly superior collective entities'.[89] T. E. Utley did not necessarily see Powell's position as inconsistent, but it was significant that his defence of Powell returned to opportunism, albeit in a qualified manner. Utley argued that it 'would be sycophantic to deny that Powell's pre-occupation with immigration (natural as it is for a Wolverhampton member and a believer in the nation state) owes something to his knowledge that this is a compelling popular theme, more so than the virtues of free enterprise or the need for a realistic defence policy'.[90]

The argument was increasingly made that Powell had no constructive proposals to deal with immigration or immigrants in Britain. This was the view of James Callaghan, as Home Secretary, in April 1968, who lamented that: 'He is unrealistic in assuming there will be substantial repatriation. He will <u>never</u> use his powerful intellect to show us how to live with this coloured group, who are with us!' Hogg was strongly in agreement, annotating Callaghan's final remark: 'This is the point. The mistakes (if they are mistakes) have given us a problem with which we must cope + can only do so on the basis of human rights.'[91] This view found an echo in Foot's book, which argued that: 'For the real problems which confront immigrants and their neighbours, Enoch Powell has no credible solution.'[92] Powell's case was not helped by the widespread confusion over whether his policy of repatriation was to be forcible or voluntary. Leon Brittan, brother of Samuel and a cabinet minister in the 1980s, told Powell: 'I know from my own friends and people in North Kensington [where he was the Conservative parliamentary candidate] that there has been genuine uncertainty on this point among many people who are generally sympathetic to your viewpoint.'[93] More damningly still, Utley's largely sympathetic book on Powell made the same point, noting a 'certain amount of ambiguity' over the question of deportation.[94]

There was, of course, a hardening of Conservative Party policy that was, in some part at least, in response to the public reaction to Powell's speech.[95] In September, Heath committed the party to removing all remaining privileges from Commonwealth immigrants and to treating them as aliens, with tighter restrictions on the entry of dependants.[96] The party also began to investigate the projected future size of the immigrant population.[97] Yet, overall, there was an attempt to draw a line between Powell and the party.

Speaking in Eastbourne in November 1968, Powell had taken issue with the fact that Heath had objected to his 'tone' in Birmingham in a speech when he also provocatively stated that: 'The West Indian or Asian does not, by being born in England, become an Englishman . . . in fact he is a West Indian or an Asian still.'[98] Yet Heath was now emphasizing policy differences, particularly positive action to improve race relations. In January 1969, Heath stated: 'I asked Mr Powell to leave the Shadow Cabinet because his views were not Conservative Party views on this matter and because I objected to the way in which he expressed them'.[99] This led *The Sunday Times* on 2 February 1969 to state that Heath had 'a genuine desire to see race relations improve' and, in contrast to Powell, 'refuses to spout the fantasies of racial purity', a reference to Powell's speech at Eastbourne. Powell took issue with this and began libel proceedings against the newspaper, with the case settled in 1970.[100] Meanwhile, the Conservative Party continued to distinguish its position from that of Powell. In mid-1969 Hogg argued that Powell 'pandered to those who think it [immigration] can be eliminated', while 'Heath's policy' was 'based upon the premise that although perhaps you can reduce it, you can't eliminate it and the first and most vital priority is to meet it and to face the problem'.[101] This view found an echo elsewhere. On the Parliamentary Select Committee on Race Relations and Immigration, the former Liberal Party leader Jo Grimond argued that Powell was 'building up a wholly hysterical attitude about this whole problem' and, considering that there would be limited interest in repatriation, contended that 'Powell has no constructive ideas whatever'.[102]

Yet Powell's stance was deliberate. He explained to Cyril Northcote Parkinson, the naval historian who was sympathetic to his viewpoint, that 'in all my own statements on Commonwealth immigration I have limited myself to the single issue of "alienness" combined with numbers. This does not mean that there are not other important aspects, but in political debate it is essential to fasten on the one vital part of one's argument and stick to that.'[103] Powell later made a similar point to the civil servant Sir Philip Allen who, in a note for the Home Secretary, recorded: 'He said that he had not himself concentrated on what could be done here about an indigenous coloured population – he had devoted his efforts to keeping down the numbers.'[104] As we have seen, the emphasis on one particular theme was an important part of Powell's strategy. Yet, on this issue, it left him exposed. On 17 January 1970, Powell argued that except 'in connection with, and as integral part of voluntary and assisted repatriation, measures of financial and other alleviation to the administration of the areas especially affected... are positively harmful in their effect because they encourage all concerned to deceive themselves for longer and longer as to the true magnitude of the prospect'.[105] Patrick Cosgrave, working at the Conservative Research Department, examined the speech for Heath and argued that it showed that Powell 'opposes any serious attempt to alleviate the effects of this concentration by Government aid'.[106] With Powell already known to be critical of regional planning, on BBC Radio 4 Heath stated that:

> [T]he conclusion, as I understand it, of Mr Powell's present speech is that – certainly the implication of it is that – we should do nothing to help the Boroughs and Cities like Birmingham and Wolverhampton which have got these problems in the hope that if only we let the housing get bad enough and the schools get overcrowded enough and the Health Service burdened enough, the immigrants will go away of their own accord and the problems will disappear.[107]

Powell told Heath that 'no one who had read the speech... could reasonably understand the conclusion or implication of it to be that which you are

Figure 6. A demonstration in London against Powell and his anti-immigration stance, January 1970.

recorded as asserting'.[108] Yet Heath's interpretation understandably resonated, being partially repeated in the *Sunday Telegraph*.[109] Powell promptly wrote to Peregrine Worsthorne, the paper's deputy editor, not just to state that 'I have said neither this nor anything to this effect' but also to express his concern about it 'getting repeated as if it were fact'.[110] There was a real danger, by this time, that Powell's influence in political circles was being undermined by his position on immigration. Harris, who—as we have seen—considered his stance on the issue was inconsistent with his economic thought, echoed a broader point when he told Powell, 'I cannot help thinking that you are missing a golden opportunity to widen and deepen your following, instead of risking the opposite effect.'[111]

'Disorder', misleading statistics, and 'national catastrophe'

From 1970, Powell made a determined effort to shape the debate over immigration, relating concerns over 'race' to fears of wider disorder. Powell had taken particular interest in the social and political unrest that had appeared to develop from 1968, collecting a file of material on it that, as he told Bill Schwarz in 1988, he had named 'The Thing'.[112] At a time of student unrest in higher education, and at a point when student protests against Powell were prevalent, he chose a dinner held by the Federation of Conservative Students at the northern universities to argue that 'university disorder... is closely, not to say, integrally, connected with that more general civil disorder or anarchy which I believe is also on the ascendant'. In exaggerated terms, Powell considered that the 'object of this minority is the destruction of authority, of the institutions of society and of society itself'.[113] In June 1970, during the election campaign, Powell argued that the political parties 'dare not discuss a subject... which for millions of electors transcends all others in importance'. In what has become known as his 'Enemy within' speech, Powell argued:

> Our danger is that the enemy has mastered the art of establishing a moral ascendancy over his victims and destroying their good conscience... Have you ever wondered, perhaps, why opinions which the majority of people quite naturally hold are, if anyone dares express them publicly, denounced as 'controversial', 'extremist', 'explosive', 'disgraceful', and overwhelmed with a violence and venom quite unknown to debate on mere political issues? It is because the whole power of the aggressor depends upon preventing people

from seeing what is happening and from saying what they see. The most perfect, and the most dangerous, example of this process is the subject miscalled, and deliberately miscalled, 'race'. The people of this country are told that they must feel neither alarm nor objection to a West Indian, African and Asian population which will rise to several millions, being introduced into this country. If they do, they are 'prejudiced', 'racialist', 'unChristian' and 'failing to show an example to the rest of the world'... It is even heresy to assert the plain fact that the English are a White nation.[114]

At the same time, Powell drew on debates over immigration statistics to contend that the people had been misled—a development of his earlier implication that, with the process being accidental, they had not been consulted. In May 1970, addressing the conference of the Institute of Population Registration, Powell praised the organization's successful call for the inclusion of the country of birth of both parents on the registration of a child's birth. Powell argued that this change produced the 'discovery that the Registrar General was gravely underestimating' the number of children of New Commonwealth origin, the natural increase. He then further suggested that 'at least one-fifth of the population of what is now the City of Birmingham will in course of time be coloured'.[115] Speaking in Wolverhampton during the 1970 general-election campaign, Powell was more forthright in saying that 'the people of this country have been misled, cruelly and persistently', and going on to state that there were already 'parts of this town which have ceased to be part of England, except in the sense that they are situated within it geographically'.[116]

Powell's stance immediately put him at odds with the new Conservative government. The party had come to power on a manifesto that pledged to end large-scale immigration by ensuring that future work permits would not carry the right of permanent settlement for the holder or their dependants and would normally be issued for only twelve months. The manifesto had also promised 'assistance to Commonwealth immigrants who wish to return to their countries of origin', while stressing that it abhorred 'any attempt to harass or compel them to go against their will'.[117] Yet there was a wider perception that Powell's more outspoken position had exposed the manner in which 'the distance between politicians and the public is great and growing'.[118] Powell was, according to the Westminster journalist Andrew Roth, now 'the most significant Tory tribune, speaking for substantial sections previously ignored by established party leaders'.[119]

The Office of Population Censuses and Surveys (recently formed from a merger of the General Register Office and the Government Social Survey

Department and led by the Registrar General) considered that Powell's charge of underestimation could 'be counteracted by making public . . . the amount of detailed work and thought we have put into this subject' but was wary of doing so because it recognized that it might be necessary to 'modify . . . assumptions about future rates of immigration'.[120] The office did, however, perceptively note a flaw in Powell's position: it included children where one parent was UK-born in 'any assimilation problem'.[121] The dispute directly fed into the feud between Powell and Heath. The newly elected prime minister was initially keen to confront Powell but was urged not to do so by Reginald Maudling, the Home Secretary, and soon resolved 'to keep as far as possible out of the "numbers game" '.[122] Aware that the official statistics did 'not give a complete picture of Commonwealth immigration' (excluding, for example, those admitted as visitors or students who decided to settle permanently having had their conditions revoked), Maudling adopted a strategy of 'trying to deal with the explosive subject of race relations' by seeking 'the avoidance of any unnecessary controversy . . . with Mr Powell'.[123]

Powell persisted. He voted with the government on the 1971 Immigration Bill, which treated Commonwealth citizens the same as those from elsewhere, meaning that they did not have the right to bring dependants and could only remain in the UK if they had lived there for more than five years. It also included provision for voluntary repatriation, with funding for travel expenses. *The Spectator* initially considered it a 'Powellite triumph'.[124] But, for several reasons, this was not the case, as Powell made clear when it was debated in Parliament. He was critical both of its failure to define UK citizenship and of its 'patrial' provision, which excluded from immigration control most of those with a grandparent born in the UK. Powell considered that it stood to introduce 'a new class who will have privilege of entry and residence' but returned once again to colour when he noted that it potentially included 'hundreds of thousands' of Anglo-Indians.[125] Powell's attack continued. In summer 1971 he cited official figures which, for the period between May 1970 and April 1971, showed a 10 per cent increase in New Commonwealth immigration on the previous year, and stated: 'Immigration is not diminishing. The Government, the Home Office, the race relations propagandists all want that to be believed; but it is not so.'[126] Later in the year, Powell criticized the government's 'back-tracking on assistance to voluntary repatriation'—about which very little had, in practice, happened.[127]

In summer 1972, events in Uganda, where President Idi Amin announced the expulsion of all Asians, further soured relations between Powell and the government.[128] As the government attempted to persuade Amin to reverse his decision, and amid speculation that Asian holders of British passports in Uganda numbered 55,000, Powell spoke about their possible arrival as 'the spectacle of national catastrophe approaching in slow motion'. He argued that 'we have no sort of special obligation to these people' and described the Ugandan Asians as 'the thin end of a very thick wedge'.[129] Powell made similar comments on BBC Radio 4's 'The World at One' on 27 August, provocatively suggesting that the Attorney General Sir Peter Rawlinson was 'misleading the country' about their right of entry.[130] In a context where a Gallup poll in September suggested 57 per cent were against Ugandan Asians being allowed to settle in Britain, Powell's stance generated difficulties within the Conservative Party.[131] Hogg, now Lord Chancellor and with a life peerage as Baron Hailsham of St Marylebone, reflected to the Attorney General that: 'It is always difficult to know what to do about these things. He gets the publicity and when one traipses round afterwards cleaning up the mess much of the damage has been done.'[132] Yet Powell was arguably more isolated than he had been in 1968. Gilbert Longden, a key ally of Powell at that time and someone who continued to call for a halt to immigration, considered that the number of Ugandan refugees was relatively small and that there were special circumstances involved.[133] Indeed, when the Labour government had made Kenyan Asians subject to the voucher restrictions of the 1962 Commonwealth Immigration Act in 1968, an assurance had been given in Parliament that any Asian citizen 'compelled' to leave the territory where they were living would be accepted in the UK.

Towards the extremes?

Powell's break with the Conservatives in 1974 was concerned with economics and, above all, with Europe, but immigration nevertheless continued to be a prominent issue. From this point on, however, Powell was battling a perception that he moved on the extremes of British politics. In the first place, there were suggestions about Powell's connections with the National Front that had been established in 1967. Powell declined a series of invitations to join the organization and to contest a seat as one of its candidates.[134] Nonetheless, suggestions about the connection persisted—even if they did not always suit the National Front. Martin Webster, one of its most prominent members, took issue with the *Daily Mirror*'s front-page article on 4 April 1977, which claimed that the National Front wanted Powell as its leader. Webster stressed that while there was agreement over immigration, Powell's free-market economics (and his opposition to capital punishment) were at odds with National Front policy.[135] Conservative circles were also pervaded by the rumours. Hailsham recorded that he had been told—at third hand—that 'it was quite certain that Enoch had agreed to lead the National Front'.[136] Developments in popular politics reinforced the impression. After Powell's departure from the Conservative Party, Bee Carthew, whose West London apartment had served as the headquarters for the association that had been established in 1970 to publish the monthly *Powellight* newsletter, had, by 1976, turned her home into the West London branch of the National Front.[137] The comments of Powell's publisher, Andrew G. Elliot, captured a sense of developments nicely. Elliot's Right Way Books had been the first to publish his Birmingham speech, with Elliot himself telling Powell that he was '1000% right on this terrifying colour problem'.[138] Now, recognizing that Powell still elicited considerable popular support, Elliot told Powell: 'I am finding it harder than ever to defend you amongst the middle or upper classes. A great number of these people seem to take the attitude that you have become an extremist, too far to what they call "The Right"'.[139]

The change was also apparent in government attitudes to Powell vis-à-vis race-relations legislation. In October 1976 Powell made a speech to the Surrey Monday Club in which, calling again for repatriation, he warned 'physical and violent conflict must sooner or later supervene where an indigenous population sees no end to the progressive occupation of its heartland by aliens with whom they do not identify themselves and who do not identify themselves with them'.[140] With no formal complaints as yet, the Solicitor General considered it 'the usual Powell type of speech' that 'will do nothing to reduce the unease and concern felt by the coloured population of this country' but added that he had 'considerable doubts however whether there is a prima facie case under the Race Relations Act 1965'—though he did note Powell's reference to limiting 'the dimension of an "alien wedge"'.[141] Sam Silkin, the Attorney General, took a different view. While not considering prosecution because it was difficult to prove intent— just as it had been in April 1968—Silkin worried that 'people will lose faith in the enforcement agencies if they do not condemn what is obviously morally wrong'.[142] Powell had again been quoting—this time from Lord Radcliffe, a prominent judge best known for the 1959 Radcliffe Report on monetary policy, who had spoken in 1969 of 'inserting into a fairly complex urban and industrial civilisation a large alien wedge'.[143] Silkin was undeterred and told correspondents who had criticized Powell's speech that:

> I have no doubt that a very large proportion of those who have made this country their home, let alone those who were born here, would rightly regard as insulting Mr Powell's description of them as 'an alien wedge' and his defeatist assumption that it is impossible for them and the non-coloured population amongst whom they live and work to do so in harmony with one another . . . I also deeply regret Mr Powell's apparent inability to appreciate that both his language and the defeatism expressed by him are themselves only too likely to damage race relations and hence to create or to exacerbate the divisions and disharmonies which he so persistently prophesises.[144]

Powell's attitude to Thatcher, as Leader of the Opposition from 1975, served to cement the sense of his separation from the mainstream of politics. Thatcher had earlier taken a benevolent line on Powell. The two of them had first met in 1948 but, despite her long-standing admiration for Powell—which grew as she was drawn to his economic arguments—Thatcher had voted for Heath in the 1965 party-leadership election.[145] Powell and Thatcher had then spent six months in the shadow cabinet together, until Powell's dismissal in April 1968. In 1970, in response to criticisms of her local Finchley Conservative Association's choice of Powell as a guest speaker, Thatcher argued that those 'who use this country's great tradition of freedom of speech should not seek to deny that same freedom to others'.[146] Nonetheless, with Thatcher at the helm, Powell continued to attack the Conservative Party's 'silence or calculated evasion' on immigration.[147] Thatcher privately sought to reassure Powell that the 'Conservative Party believes that the present level of immigration is too high and must immediately be reduced.'[148] And in January 1978 she famously told Granada Television's 'World in Action' that the British people feared they 'might be rather swamped by people with a different culture'.[149] Thatcher's remarks were widely considered to have pandered to popular prejudices.[150] Yet, in reality, the position was more complex. In addition to using concerns about immigration to gain political advantage, the party had also begun, from 1976, to make concerted efforts to secure the support of black and Asian minority voters.[151] This was why, as Powell himself noted, the party sought to minimize the impact of Thatcher's comments by stressing that she was simply echoing established party policy.[152] Nevertheless, Thatcher's speech prompted calls for Powell to offer her support from, for example, Patrick Donner, the former Conservative MP.[153] Powell's sharp reply echoed his dismissive attitude towards her on economic policy: 'I am naturally watching what is happening with sardonic interest; but Mrs Thatcher has evidently a long way to go before she even understands the matter, let alone is in a position to give any lead on it. In any case, no measure of less than heroic dimensions could now produce any impression on the future problem.'[154] Powell was soon equally critical in public, saying that it was 'the cruellest folly or deception to induce people ... to imagine' that immigration could be stopped with anything other than 'a policy for reimmigration and resettlement'.[155]

With the Conservatives in government, and against the backdrop of urban disturbances in 1980, 1981, and 1985, dubbed 'race riots' at the time, Powell remained as apocalyptic as ever, but, in the main, his arguments did not resonate. As rioting in St Paul's in Bristol in April 1980 was reported to the House of Commons, Powell asked the Home Secretary, Willie Whitelaw, if he was 'surprised by these events'.[156] This swiftly drew a response from the Conservative MP for Bristol West, William Waldegrave, who spoke dismissively on BBC Radio 4 of how 'people like Enoch Powell are rubbing their hands with glee', prompting Powell to take umbrage.[157] Yet Waldegrave, who told Powell of his admiration for his contribution to Conservative thinking, insisted that 'predictions of widespread racial violence have some self-fulfilling power in them'.[158] The following year, 1981, after rioting in Brixton, London, in April and in Toxteth, Liverpool, in July, Powell tried to interest the publisher Elliot in 'a paperback assembling the principal items— and very up to date some of them are! – of what Enoch predicted', suggesting that this 'would have a market right now'.[159] However, Elliot turned Powell down, telling him frankly that 'your other books are not easy to sell'.[160] In the same year, Powell welcomed the passage of the British Nationality Act, which reclassified the UK and Colonies Citizenship into British Citizenship, British Dependent Territories Citizenship, and British Overseas Citizenship, with only British Citizenship giving automatic right of settlement. Powell was pleased that 'the word "British" is for the first time in the law of the United Kingdom used to describe the United Kingdom and the United Kingdom alone', meaning that the 'United Kingdom is therefore declaring, for the first time, that it is a nation'.[161] Yet, in the main, he continued to be dissatisfied as he saw himself at odds with the overall public mood. The Scarman Report, commissioned after Brixton and published in November 1981, argued that it had been a spontaneous outbreak of resentment, derived from an underlying social and economic situation in which 'racial disadvantage' needed urgent attention. In 1982 Powell called for 'the British people and their government and political parties to snap out of the fatalistic resignation with which millions now watch their cities and their country sliding towards the abyss'.[162] Continuing to fear 'civil conflict of awesome scale and intensity', Powell called this a 'spell of silence and pretence'.[163] Where the Scarman Report had argued for improvements in policing (which had been decidedly heavy-handed towards the black community), Powell returned to repatriation in a form that strongly implied the application of pressure to leave. Amid much discussion of training and retraining in a context of high unemployment, Powell asked whether 'among the New Commonwealth ethnic population [it] ought not to be deliberately and systematically related to the needs and prospects of their home countries'.[164] When rioting broke out in Handsworth, Birmingham, in September 1985, Powell rehearsed old themes, foreseeing 'a Britain unimaginatively wracked by dissension and violent disorder, not recognisable as the same nation as it has been, or perhaps as a nation at all'.[165] Powell also saw a new version of the old danger of aggressive immigrant groups. Expressing concern that those in Hong Kong, who had acquired British Dependent Territories Citizenship as part of the 1981 British Nationality Act, would be given some form of British nationality, with accompanying right of UK residence, after Hong Kong was transferred to China in 1997 (in a process shortly to be agreed under the terms of the Sino-British Joint Declaration of December 1984), Powell called for great vigilance. He warned that the Chinese population in Britain would undertake 'a major, sustained operation in the next fifteen years and after to transfer the maximum population from Hong Kong to Britain'.[166]

Powell also now developed the arguments—which he had first sketched out thirty years beforehand—about the manner in which immigration could undermine democracy. In 1978, in an article translated from German and published in the *New Statesman*, Powell had suggested that the 'presence of coloured MPs' could 'become incompatible with the functioning of the British parliament', but, at this time, he placed the danger below that of the threat from the European Community and from nationalism, especially in its Scottish form.[167] In 1985 Powell took issue with an article in *The Times* by Roger Scruton, the Conservative philosopher, editor of the *Salisbury Review* and a lecturer at Birkbeck College, London, arguing for a quota of ethnic-minority representatives of ethnic electorates in the House of Commons (on the basis that this would bolster Conservative forces), at a point when the Labour Party was debating setting up 'black sections' to ensure proportional representation at all levels of the party.[168] In a context where equal opportunities provisions had increased, Powell argued:

> These are symptoms of approaching crisis; for where numbers are political power, as, supremely, in Parliament, the numbers game of ethnic monitoring and quotas becomes a matter of life-and-death that will disturb even the pacific complacency of the British public, which has been content, with no more than private murmurings, to observe the spread of this epidemic folly. Dr Scruton flies in the face of human nature when he imagines that fifty or sixty Members of parliament differentiated from and privileged above by the acknowledged right of race will not know how to use that capability to attract power from the rest who are bidding and counter-bidding for their votes.[169]

Powell expanded on this point in 1993, on the twenty-fifth anniversary of his Birmingham speech, grappling not with the prospect of an imagined quota but with the real impact of the geographical concentration of parts of the immigrant population, arguing: 'It is here that the compatibility of such an ethnic minority with the functioning of parliamentary democracy comes into question.' Powell continued:

> Parliamentary democracy depends at all levels upon the valid acceptance of majority decision, by which the nation as a whole is content to be bound because of the continually available prospect that what one majority has decided another majority can subsequently alter. From this point of view, the political homogeneity of the electorate is crucial.[170]

Yet, by this stage, the reality of British society did not appear to fit Powell's prognosis—if indeed it ever had. Immigrants from the New Commonwealth (principally India and Pakistan) had always been divided in a range of ways—not just by place of origin and religion but also, for example, by generation and social status in Britain. By the 1990s, moreover, it was the 'rich diversity of Britain's immigrant mix' that was striking in a situation where ethnic minority groups were fragmented, where there had been also been a considerable rise in European-born immigrants, and where there was some—albeit varying—degree of participation in party politics. This was the backdrop to increased talk of a (not always neatly defined) pluralistic 'multiculturalism'.[171] This development stood to undermine Powell's arguments, as he had to accept, acknowledging that:

> What we do not, as yet, know is whether the voting behaviour of our altered population will be able to use the majority vote as a political instrument and not as a means of self-identification, self-assertion and self-enumeration. It may be that the United Kingdom will escape the political consequences of communalism; but communalism and democracy, as the experience of India demonstrates, are incompatible.[172]

4

Europe

The recurring debate over how to respond to closer European integration—in which Powell played a full and dramatic part—has had a far-reaching impact on British politics in the years after 1945. Time and again, it had, as the prominent journalist Hugo Young put it in 1998, a particular 'fissile effect' of creating divisions within political parties.[1] And in 1975 it produced the first-ever national referendum—putting the question of continued European Community membership, which had only been secured two years beforehand, directly to the people.[2] Yet the issue was far from settled. Indeed, the 2016 referendum on European Union (EU) membership—and its ongoing consequences—has shown just how contentious, at a political and wider public level, the issue continues to be. Powell is firmly recognized as one of the foremost opponents of British membership, but we are also aware that he had once supported it—and not simply on the basis that it was an economic grouping. We appreciate too that it was his fears about the loss of parliamentary sovereignty which came to underpin his position as he argued that joining the European Community threatened the very existence of the British nation.

Powell presented his opposition to Community membership, including his attempt to draw parallels between it and immigration, as a populist cause that saw the people ignored, and even manipulated, by party elites. As he did so, Powell's awkward endorsement of a referendum, and his more frequent demand for the people's wishes to be considered—especially if they differed from the views of their elected representatives in Parliament—exposed the tensions in his thought between parliamentary and popular sovereignty. Powell made a further argument that over Europe the party system was failing in its fundamental job of offering a choice to the electorate—a particular type of decline but also a response to finding himself adrift in British party politics. This was the context in which Powell began engaging, albeit sporadically, with pressure groups calling for British withdrawal from the European Community and eventually came, in the early 1990s, to endorse parliamentary candidates from the Anti-Federalist League (AFL) and the United Kingdom Independence Party (UKIP) into which it evolved.

Britain in Europe

Until the end of the 1960s, Powell viewed issues about Europe in terms of other areas we have already examined: international relations and economics. He had, however, already fluctuated in his opinions. In 1950, as the Labour government rejected the French ultimatum to decide promptly whether to join the European Coal and Steel Community (ECSC), Powell was one of six Conservative MPs who abstained when the Conservative Party opposed the government's decision.[3] The overall Conservative position was based on an acceptance of European unity as a check against communism, a view that aligned it with the United States.[4] Powell's concern was the Empire. He was opposed to 'any pooling of sovereignty with the European countries which would automatically result in severing her from the non-European countries of the Empire'. He further argued that, 'unlike the countries of the continent, Britain's main defence obligations lie overseas in the countries of the Empire or those bordering upon it'.[5] Subsequent events moved quickly, but Powell's attention was elsewhere. With the United Kingdom standing aloof, the six West European states already in the ECSC (West Germany, France, Italy, Belgium, the Netherlands, and Luxembourg) convened at Messina in Sicily in 1955 and agreed to form the European Economic Community (EEC), with a common market and customs union, which was enacted in the Treaty of Rome (1957) and came into being in 1958.

After the Conservative government under Harold Macmillan applied for membership of this new European grouping in 1961, Powell embraced economic arguments in favour of joining and used them to attack Labour. With the government keen to benefit from a shift in British trading patterns away from the Empire/Commonwealth and towards Western Europe in the previous decade, Powell criticized Labour's 'dithering and ambivalence' at a time when the party was divided over membership and its leader Hugh Gaitskell notably opposed.[6] Powell's assault on Labour continued even after the French President Charles de Gaulle vetoed the UK application in

January 1963. Developing his case for a 'free economy', Powell argued that
Labour's main priority—in contrast—was 'to keep our economy sufficiently
insulated from the outside world to be in the control of the national planners',
which was 'the root of their antagonism to the Common Market'.[7]
Significantly, Powell was also dismissive of those in the Conservative Party,
such as Victor Montagu (formerly Viscount Hinchingbrooke), who argued
that British membership would damage trade with the Commonwealth.
Back in 1950, Powell had himself sought to prioritize trade with the Empire
but, having argued that the Empire's break-up was inevitable and that the
Commonwealth was a pretence, he now blasted the (numerically diminishing)
grouping 'which remains irreconcilably opposed to a European alignment
and still worships at the deserted shrine of Commonwealth preference'.
Powell's overall view was that there was a recognition, across the board, of
the potential benefits of British membership: from industry anticipating
increased trade; from agriculture expecting to flourish under the managed
prices of the Common Agricultural Policy (CAP); and from the public that
was beginning to perceive advantages in the large European market.[8]

Importantly, at this stage Powell sought to minimize concerns about the
diminution of British sovereignty. During the House of Commons debate
over the UK application in August 1961 the Conservative Derek Walker-
Smith, the former Minister of Health, had explicitly argued that European
political union, which he held to be the long-term goal, would undermine
sovereignty.[9] On the Labour side, Douglas Jay, Michael Foot, and Peter
Shore soon echoed similar concerns.[10] From his involvement in the shadow
cabinet in 1965, as shadow Transport Minister before becoming shadow
Defence Minister in the summer, Powell could have been in little doubt
that the Common Market was regarded as a 'political and military as well as
an economic grouping'.[11] Yet he argued:

> The instinctive resistance of the British to anything which would limit their
> treasured independence and national sovereignty has been much softened.
> They have become accustomed to the notion that the decisions of
> international bodies on which Britain is represented but which she does
> not control might be accepted without abandoning their pride that 'Britons
> never shall be slaves.'[12]

Powell saw membership of the European Community as a means of checking
British economic and international decline. Powell had, of course, taken
issue with what he saw as the fixation on comparing British economic
performance unfavourably with that of other, especially West European,

states. Yet, while he disagreed with the left-wing analyses of the economists Andrew Shonfield and Michael Shanks, with their calls for more state planning, he agreed with them, at this stage, that it would be economically beneficial to join the Community—albeit on the basis that this would facilitate greater competition. Arguing that it was necessary to 'see the outside changing world in its true light', Powell argued that 'Europe, regarded economically rather than politically, is the greatest industrial and technical power in the world', capable of challenging 'the Russo-American monopoly of the most advanced and powerful techniques'. He went on:

> It is as a European power, utilising what is unique in our European situation and endowments, and testing our achievement and performance under the most competitive and rewarding conditions we can find, that we shall work out a Britain in the 1970s which does not need make-believe to bolster its self-respect... This is Britain's world-wide role, no less than that of France or Germany, to be herself, genuinely and fearlessly, in the Europe and the world of the 1970s. The real isolationism and renunciation is to wrap ourselves round with illusions, such as the illusion of our 'special relationship' with the United States, or the illusion that the Commonwealth exists as a political force.[13]

Defence played an increasingly important part in Powell's arguments. As he called for a withdrawal from East of Suez and a concentration on Western Europe, Powell reflected that the post-1945 presence of British land and air forces on the Continent appeared 'to convey in an instinctive, uncomplicated way a popular recognition that somehow Britain henceforward belongs with Western Europe'.[14] This was a striking comment made as a Labour prime minister submitted the UK's second application for European Community membership in May 1967. The application was promptly rebuked by de Gaulle, but Powell was undeterred. In autumn 1966, amid government discussions about reducing the size of the British Army of the Rhine (BAOR), Powell told Sir Evelyn Shuckburgh, the new British Ambassador to Italy, that the 'withdrawal of British forces from Germany was quite incompatible with the Government's new drive to enter Europe' and 'merely gave the Europeans proof that we were not Europe-minded and were ready to seek the first opportunity to detach ourselves from the Continent'.[15] With his long-standing opposition to the US alliance bolstered by French questioning of the commitment to NATO, he argued that while 'the security of the British Isles is bound up with Western Europe', the North Atlantic Alliance was—in his balance of power analysis—'an affiliation which corresponds with a less fundamental and more temporary grouping of powers'. From this, Powell boldly concluded that: 'Political unity is inseparable from defensive unity, and to move towards the one is to move towards the other.'[16]

Party, people, and sovereignty

Powell dramatically changed his position in March 1969. He was, of course, outside the shadow cabinet by this point, and we should remember that Powell was far from alone in changing his views on the issue of European Community membership. For example, Tony Benn, who became one of the most prominent Labour opponents of British membership in the 1970s had, at one stage, spoken of the possibilities of technical cooperation in the large market of the Community.[17] Nonetheless, it is clear that Powell disingenuously attempted to gloss over his earlier record. He said he had 'supported, as being right on balance at the time, the decision of Harold Macmillan to seek membership of the European Common Market'. He claimed that when 'Harold Wilson decided to renew that attempt two years ago, I was far less sure either of the wisdom or the prospects; but I did not see how Edward Heath and the Tory Party could creditably do other than wish him success'. Yet Powell argued that the situation was transformed as the likely rejection of the application became clear. Powell now saw leaving it 'on the table' as a 'humiliation'. Where he had previously emphasized Britain's connectedness with Europe, Powell now struck a different note, identifying objections to Community membership about both economics and sovereignty. He argued that 'being an island, we are a commercial nation with the maximum number of options open' and that the 'ideal thing for us would be freedom of trade with as many countries as possible'. He thus identified the European Community's common external tariff as one of its disadvantages for the UK.[18]

In a context where Powell argued that public opinion required a 'clear, definite and cast-iron case be made' for entry, he set out to prevent this mood from developing. Having previously welcomed the potential impact of Community entry on British agriculture, Powell now launched a scathing attack on the operation of the CAP—an issue that was to assume greater significance in the years to come. He argued that it was politically driven and served to maintain 'relatively inefficient agriculture', fixing 'common internal prices ... so high as not only to keep the existing agricultural labour on the land but to cause it to produce more than the consumers will buy, resulting often in large surpluses which the tax-payers have to buy up'.[19] These economic issues were echoed in the Conservative Party as a whole, but Powell was more distinctive (though not alone) in the emphasis he gave to concerns about sovereignty. He argued that the European Community involved a 'series of complex, bureaucratic institutions not easy to reconcile with our own very different system of administration under parliamentary control', which was all the more worrying because the Community's founding document, the Treaty of Rome, 'envisaged a progressive increase in the power and importance of the central bureaucracy of the Market'. At this stage, Powell did, however, hold out hope that the Community itself would change as a result of the position of France, one of its two principal members, where de Gaulle had called for a 'Europe of nations', seemingly joined in some kind of free-trade area. Powell was emphatic that this was 'the only Europe to which Britain, so long as she herself remains a nation, could belong'.[20]

With Powell's hopes subsequently thwarted as de Gaulle left office in April 1969, he now focused on the proposal for the creation of a directly elected European Parliament, which he saw starkly revealing both the extent of the European Community's political ambitions and the mistaken nature of them. Considering Parliament a core component of the British nation, Powell was clear that this did 'not mean that a politically united nation can be created or promoted by creating an elected parliament'. His firm view was that an 'elected parliament cannot work unless, and until, and as long as, those who do the electing regard themselves as a single whole, all of whose parts will ultimately see their separate interests as subordinate to the interest of the whole'. In keeping with his broader understanding of how nations emerged, he stressed: 'I am not saying that no such nation or sense of iden- tity could ever come into existence.'[21] Yet Powell was quick to assert that this meant a 'single electorate' where 'divisions would be on the basis of party, and not nationality'.[22] At this point, Powell's emphatic view, as he told the Conservative Parliamentary Foreign Affairs Committee, was that 'a majority of British people did not see how they could become part of a political union'.[23]

By the time of the 1970 general election—even amid the ongoing furore over immigration—Powell was arguing that 'the question of joining the Common Market is the most fundamental of all'. Powerfully, he went on: 'It is a question not merely, what sort of a nation are we to be but what nation are we to be?' With the European Community having recently adopted a

target of establishing a common currency by 1980, Powell argued that a
'single currency means a single government'. He took the basic agreement
between the Conservative and Labour manifestos on the Community to
signify the 'failure of the party system', which appeared 'no longer to do its
work of offering a choice between policies'. In this context, Powell argued
that it was 'not surprising' to hear demands for a referendum, which had
gathered increasing momentum, especially in Labour circles, from 1968.
Powell made it clear that he had substantial reservations. He asserted that it
was 'inconsistent with the responsibility of government to Parliament and
to the electorate' because, if the referendum vote went against the course
advocated by the government, the 'result...would be, quite literally,
irresponsible government'. In practical terms, Powell also argued that a
referendum would be unhelpful to those who, taking a different view to
himself, considered that the decision to join should depend on the terms—
which would not be clear in advance. Even with the party system working
inadequately, Powell's preference was for 'close and continuous debate' on
the issue in Parliament.[24]

Powell's attack soon turned increasingly to the Conservatives—and, in
particular, to Heath. Twelve days after victory in the 1970 general election,
Heath launched the third application. Despite the commitment to open
negotiations, the Conservative manifesto had 'avoided an overt commitment
to entry', but Heath now took the view that his thirty-seat majority was a
'sufficient mandate'.[25] In January 1971, Geoffrey Rippon, the Chancellor of
the Duchy of Lancaster, who had been given the job of negotiating entry,
struck a pre-emptive blow at Powell, noting his earlier change of position in
the House of Commons.[26] Powell hit back in April, accusing the government
of 'sleight of hand'. He contended that instead of the negotiations being
about 'the terms on which Britain would agree to be a member of the
Community', they had begun with the government 'accepting the Community
and its rules and principles, exactly as they stand' and were now 'merely...about
what would happen in the transition period'.[27] Powell had a point, but this
was dramatic language that even prompted a call for Powell to resign from
the party.[28] In a context where the government was concerned about public
attitudes towards European Community entry, with polls suggesting the
electorate was either against or apathetic, Powell pressed his arguments
further. He did so in a high-profile speech at The Hague in May—with the
Foreign Office having worried in advance that Powell would place the
British Embassy in an awkward position by contradicting the official

Figure 7. Powell at his desk at home in Belgravia, London, March 1971.

government line as negotiations with the European Community neared conclusion.[29] Powell did just that. Exaggerating the clarity of public attitudes, he argued that 'opinion in Britain is preponderantly hostile to British membership and is steadily becoming more and more hostile', adding that the 'objection went to the very root of the Community's professed political objectives'.[30] With the conclusion of the negotiations in June 1971, and a government White Paper published the following month, Powell argued that opinion 'has been right to fasten upon sovereignty as the central issue', because entry meant 'a declaration of intent to surrender this country's sovereignty, stage by stage, in all that matters to a nation, and makes a nation'. Powell argued that what he saw as public opposition to European Community membership was part of a broader desire 'to get back our pride and our confidence in ourselves'.[31]

Powell was now clear that concerns over the loss of sovereignty overrode economic considerations in importance. He contended that even 'if the economic effects of British membership were as beneficial as I believe them to be the reverse, they would still weigh lightly in the scale against the political consequences'.[32] Even so, at a point when he was increasingly critical, from a free-market perspective, of the direction of the Conservative government's economic policy, Powell stressed that through membership Britain would lose 'the vital principle of her commercial policy – the ability to seek, through the free choices of her citizens, that pattern of external trade which at any time accords most nearly with her own best interest'.[33]

Powell also extended his attack by comparing the government's handling of the European issue with immigration. He contended that, as in the latter case, the public were 'fearful' that 'another alteration, as large and as unwelcome in its effect upon Britain, might similarly come about without consent and without consultation'. In heavily populist terms, Powell argued that 'the pattern has every appearance of being the same: a minority, perhaps a small minority, determines the question over the heads of the majority, and then the majority is presented with a *fait accompli* and told that it is good for them and that anyhow it is too late to argue about now'. Returning to his argument about the electorate's inability 'to find the alternatives personified and dramatised by the parties' on 'questions . . . of most crucial and lasting importance', Powell now called this 'tacit connivance between the two great parties in the state' and used it to justify his increasing criticism of his own party:

> For the individual Member of Parliament it creates a new duty and responsibility. He can no longer be just a representative in local or sectional concerns but, in anything beyond those, claim that merely by virtue of adherence to party he is playing his part in the political debate on behalf of the constituents who elected him. As the storm centre of politics has deserted the dead ground between the parties, so the Member's personal responsibility has been elevated to the national plane, and he finds himself called upon to perform a duty, and fulfil a function as an individual, which for the time being Parliament and party have collectively abandoned.[34]

As the likely extent of parliamentary support for European Community membership became clear, Powell spoke of 'a perilous dichotomy between Party and Parliament on the one side and public opinion and the people on the other side'. Having rejected the constitutional need for a referendum in July 1971, Heath had agreed to a free vote in the House of Commons, which, on 28 October, approved entry by 356 to 244—a margin over three times the size of the Conservative majority. Powell had already outlined why he considered this outcome a problem:

> There should be no misunderstanding in this context about the special, in fact the unique, nature of the Common Market issue. On the great mass of matters where Government and Parliament must take decisions, there is not only no requirement that they should sedulously conform with the balance of opinion in the country at any moment but it would be destructive of our Parliamentary

democracy and of responsible government for them to do so....Without this there could be no consistency of policy or stability of administration. From time to time, however, there arise issues where this principle does not hold good, but where on the contrary it is both impossible, and wrong to attempt, to proceed without the support of the mass of the people.

Powell argued that Heath had recognized this when he spoke about the need for the 'full-hearted consent of Parliament and people' in May 1970, before the general election. Unlike other decisions taken by governments or Parliament, which could be rejected at the next general election, Powell considered that joining the European Community was 'an irrevocable commitment which only the willing and manifest consent of the people at large can validate'. He now argued that the 'irreversible' nature of the 'commitment to ever closer self-identification, political as well as economic', did 'not derive from the mere wording of the Treaty [of Rome, 1957]' but was 'implicit in the nature of the Community itself and in the very grounds which are urged for joining it'.[35]

Towards Labour and a referendum

In October 1971 Powell also took the momentous step of talking more favourably about Labour as a way out of this impasse. He argued it was 'the Labour Opposition, in spite of its divisions, which has assumed the role that otherwise was vacant: the role of ensuring that the preponderant voice of the people of this country is heard and listened to upon the gravest decision which a nation can face in time of peace'.[36] At this point, 'the Conservatives had become the party of Europe'.[37] Yet, for all his differences with his own party, there were inherent problems with Powell's (even tentative) resort to Labour. In principle, Labour's opposition to the 'Tory terms' of entry, calling for changes to the financing of the European Community budget, including the CAP, alongside the retention of sufficient parliamentary powers to undertake effective regional, industrial, and fiscal policies, chimed with Powell's critique of Heath for simply accepting European Community terms as they stood. Yet, in reality, the 'Tory terms' argument was an attempt superficially to unite a deeply divided party.[38] Indeed, in the 28 October debate, sixty-seven Labour MPs voted with the government and a further twenty abstained. Most importantly of all, Powell—despite his comments about the need for the consent of the people—did not support a referendum on membership of the European Community, a proposal that was gaining ground in the Labour Party.[39]

Powell's persistence on the European Community, and his nod towards Labour, had immediate political ramifications. Some of his noted Conservative allies urged caution. John Biffen, upset that Powell was being 'vilified' within the party, told him: 'There is more than one road away from Rome . . . I shall not be a root and branch opponent of the enabling legislation, but will be looking for more Fabian tactics.'[40] Patrick Donner disputed Powell's reading of public opinion, arguing that 'the mood of the country has changed to one of tacit acquiescence and a new desire to get down to brass tacks and to make a success of it if we can'.[41] As the government embarked on the legislative process of joining the Community in the first half of 1972, Powell also began working with Labour MPs who were hostile to British membership, such as Bob Mellish, Peter Shore, and Michael Foot, in an attempt to overturn the decision.[42]

All the while, Powell's position appeared at odds with his continued resistance to a referendum. As Heath prepared to sign the Treaty of Accession, Powell argued forthrightly that the government had 'no moral right' to do so.[43] Speaking on 24 January in Brussels, where Heath had signed the treaty two days beforehand, Powell contended that 'in any democratic state . . . it is dangerous if not disastrous to sign a treaty without the concurrence of general opinion'.[44] Powell subsequently argued: 'The power is still the people's if they have the will to use it.'[45] With the second reading of the European Communities Bill carried by 309 to 301 on 17 February 1972, Powell dramatically stated that 'the "compact of government with people" has been decisively broken', meaning that the 'Government and the nation are set on collision course'. Powell argued, however, that it was the House of Commons that could prevent 'that disaster'.[46] He took this line as calls for a referendum intensified. In April, Neil Marten, the Conservative MP who was prominent in opposing entry, suggested an amendment to the European Communities Bill that called for a consultative referendum. The amendment was unsuccessful, but it was significant that it gained Labour backing (albeit in a manner that exposed divisions on the issue). Powell seemingly continued to hold out hope that Parliament would reject the bill. In late February, he had written to the British Ambassador to France, 'to impress on him that the European Communities Bill would not be adopted by Parliament, and urging him to advise Paris accordingly'.[47] In May Powell even wrote to the Queen, asking that during her visit to France 'great care . . . be taken to avoid all expressions on her part which could be interpreted as assuming, still less approving, this country's membership of the European Economic Community, at a time when the House of Commons still has the European Communities Bill before it'.[48]

Powell continued to resist calls for a referendum after the European Communities Bill received its final approval in July 1972. He argued that there was 'no need' for a referendum because the British people 'have it in their power to conduct a continuous referendum upon Britain and the Community by the attitude which they take, and which they persuade their representatives to take, towards all the practical and concrete implications for Parliament and this country'.[49] Powell continued to see general elections as critical, arguing that they were 'the meeting of minds between parties and people', the process through which 'the nation does, in some complex, collective way, choose a direction, a purpose and even a faith'. He added: 'If leadership is the function of politicians and parties, then elections are the supreme moments at which the function of leadership is exercised.'[50] This was not just philosophical musing. Powell was preparing the ground for an endorsement of Labour at the next general election.

In June 1973, Powell urged voters to have faith in what he saw as the Labour Party's opposition to the European Community. He stated (slightly cryptically and long-windedly) that 'if they were presented, with two opposing parties which offered a choice between the option they desired and the option they did not desire, electors would be perverse indeed to choose what they did not want for fear that those who promised what they did want would not perform it'.[51] During a subsequent BBC radio interview, Powell was more explicit about his own position—saying that, in certain circumstances, if parliamentary sovereignty was preserved, he would be prepared to see 'Labour administrations for the rest of my lifetime'.[52] It was this line of thinking that led Powell, more cautiously, to tell the Cambridge economist Nicholas Kaldor—who, taking a different approach on economic affairs to Powell, had been an advisor to the Labour governments in the 1960s—that '[m]embership on present terms is not yet one of the inevitabilities'.[53]

Powell presented his position as a response to an internal conflict within the Conservative Party, which went to the heart of the nature of party itself. Viewing party as 'the embodiment of a principle or a coherent set of principles' as well as 'a means of carrying on government' by 'binding together the majority as a tolerably stable basis for the exercise of power', Powell considered it 'normal that the principles and professions of a political party take on a motley and less distinctive aspect when that party has been sustaining a government in office for a period of years', but he ominously contended that there were 'limits':

> Principle and practice may overlap rather than coincide, but there is a point at which they lose contact with one another altogether or fall into direct conflict. When that point is reached or passed, a total change comes over the nature of party, and instead of maintaining the mutual compact and confidence of government and people, it undermines and destroys them. The re-assertion of party principles then ceases to be an evidence of failure to understand and recognise the two-fold function of the party system. It becomes a pressing and overriding duty, on which the continued health of the body politic depends.

Powell was at odds with the Conservative leadership over economics and immigration, but Europe was the tipping point:

> If the electorate were ever compelled to look to the Conservative Party's political opponents in order to assert the British people's right to be heard before its parliamentary self-government and separate existence as a nation disappear, the whole structure and meaning of political parties in this country would have been altered beyond recognition, and he would be a rash prophet that would dare to foretell the outcome.[54]

Powell's position caused tensions in his constituency, and prompted the Tettenhall Wightwick ward branch to make a formal complaint to the Annual General Meeting (AGM) of the Wolverhampton South West Conservative Association, directly asking Powell if he intended to stand as a Conservative candidate in the next general election.[55] Powell's reply, that a 'party is not the private property of its leader', made clear the depth of his dispute with Heath but was also an attempt to dodge the question.[56] By early 1974, Powell had made up his mind not to stand. Expecting a general election at any point, Powell drafted a letter to the chairman of the Wolverhampton South West Conservative Association in which he stated that 'no-one who puts the maintenance of this country's political independence and of the supreme authority of Parliament above all other considerations can, in my opinion, support the return of a government which has purported to take Britain into the European Economic Community without the consent of her people'.[57] Also at odds with the government over economic policy, Powell's actual letter refusing to stand—once a general election had been called—gave more emphasis to these other concerns, but this should not detract from our understanding of the importance of Europe in this decision.[58]

Powell's decision left him marooned in British party politics. He began to engage with pressure groups opposed to British membership.[59] He turned down the chance to address a meeting of the Anti-Common Market League in London, arguing that 'the impact would be greater in the provinces', nearer to his own political base, and opted instead to address Get Britain Out in Birmingham and the West Riding.[60] Having held clandestine meetings with Labour leader Harold Wilson since June 1973, Powell also kept the Labour Party informed, through an intermediary—the journalist Andrew Alexander—that he intended to call on Conservatives to vote Labour in his speeches, with the second being 'hotter' in this regard.[61] Speaking at the Bullring in Birmingham on 23 February, Powell argued that the electorate was faced with 'a conflict between the call of country and that of party', where 'the call of country must come first'. With Labour promising to renegotiate the terms of entry, and then submit the outcome to a referendum, Powell argued that this was a 'clear, definite and practicable alternative' offered by 'a political party capable of securing a majority in the House of Commons and sustaining a government'.[62] Two days later at Saltaire, Powell explicitly addressed those who 'would not otherwise give their vote to the Labour Party' and spelled out the full implications of doing so:

> He must, for that Parliament, accept or acquiesce in the whole consequences of his choice; for party is the mechanism of parliamentary democracy, and we act by choosing parties not individuals. The elector must therefore decide which issue is for him to be the one of overriding importance .... in this case the choice, humanly speaking, is between what is reversible and what is irreversible.

Powell argued that his fundamental beliefs had not changed but that those of his party had:

> I was born a Tory, I am a Tory, and shall die a Tory...I never yet heard that it was any part of the faith of a Tory to take the institutions and liberties, the laws and customs, which his country has evolved over centuries, and merge them with those of eight other nations into a new-made artificial state and, what is more, to do so without the willing approbation and consent of the nation.[63]

Powell was subsequently subjected to a range of pressures. The chairman of the Wolverhampton South West Conservative Party, George Wilkes, told Powell that his decision not to stand 'was respected by us all until you announced your decision to vote Socialist'.[64] Powell had certainly caused a stir—gaining newspaper front-page coverage on five of the twenty-one

Figure 8. Powell speaking at the 'Get Britain Out' rally in Birmingham on 23 February 1974.

days of the election campaign.[65] Yet, by the summer, some of those close to Powell questioned the political acumen of his stance. Back in June 1973, Biffen had told Powell frankly that he would not 'endorse any appeal to vote other than Conservative'.[66] Now Biffen advised him that opposition to Community membership was 'not a topic on which you can successfully appeal for a transference of popular votes'.[67] Nicholas Ridley, who was later a Cabinet minister under Margaret Thatcher and who agreed with Powell on economic matters, initially considered that he had made the 'right decision' in not contesting his seat.[68] Yet now, writing admittedly 'biased as a pro-European', he suggested that Powell had placed too much faith in Labour. Ridley argued that it was 'becoming more and more obvious that Labour intend to stay in the Market. Although they will "re-negotiate"... the sovereignty issue is no longer up for renegotiation.'[69] Powell was sufficiently concerned to press Foreign Secretary James Callaghan on the matter. Callaghan did not have particularly strong views on Europe.[70] Powell was, however, seemingly reassured by Callaghan's insistence that he was committed 'to form a judgment on the package as a whole including especially issues of sovereignty and whether the degree of control that Parliament will be asked to relinquish (if we remain a member of the Community) is acceptable to me personally and in line with our policy'.[71] Also enjoying close relations with Michael Foot and Douglas Jay, Powell told a correspondent that: 'So far as one man can know another's motives, I know those of the leading Labour Members in alliance with whom I fought and fight membership of the E.E.C as at present. They are the same motives as my own.'[72] As a result, and with another general election in the autumn, Powell continued to endorse Labour, describing it as the 'one major party at this election ... which offers Britain the prospect of regaining and preserving its parliamentary self-government and political independence'.[73] Moreover, Powell was willing, if not positively to endorse, at least tacitly to accept, the prospect of a referendum, albeit with the important qualification that its result, which the Labour manifesto described as 'final', would only be binding for that Parliament—on the basis that no Parliament could bind its successor.[74]

With Labour increasing their number of parliamentary seats to secure a very slim overall majority in the October 1974 general election, Powell's engagement with the referendum campaign intensified the following year. As the Labour government now undertook negotiations with the European Community, Harold Wilson publicly committed to a referendum on 23 January and, in March, set the date for 5 June. In late February Powell addressed a meeting of the National Referendum Campaign (NRC), which sought to coordinate the 'no' campaign.[75] He also joined its committee, which had the Conservative Neil Marten as chairman, Labour's Douglas Jay as one of its vice chairmen, and counted Michael Foot, Peter Shore, and Barbara Castle among its prominent Labour members.[76] Powell played a part in ensuring that, while high food prices formed part of the case against Community membership, the threat to sovereignty was also prevalent during the campaign.[77] On a Radio 3 debate with Lord Hailsham, chaired by Robin Day, Powell spelled out in practical terms—in line with NRC advice—his argument that European Community membership meant 'accepting law made and taxes imposed by an authority external to the United Kingdom'. Yet Hailsham made a powerful counter-case for the ultimate retention of sovereignty by Westminster. He argued that 'the only authority which the commission has, or indeed the treaty has, in domestic law, derives from the Act of Parliament which enabled us and caused us to accede to the community'. He pointedly added, 'the fact that we're holding a referendum shows that that Act of Parliament can, so far as domestic law is concerned, be repealed and then we should leave the community'.[78] More generally, arguments were made that some degree of pooling of sovereignty was necessary to increase the UK's influence in the world. In the end, it appeared that the issue of sovereignty—in contrast to food prices and other economic issues—did not resonate with the voters.[79]

If Powell's arguments were sufficiently countered in this respect, he still made his boldest bid yet to connect European Community membership with national decline. He argued that the 'sense of dejection which has grown over Britain during the years since the War has deepened in the recent past into something not far from despair', with acquiescence in joining the Community as 'the most striking symptom of this moral collapse'. In dramatic terms, he contended that 'belonging to the Common Market...spells living death, the abandonment of all prospect of national rebirth, the end of any possibility of resurgence'.[80] Powell argued that the referendum choice was whether Britain possessed 'the will and the power to remain a nation'.[81] In a context where there was already a greater sense of a 'class struggle' than ten years earlier, Powell suggested that the nature of the debate over the Community was 'producing in British politics a division and polarization by class which has been mercifully lacking for the past generation but which is not likely to end tomorrow or on referendum day'—with disastrous consequences for the nation and the Conservative Party.[82] With the party leaders all supporting the 'yes' campaign, with widespread newspaper support, and with higher socio-economic groups more likely to vote to remain in the Community, Powell argued:

> The issue of Britain and the Common Market is...being turned into an issue between the classes, where to be pro-market and anti-referendum is regarded as the badge of the middle and upper ranks of society who feel more affinity with the management of the new super-state than with their own fellow citizens... This recrudescence of class-consciousness under the influence of the Common Market controversy is something of evil portent not only for the nation as a whole but in particular for the Conservative Party... There are two things which are absolute death to the Conservative Party in Britain. One is to cease to be identified with the nation, with its pride in its institutions and its confidence in the rightness of its popular instincts. The other is to come to be identified with the division of the classes.[83]

'The party system has broken in our hands'

The outcome of the referendum, which saw 67 per cent in favour of accepting the renegotiated terms and remaining in the European Community, changed Powell's stance in several ways. Like others, such as Marten, he now focused on opposing direct elections to the European Parliament, which had been agreed in principle in 1974. Powell argued that if these elections took place, it would 'no longer be possible to pretend that Britain has not ceased to be a nation' because those elected would 'derive their authority from the same electorate and by the same process as Members of Parliament derive theirs'.[84] With the candidates not belonging to Community-wide parties, Powell made the reasonable point that they would be elected on the basis of party affiliation in the UK. Yet Powell took this further to suggest a particular danger: when decisions were taken by the Community as a whole that were at odds with the interests of the British electorate, or sectors of it, the elected representatives could simply claim that the outcome had been beyond their control. For Powell, this meant that direct elections would 'strengthen the arbitrary and bureaucratic nature of the Community by giving a fallacious garb of elective authority to the exercise of supranational powers by insti-tutions and persons who are – in the literal, not the abusive, sense of the word– irresponsible'.[85]

In the aftermath of the referendum, Powell also had to react to an 'alarming' situation where Labour and the Conservatives were committed to remaining in the European Community.[86] He now joined the National Executive Committee of the Safeguard Britain Campaign (SBC), the successor to the NRC, which held its first meeting in mid-December 1975.[87] Yet, at times, he had an awkward relationship with the campaign, which related to the way that Powell was now perceived as moving on the extremes of politics. Tellingly, in mid-1976 the acting chairman of the SBC in the north-east wrote to Powell asking him not to speak at their meetings because 'the National Front regard you as their patron saint and will seize upon these meetings to the disadvantage of the anti-Market cause'.[88] Nonetheless, Powell chose a public meeting of the SBC in June 1978 to outline his new position vis-à-vis the party system and its requirements on the electoral behaviour of individual voters. Back in 1970, before he had begun to place his hopes in Labour, Powell had argued that the system was failing to provide choice. Now, in a situation where those opposing British membership of the European Community could 'no longer vote for either party, for either government, as a means to our end', Powell argued:

> The party system has broken in our hands. We will appeal above its head to the electoral system itself, the electors' right to vote for the candidate who offers what he, the elector, wants and to vote for no other. Those candidates, and only those candidates, ought to receive our vote at the next general election

who are individually committed, irrespective of personal consequences...to vote on all occasions and all subjects in such a way as to terminate Britain's present membership of the Community...from ministers or shadow ministers to the run-down agent's office in the hopeless seat, the effect would be felt, the prospect would begin to transmute the attitudes and behaviour of our rulers.[89]

On the face of it, this was a striking position for Powell, who described himself as 'an almost fanatical advocate of party in politics', to adopt.[90] Yet it was understandable in terms of his already detached position from British party politics—a development that had been reinforced by his status as an Ulster Unionist MP after 1974. Certainly, Powell resisted pressure to rejoin, or to collaborate closely with, the Conservatives. Thatcher herself had made it plain in February 1976 that his call to vote Labour prevented 'any prospect' of this happening.[91] Yet, behind the scenes, others who hoped to have an influence on Powell broached the subject. The historian Maurice Cowling, a founder of the Salisbury Group, had been supportive of Powell since at least early 1968 when Cowling had asked if he could suggest Powell's name for the Mastership of Peterhouse, Cambridge.[92] Cowling had supported Powell's decision not to stand in Wolverhampton South West in 1974.[93] But in June 1975 he had argued that Powell and Thatcher should work together, with Powell rejoining the party.[94] In March 1977, Cowling made the same argument privately to Powell, emphasizing not just that, under Thatcher, the party had moved in a more amenable direction but also powerfully adding his assessment that 'the strength of your position has lain in the past in the fact that you are a Conservative politician with a very much wider appeal than any other Conservative politician'.[95] Significantly, in June 1978, just after Powell had argued that the party system was 'broken', he had dinner with Keith Joseph and Alfred Sherman, a former communist who had embraced free-market economics and taken part in setting up the Centre for Policy Studies, in an attempt to find the 'basis of a possible arrangement'. Sherman and Joseph tried to meet Powell's objections about the Conservative position on the European Community but, in doing so, also revealed the gap between them. Making a familiar argument from the referendum campaign but ignoring Powell's stance towards the US, Sherman stated that 'we do not begrudge any minor concessions of sovereignty to the Community, any more than we do to NATO, which remains our primary commitment'.[96] The meeting came to nought, with Sherman considering that if Powell was 'to mute his antagonism, or even show some moderated benevolence towards us during the election period, while leaving open the possibility of some post-electral [*sic*] arrangement that would be the most we could hope for'.[97]

Indeed, at the 1979 general election, Powell repeated his call to 'go above and beyond party and get our way' by voting for 'a publicly pledged and dedicated opponent of the E.E.C.' Powell made clear what this meant in practice, including possible abstention:

> In some constituencies there may be two or more candidates who would deserve our vote on these terms. In that case it is no business of mine on whom the favour falls. In other constituencies the only candidate who deserves our vote in the context of the Common Market may be one who forfeits it on other grounds. In that case a vote withheld is a vote well used: abstention can in itself be an exercise, and an effective exercise, of the franchise.[98]

Powell had less influence on British politics by this stage, but he retained a sufficiently large profile to ensure that Thatcher—at an election press conference—was forced to argue that his position would not affect the Conservative vote.[99] Yet Powell's position itself also appeared unclear, and even contradictory, because at the first direct elections to the European Parliament, held on 7 June 1979, Powell actually endorsed Labour.[100] In one sense, Powell's tack was understandable. Where Labour's general-election manifesto, emphasizing the importance of national sovereignty, had called for 'fundamental and much-needed reform of the EEC', at the European election the party manifesto went further (under the influence of Tony Benn) to state that if this was 'not achieved within a reasonable period of time, then the Labour Party would have to consider very seriously whether EEC membership was in the best interests of the British people'.[101] Even so, Powell still found himself in a tangle when, with the European election in mind, he made the wider argument that a boycott was 'never a satisfactory form of electoral self-expression' because it was not possible to 'deal with an accomplished fact by shutting your eyes and pretending not to know that it exists' and that there was a danger that 'non-voting will be interpreted as consent'.[102]

With the Conservatives in government, Powell took his criticism of the party in a new direction, arguing that foreign policy coordination 'was now the chosen route to unification'. He made this argument on the SBC Executive Committee—where he was taking a more active role—and cited the response to the Soviet invasion of Afghanistan as a prime example.[103] Peter Carrington, the Foreign Secretary, had indeed been keen to work closely with the European Community but Thatcher was, above all, determined to align British actions with those of the United States.[104] Powell's concern was that membership of the Community 'for which the Foreign Office worked through dedicated year after dedicated year, has in itself made the Foreign Office the key department of state'.[105] Powell argued that for 'the Foreign Office, the E.E.C. has been a sort of new kingdom, a surrogate of lost imperial power'.[106] Notably, Powell was able to persuade the SBC to take a (moderated) version of this line in its declaration to the European Community Heads of Government meeting in London in November, which lamented 'the progressive transfer to the Community or to institutions under its aegis [of] the formation of foreign and defence policies'.[107]

Powell continued to see the European Community as the core dividing line in British party politics and it continued to see him fluctuate in his endorsement of Labour, whose own position on Europe vacillated. Powell called the Social Democratic Party (SDP), formed in March 1981 by four senior Labour figures—Roy Jenkins, David Owen, Bill Rodgers, and Shirley Williams—'the extreme pro-European party, whose one common characteristic and undisputed stance is devotion to the destruction of Britain's Parliamentary independence'.[108] As Shirley Williams contested the Crosby by-election for the new party in a high-profile campaign later in the year, which saw her become the first MP elected under the SDP label, Powell argued that the SDP sought 'to deny and denigrate Britain's nationhood'.[109] Yet Powell's verdict was exaggerated in the attention it gave to Europe. Labour's conference in January 1981 had indeed committed the party to withdrawal from the European Community, but the SDP had emerged in response to the general leftward swing in the Labour Party. With a total of twenty-eight Labour MPs defecting, political scientists Ivor Crewe and Anthony King have argued that the defectors were actually united by their shared, and bleak, assessment about the prospects of Labour's Right within the party.[110] At the same time, Powell warmed to Labour, which was led from late 1980 by Michael Foot and increasingly entrenching its opposition to European Community membership.[111] In February 1982, in fulsome terms, Powell stated that:

> It is not my party. It has never been my party. But that does not blind me to the unique service that the Labour Party alone has it in its power to perform for this country .... Patriotism requires of a man or woman that they should distinguish the one thing that is essential for their country from all the inessentials, great or small, and that they should make that one thing the object to which, if necessary, they were prepared to sacrifice everything else.[112]

The timing of Powell's endorsement was apposite, coming just before the outbreak of the Falklands War that saw Powell reflect admiringly on Thatcher's actions. Even afterwards, however, Powell was emphatic that Europe remained 'the question precedent to all other questions, the be-all and end-all of all political activity and belief, an issue literally of life and death'. He still considered that 'it would be a monstrous frivolity, a moral suicide, to offer political allegiance to a party committed to the principle that this country's laws ought to be made, its taxes imposed and its causes judged by an external authority'.[113] Powell found Labour's position more palatable, even as its 1983 general-election manifesto explicitly sought European Community withdrawal to pursue 'radical, socialist policies for reviving the British economy'.[114] Yet, in a familiar pattern, Powell's position changed again after the 1983 general election. With Foot departing as Labour leader and the party soon moving, under new leader Neil Kinnock, from October to an acceptance of Community membership for the time being, Powell told a meeting of the British Anti-Common Market Campaign (the name adopted by the SBC in 1982) that the issue had 'become de-politicised, in the sense of being divorced from every other issue of inter-party division. The cause is now everybody's and anybody's.'[115]

'Bruges and all that'

From 1987, Powell argued that 'the big changes now on foot in the relations between Britain, America, Russia and the other continental nations can-not...fail to reduce the pressures which have been pushing our governments and parliaments down the road to a European political mission'.[116] As we saw in Chapter 1, at this stage he saw the influence of the United States declining, alongside the rise of 'Mittel-Europa' and the growing awareness of the need for an understanding between Britain and Russia. Thatcher's role in this was crucial as she established warm relations with Soviet leader Gorbachev. Her speech in Bruges, on 20 September 1988, was equally sig-nificant in prompting Powell to move towards support for the Conservatives for the first time since 1974. With Jacques Delors, the President of the European Commission, pledging that he would require member states to introduce labour legislation, Thatcher argued: 'We have not successfully rolled back the frontiers of the state in Britain, only to see them re-imposed at a European level with a European super-state exercising a new dominance from Brussels... To try to suppress nationhood and concentrate power at the centre of a European conglomerate would be highly damaging.'[117] Powell now embraced a 'transformed' situation in which Thatcher 'has announced herself opposed to the transfer of powers from our national parliament to the institutions of the EEC' and where a 'new Europe is emerging before our eyes, a Europe of nations'.[118] Proclaiming the Conservatives 'the national party' once again, Powell argued that for Labour, which increasingly welcomed its social legislation, 'the European Community now fills the place in socialist thinking which used to be occupied by the Comintern'—a poignant argument at the end of the Cold War.[119] With Thatcher stating that she was 'not prepared to see Parliament's powers in the crucial areas of economic and financial matters diminished' as the European Council meeting in December 1989 discussed economic and monetary union, Powell wrote to offer 'respectful congratulations' and to say that she 'both spoke for Britain and gave a lead to Europe'—comments that left Thatcher 'deeply touched'.[120] It was also a revealing indication of Powell's changed stance that he wrote to Nicholas Budgen, who had succeeded Powell as Conservative MP for Wolverhampton South West, stating: 'If developments in the Conservative Party enable me, on grounds of the EEC, to commend it to the electors at the next General Election, I can think of nowhere better to do so than Wolverhampton South West.'[121]

Powell also became more involved with groups calling for British withdrawal from the European Community or for a substantial rethinking of the nature of the Community. Powell signalled his interest in being associated with the Bruges Group, the think tank that took its inspiration from Thatcher's speech, even before it had held its first meeting in February 1989.[122] The group enjoyed substantial academic support and included, among its council, the historian Professor Norman Stone, the economist Professor Patrick Minford, the political scientist Professor Kenneth Minogue, the philosopher Professor Roger Scruton and the political philosopher Dr John Gray. Its chairman was, moreover, the IEA stalwart Ralph Harris.[123] Despite this distinguished company, Powell was determined that his own views would not be subsumed by those of the group. Given his earlier disagreement with Harris over immigration, Powell made it clear that, while he supported the group's 'campaign for a Europe of Sovereign States', he considered it necessary to emphasize that 'freedom of trade, of which I am in favour, does not involve – is indeed an alternative to – the free movement of persons for settlement'.[124] Powell was also willing to be co-opted back on to the Committee of British Anti-Common Market Campaign, which was to become the Campaign for an Independent Britain (CIB).[125] Powell explained to its honorary secretary, Sir Robin Williams, that he had 'ceased to seek co-option to your Committee two or three years ago', finding 'its meetings inadequate justification for the time employed', but he now considered that 'Bruges and all that has opened a new chapter'.[126] That said, Powell turned down the chance to become CIB president.[127]

Powell's focus remained national party politics. In autumn 1990, as Thatcher's position came under threat, Powell gave her explicit support. Divisions within the Cabinet had become starker following the Rome Summit in October that called for an intergovernmental conference on monetary and political union (which would culminate in the Maastricht Treaty). Geoffrey Howe, the former Foreign Secretary and now Deputy Prime Minister, took objection to Thatcher briefing journalists in a manner that was more critical of this summit's proposition than the official Foreign Office line. Howe was then prompted to resign when Thatcher made her 'No, No, No' speech in the House of Commons attacking Delors and his plans to make the European Parliament the legislature for the Community and the Commission its executive. With Thatcher—seemingly in uncompromising mood—challenged for the leadership by Michael Heseltine, Powell now called on the Conservative Party to fight a general election in which they 'champion the right of the British people to govern themselves through their own House of Commons'.[128] Powell subsequently went further as Thatcher defeated Heseltine, but not by enough votes to secure re-election, and the contest went to a further round. He told a public meeting of the Monday Club in Surrey that 'if Mrs Thatcher continues to lead the Party, I intend to apply to be re-admitted to it and to be given the opportunity at the next General Election to urge my fellow countrymen to vote Conservative for Britain to remain under a self-governing nation', relaying this to Thatcher through her close supporter, and former Cabinet Minister, Norman Tebbit.[129]

With Thatcher resigning in late November 1990 and replaced by John Major, Powell intensified his opposition to the UK joining the European Exchange Rate Mechanism (ERM), which had been introduced in 1979 as part of the European Monetary System to reduce exchange-rate volatility in preparation for economic and monetary union and the introduction of a single currency. In May 1988 Powell had expressed concerns about the UK joining the single currency and suggested that recent rises in interest rates had not been, as Nigel Lawson, Chancellor of the Exchequer, said, to counter inflation but instead to help the value of the pound sterling to 'converge' with other Western European currencies.[130] Powell celebrated Thatcher's initial opposition.[131] Yet, at the European Council meeting in Madrid in June 1989, Thatcher—under pressure from Lawson and Howe—had made an important concession. She agreed that sterling would join the ERM, converging within 6 per cent of the value of a weighted basket of the member states' currencies, and secured in return an agreement that the later stages of the Delors plan for a common currency would be postponed until further discussions had taken place. Now, after Thatcher's departure, Powell contended that the 'convergence' required for participation in the ERM would hinder trade and economic development—on the basis not just that international trade thrived on differences between states but also that it was 'through the differentiation and competition between its various groups that humanity has progressed and developed'.[132] The following year, 1991, Powell powerfully applied this argument to the position of the former communist countries in Eastern Europe. Amid widespread triumphalism in their movement towards capitalism, he argued that they were 'desperate to produce what they can freely trade with the outside world, and especially with their Western neighbours' but were prevented from doing so by the European Community's mistaken insistence that they 'converge first'.[133] Alongside this, Powell repeated his argument—first made in the late 1960s— that fixed exchange rates were a means of controlling citizens, 'the invariable mark of a tyranny'.[134]

Powell's disappointment with Conservative European policy under Major led him to argue that the government had 'abrogated' Thatcher's policy, dating from Bruges, 'to allow no diminution in the right of the people of the United Kingdom to be ruled by and under Parliament'.[135] As a result, Powell now reverted to his position of encouraging electors to vote for the candidate if they opposed British membership of the European Community.[136] In agreeing to the Maastricht Treaty in December 1991, Major secured the ability to opt out of both the single currency and the Social Charter as well as the removal of the commitment to federal union from the text of the treaty. This significantly reduced Conservative opposition to the government in the House of Commons. Yet these concessions did not appease Powell. With a general election imminent and with the

Maastricht Treaty signed and due to come into force in November 1993, forming the European Coal and Steel Community and the EEC into the EU, he argued:

> That fight is a sham fight. The opponents are in reality joined in a conspiracy to insult and cheat the electorate – a conspiracy no less real for being tacit. They purport to be about to submit to the electorate for decision alternative policies on matters of taxation and the economy, while all the time their intention and aspiration is that those very matters shall in the foreseeable future be withdrawn altogether from the control of the House of Commons and therefore from the control of the electors of the United Kingdom.[137]

In a significant change to his position, Powell was now willing to endorse the parliamentary candidates of the AFL (Anti-Federalist League), a single-issue party specifically opposed to membership of the European Community in its current form. The AFL had been formed in November 1991 by Alan Sked, a historian based at the London School of Economics who was also a founding member of the Bruges Group, to defend 'British sovereignty' amid the Conservative and Labour agreement over the Maastricht Treaty that it considered would make the 'process of unification irreversible'.[138] Back in 1979, Powell had refused to lend support to the United Anti-Common Marketeers. Considering the electorate likely to vote 'to ensure that their own party makes a good showing', Powell had argued that those 'standing simply as anti-market will therefore receive few votes, and this will then be misrepresented as indicating low antipathy among the public to British membership'.[139] Powell now considered that the climate had changed. He took issue with 'the ambiguity of the terms "federalism"', being clear that 'the European Community aims at being a unitary state and not a federation'.[140] Even so, he endorsed Sked as the AFL parliamentary candidate at Bath. But he was more cautious in his endorsement of other AFL candidates, telling Sked that 'I obviously do not know the "record" of any other candidate merely because of his membership of some organisation.'[141] Powell also selectively endorsed the candidates of UKIP, the name adopted by the AFL in September 1993. Nigel Farage sought his backing when he was standing in the Eastleigh by-election in 1994, but Powell declined.[142] Yet, later in the year, he gave his support to the UKIP candidate, Malcolm Floyd (who enjoyed the 'full confidence' of Sked), in the West Dudley by-election.[143]

However, Powell took a different stance to Sked over contesting European Parliament elections. In 1978, Powell had argued that the 'place and the body to end Britain's membership – the place for resistance, obstruction, agitation – is Westminster, because that is where the power to take the decision lies'. Pointedly, Powell argued that a 'candidate who stood and was elected to the European assembly as an opponent of British membership with the object of bringing that membership to an end would be as silly as an Irish Nationalist who got elected to Westminster when there was already a national parliament in Dublin with acknowledged power to dissolve the Union'.[144] Powell's argument seemingly only applied to single-issue anti-European Community parties. In the 1990s, Powell continued to argue that it was best for them 'simply to boycott' European parliamentary elections. In contrast, UKIP policy was, as Sked put it, 'to contest European parliamentary elections as exercises in mobilising our members and attracting political attention', though—at this stage—without intending to take up the seats.[145] It was, therefore, unsurprising that Powell turned down Sked's invitation to be the UKIP candidate for Central London in the 1994 European Parliament election.[146] By 1995 Powell was, in any case, distancing himself from UKIP. When a newly established Nottingham University branch asked for Powell's support, he replied, 'I am sure that there is a movement of public opinion on a large scale against Britain's membership of the European Union; but this can only be expressed through a party likely to win a majority at a general election.'[147]

Powell had, by this stage, strengthened his connections with senior 'Eurosceptic' figures in the Conservative Party, a term that was increasingly used to mean opposition to policies emanating from EU institutions and/or full-blown opposition to membership of the EU.[148] In 1990 Peter Lilley, the Financial Secretary to the Treasury, told Powell that on 'matters European...I increasingly share your forebodings'.[149] Frustration over the ratification of Maastricht in 1993, combined with the government's forced withdrawal from the ERM in September 1992, gave further impetus to these forces.[150] More widely, the end of the Cold War had quietly undermined the view that European integration was necessary as a bulwark against communism.[151] By 1994 Jonathan Aitken, newly promoted to the Cabinet as Chief Secretary to the Treasury, told Powell that:

> The vision of Enoch is shared by at least four of your disciples who now sit at the Cabinet table. This, I trust, should give a flicker of hope to those who care deeply about the sovereignty of the United Kingdom and the Crown in Parliament. The crunch in Britain's relationship with the European Union is

surely coming. I shall prepare in readiness for this momentous and historic challenge.[152]

The Cabinet, by this point, included Lilley as Secretary of State for Social Security, Michael Portillo as Secretary of State for Employment, Michael Howard as Home Secretary, and John Redwood as Secretary of State for Wales. It is, of course, unclear precisely how far any of them—apart from Aitken—were influenced by Powell's arguments.[153] Nonetheless, following Redwood's unsuccessful leadership challenge to Major in summer 1995, Powell certainly still held long-term optimism for 'those of us who want to keep Britain independent and self-governed'.[154] Powell was also in touch with the Conservative backbench rebel Teresa Gorman.[155] And he was in dialogue with Bill Cash, the chairman of the European Foundation, and Daniel Hannan at the European Research Group.[156]

Yet if Powell's views on Europe were resonating more widely in the Conservative Party at this time, there was still a wariness of his connection with immigration. Two examples make this point well. In 1995, Niall Ferguson, then an increasingly prominent historian who was supportive of the Conservative Party, praised Powell's economic liberalism and added 'how right he had been about the constitutional implications of the European Communities Act' involving 'the fundamental diminution of the sovereignty of Parliament'. But Ferguson added, 'I detest his views on race, and will fight every attempt to introduce them to British Conservatism.'[157] At the 1997 general election, Powell publicly endorsed Nicholas Budgen in Wolverhampton South West as a candidate who would 'vote to uphold the independence and sovereign parliamentary government of Britain'.[158] In an earlier draft of his statement, Powell had added: 'Your determination to keep immigration policy at the forefront of the campaign is also right. If a Labour Government is elected its willingness to relax immigration controls can only harm the interests of all British citizens.'[159] Budgen was evidently relieved when this passage was dropped. Pam Powell, Enoch's wife, left a telephone note: 'Nick rang – happy no mention of imm[igration] in E's letter.'[160] Budgen's agent also considered that 'the tone and the message was just right'.[161]

Towards the end of his life, Powell remained upbeat about the prospect of Britain breaking with Europe—even after the Conservatives suffered a landslide defeat to Tony Blair's professedly pro-EU New Labour in May 1997. He told a correspondent that the 'recent goings-on in the Conservative

Party have continued the trend towards opposition of our membership of the European Union, which is only a means of prejudicing our own nation-hood'.[162] Indeed, under William Hague as leader, the Conservative Party moved towards a more critical stance on the EU, which was in line with the startling statistic that 75 per cent of the parliamentary party were Eurosceptics to some degree.[163]

5

Northern Ireland

As an Ulster Unionist MP after 1974, Powell offered a controversial solution to the seemingly intractable Northern Ireland Troubles, which lasted for thirty years, claimed over 3,500 lives, and generated worldwide attention. Governing Northern Ireland in the same way as the rest of the United Kingdom—a policy of integration—would, Powell argued, put its constitutional status beyond doubt and remove the ambiguity that, in his opinion, fuelled the political violence. It is, of course, highly debatable whether integration would have achieved Powell's predicted outcome. At the time, it certainly put him starkly at odds with the bulk of Ulster Unionist opinion pursuing the restoration of devolved government. It also meant that he was also out of line with British government strategy, which—under both Conservative and Labour direction—consistently sought a power-sharing arrangement between the local constitutional parties and increasingly envisaged Republic of Ireland involvement in the resolution of the conflict.[1] In general terms, Powell's involvement in British politics has been more fully investigated than his time in Northern Ireland.[2] From the existing studies of Powell we do, however, have a clear sense of how integration related to his commitment to parliamentary sovereignty, with all power flowing from the centre, and to his opposition to devolution in Scotland and Wales.

In the context of Ulster Unionist politics, Powell had to be cautious and, at times, disingenuous in his advocacy of integration—obscuring the clarity of his position. There were real tensions in Powell's thinking over the competing claims of parliamentary sovereignty on the one hand and popular sovereignty on the other, which, in the case of Northern Ireland, turned on the question of who had the power to break the Union. This issue, one of perennial significance within Ulster Unionism, brought Powell face-to-face with the conditional allegiance to Britain exhibited especially by Ulster Loyalist (as distinct from British Unionist) elements, including paramilitaries.[3]

Powell found this difficult to accept—and it certainly undermined his argument that Ulster Unionism, in its commitment to the British nation, stood to counteract the prevailing loss of national confidence. This chapter also examines Powell's private, and brief public, support for British party political organization in Northern Ireland: electoral integration. As we will see, a range of political pressures inhibited him from pursuing this course fully, but it was nonetheless central to the case he made for Parliament—sustained by national political parties—as a protector of minorities.[4]

Integration

As nationalist parties gained momentum in Scotland and Wales in the late 1960s, and as discussion of some kind of devolution there intensified, Powell was adamant that Northern Irish self-government should not serve as an example of the form of semi-autonomous 'halfway houses' it was possible to construct within the United Kingdom. Powell's overall concern was to dismiss devolution as a compromise solution on the basis that nationalism, 'if it is real, cannot be bought off with less than the complete article'. Ignoring the fact that Ulster Unionists had since embraced devolved power, Powell rightly emphasized that it had only 'emerged by a sidewind during the tangled process' of the creation of the Irish Free State.[5] Powell's argument here was a rebuke of the thinking of, among others, the pro-devolution Scottish Labour politician and politics academic John P. Mackintosh, who sought to bring Northern Ireland into the debate.[6]

Against the backdrop of the deepening Troubles, Powell adumbrated his policy of integration in 1970, with the first hint that he did not agree with the existence of the Northern Ireland Parliament coming in a speech given in February at Enniskillen. At a time when the most prominent opposition to Stormont's continuation came from Republican circles, Powell stated that the 'Stormont Parliament itself...though rendered familiar and habitual by the use of nearly fifty years, is the fragment of a structure, of which the remainder never came into existence'.[7] This was a reference to the fact that in 1920 the British government had sought to establish two home-rule parliaments in Ireland. Powell's conclusions were guarded but, in a BBC interview the same day, he was sufficiently explicit to earn a public rebuke from Conservative shadow Home Secretary Quintin Hogg. Powell stated: 'I think there could come a time, and I think perhaps it would be right for our fellow citizens in Northern Ireland to be reflecting on this, when their assertion of oneness with the rest of the United Kingdom – which they passionately, clearly passionately, want to make – would be at odds with their assertion of this parliamentary independence.'[8]

At the same time, Powell sought to draw a clearer line between the Republic of Ireland and Northern Ireland as part of the United Kingdom, voicing objections to the fact that citizens of the Republic, if they lived in Britain, were given the right to vote and otherwise treated as British citizens. Holding that this arose from a mistaken assumption that not just the Irish Free State, itself a Dominion, but then the independent Republic of Ireland after 1949, 'was still within the allegiance' as part of the British Commonwealth. Powell argued that its practical effect was that 'the belonging of Northern Ireland and the not belonging of the Republic are at present obscured'.[9] Powell also saw a particular challenge ahead. Arguing that the European Community involved 'full-scale political unity', he argued that, British entry—at the same time as the Republic of Ireland—would mean 'the political unification of Ulster with the Republic'.[10]

Significantly, Powell had entered the debate at a time of considerable flux in Northern Irish politics and increasing uncertainty over the jurisdiction of the Northern Ireland Parliament at Stormont that operated on the basis of Unionist majority rule. The moderately reforming Northern Ireland Prime Minister Terence O'Neill had resigned in April 1969 amid rising sectarian tension, discontent with his leadership from within the Unionist Party, and criticism from the Reverend Ian Paisley outside the party that was proving increasingly difficult to dismiss. The founder of the Free Presbyterian Church, Paisley articulated a powerful fusion of anti-Catholic, evangelical Protestantism with intransigent opposition to change in Northern Ireland, which fed into long-standing Loyalist sentiments. O'Neill was succeeded by James Chichester-Clark, but his premiership was soon challenged by the same set of pressures, which, together with intervention from Westminster to reform local government and public-housing allocation (areas identified by the civil rights campaign as prone to discrimination), made Stormont's authority appear increasingly fragile.

Over the next couple of years, Powell sketched out his position. In his first speech on Northern Ireland in the House of Commons, in April 1970, he argued for 'a greater amalgamation and uniformity of administration, government, policy and economy in the six counties and in the rest of the United Kingdom'.[11] The following year his criticism of Stormont gathered pace, as he attributed to it some responsibility for sustaining the tensions by giving the impression that Northern Ireland's constitutional status was ambiguous. Just before a short speaking tour of Northern Ireland, he stated in a widely reported interview with a Dublin current-affairs magazine that: 'Stormont itself is a threat to the British link because it is an assertion of separateness... Anything which blurs the status of Northern Ireland as part of the UK does practical harm in that it maintains or helps to maintain this basic fuel of disorder and disruption.'[12] Just weeks before Labour leader Harold Wilson spoke in the House of Commons in November 1971 about his plan for a united Ireland, with entry of the Republic of Ireland into the Commonwealth and the introduction of an oath of allegiance, Powell conjured up the spectre of national decline, contending that the 'future for a nation which failed or abandoned a million and a half of its own citizens on its own soil would be dark indeed... the ignominy would be irreparable'.[13]

Despite his commitment to integration, Powell opposed the prorogation of Stormont in March 1972 by Heath's government because of the simultaneous introduction of direct rule. The British government hoped that this would be a temporary measure to bring a swiftly deteriorating situation under control and to provide time for the local political parties to reach agreement on some kind of reformed devolution in the future. After replacing Chichester-Clark as Northern Ireland prime minister in 1971, Brian Faulkner had, with backing from the British Cabinet, introduced internment in a heavy-handed manner against those suspected of Irish Republican Army (IRA) involvement. This produced a backlash in terms of a spiral of Republican and Loyalist political violence and a series of anti-internment rallies, most notably one in Derry/Londonderry on 30 January 1972, subsequently known as 'Bloody Sunday', when the killing of thirteen unarmed civilians by British soldiers attracted worldwide attention. Powell's objection to direct rule was, of course, an obvious way of opposing Heath, but it was also based on disagreement with the fact that Northern Ireland—unlike the rest of the United Kingdom—was to be governed by ministerial decree. In the absence of a devolved Parliament, he called for an increase in the number of Northern Irish parliamentary seats at Westminster. At a point when integration was being more widely mooted in Unionist circles, particularly by Paisley and his recently formed Democratic Unionist Party (DUP), Powell labelled this 'full integration' and said that it was 'what Unionism in Northern Ireland should demand and work for'.[14] In one sense, Powell did not therefore disapprove of the overall direction of British policy, emotively telling the

Commons that Northern Ireland had 'come home to this House'.[15] Yet he did dislike the way in which direct rule was operating. Indeed, after Orders in Council were introduced in 1974 as a means of carrying through legislation, he was critical of them for inhibiting parliamentary debate on Northern Irish issues.[16]

Powell's argument for integration, based on the premise that Northern Ireland was part of the British nation, also involved the repudiation of any kind of Ulster separatism. In 1972 and 1973, as the Vanguard Movement, a pressure group within the Unionist Party led by William 'Bill' Craig, began calling for semi-independence, Powell promptly argued that this would have meant 'turning unionism into that denial of itself, isolationism'.[17] Directly refuting the implications of the Vanguard publication *Ulster – A Nation*, Powell emphatically did not accept that there was any such thing as 'an Ulster nationality' or 'Ulster nationalism'.[18] As he later explained, Powell did not dispute the existence of an 'Ulster dimension' but saw this as akin to 'other regional dimensions in Britain, profound, historic and self-conscious'.[19]

From Powell's perspective, integration stood to provide Unionists with an overarching theme. Yet, as his involvement in Northern Irish politics increased, he was not only unable to persuade the Unionist Party to adopt it but also often had to word his proposals in ways that did not offend entrenched pro-devolution attitudes, obscuring the clarity of his position. Powell had been close to Jim Molyneaux, the MP for South Antrim, for several years.[20] The two of them now spoke on the telephone on 10 February 1974—just three days after Powell revealed that he would not stand as a Conservative. Powell's note of their conversation showed his high expectations. He authorized Molyneaux to state that 'only if the "loyal" Ulster Unionists invited me to be their leader and to represent them at Westminster, would I be prepared to consider any approach from Northern Ireland'. His view was that, 'having declined to stand as a Conservative candidate... I would need to be in personal control of the grounds and policy on which I might otherwise stand for Parliament in present circumstances'.[21]

In the event, of course, Powell's hopes were thwarted amid a complex political situation in Northern Ireland. By this stage, the United Ulster Unionist Council (UUUC), an electoral coalition comprising the Unionist Party, the DUP, and the Vanguard Unionist Progressive Party (the successor to the Vanguard Movement), had been set up in order to oppose the 1973 Sunningdale Agreement, which envisaged a power-sharing Northern Ireland

Executive and a cross-border Council of Ireland. In practice, this meant that
the UUUC was pitted against the pro-agreement parties making up the
Executive: those Unionists supporting Faulkner (who had been forced to
resign as leader of the Unionist Party and replaced by Harry West); the constitutional Nationalist Social and Democratic Labour Party (SDLP), formed
in 1970 and closely related to the civil rights movement; and the cross-
community Alliance Party, also formed in 1970. Powell shared the UUUC
opposition to power-sharing, but his reasons for doing so were quite different. The UUUC's main concern was the extent of the role of the Council
of Ireland, but this was underpinned by a widespread Unionist desire to see
the restoration of the old Stormont. In contrast, Powell argued against
power-sharing on the integrationist grounds that no other part of the United
Kingdom possessed it, readily adding that he remained fully committed to
the 'undivided sovereignty' of Westminster.[22] Powell was invited to attend
the UUUC conference at Portrush in late April 1974 and made a case strongly
for 'total integration' but, in the end, the conference endorsed a policy of
devolution for Northern Ireland within a future federal United Kingdom.[23]

Despite this difference, Molyneaux remained keen to secure Powell a
Northern Ireland parliamentary seat and sought to find alternative employment in business for Lawrence (Willy) Orr, the MP for South Down who
was amenable to the idea of not standing.[24] Molyneaux then arranged for
Powell to meet Craig, Paisley, and West on 4 July 1974 at his home in
London.[25] The leadership was clearly not on offer, but by the end of the
month, as he left for holiday, Powell gave Molyneaux 'full authority to accept
formally ... the offer of candidature for a parliamentary seat in Northern
Ireland'.[26] In a fast-moving situation, in which Orr 'simply disappeared' and
West did some 'ground work' on Powell's behalf, he accepted the South
Down nomination in late August.[27]

As he prepared to contest the October 1974 election as a candidate for
the Official Unionist Party (OUP), a name adopted to distinguish it from
Faulkner's newly formed Unionist Party of Northern Ireland, and with the
Executive having been brought down by the Loyalist Ulster Workers' Council
strike, Powell claimed to be 'entirely in accord' with the recently agreed
'Portrush Declaration'.[28] He was clearly being disingenuous. As recently as
May, the month after the UUUC conference, Powell had told an audience
in Wales that '[w]hat is not possible rationally, is to demand that the inhabitants of such an area shall exclusively decide how they are to be governed
in some respects, while sharing in other respects in the common decisions

Figure 9. The Official Unionist candidate for South Down with Ian Paisley, MP for North Antrim, outside the Stormont Parliament Buildings in Belfast, 25 September 1974.

and policies of a larger unit' on the basis that 'administration can be devolved, but the decisions that really matter cannot be decentralised'.[29]

Yet the broader context allowed Powell some latitude. This was a period of increasing constitutional debate, and hence uncertainty, when previous assumptions about the United Kingdom's status as a unitary state, which had been reflected in the report of the Royal Commission on the Constitution (often known as the Kilbrandon Report) as recently as 1973, were being called into question.[30] More importantly still, there was frequently a looseness of meaning in discussions of federalism that technically involved dividing, not devolving, power between Westminster and regional or provincial governments.[31]

'Playing the Northern Ireland question long'

Once elected, Powell mounted a surreptitious campaign against devolution. Publicly he pressed for increased parliamentary representation and democratic local government.[32] This was the first occasion on which Powell had

Figure 10. Powell's South Down general-election literature, October 1974.

mentioned an expanded role for local government, but it was consistent with an integrationist approach, as the scope and powers of local authorities had been restricted under devolution. It was also another criticism of the working of direct rule because, at the point of Stormont's prorogation, many responsibilities had been transferred from local councils to executive bodies.[33] Privately, Powell used his influence on Prime Minister Wilson, whose party he had endorsed over Europe, to argue that 'Stormont was receding in the mind of the general public, who were increasingly looking to Westminster' and were 'willing to accept a degree of devolution no greater than that worked out for Scotland and Wales'.[34] Powell may have misread the public mood in Northern Ireland, but he was arguably more perceptive in commenting that the 'Devolution Debate on the rest of the United Kingdom... provided a fortuitous opportunity of playing the Northern Ireland question long,' allowing for the possibility that, 'as the power of local government increased, the spectre of Stormont would gradually be banished'.[35]

Powell's approach initially yielded some results as he pushed party leader West to make his policy demands (expanded local government and increased parliamentary representation) a priority and as he worked with Molyneaux, who was increasingly persuaded by Powell's arguments, to derail any momentum for devolution outside the federal context.[36] Indeed, with Powell having privately lobbied Harold Wilson and Jim Callaghan over the issue, the principle of increased representation of Northern Ireland at Westminster was agreed in 1978.[37] Yet, at the same time, Powell's statements about devolution, especially in Scotland and Wales, had generated unease among Unionist opinion. In May 1976 West urged Powell 'to reassure' his constituents about his commitment to 'our declared policy for the return of a devolved Government to Northern Ireland'.[38] Furthermore, by the summer certain parts of the South Down Constituency Association became worried that Powell was not '100% behind devolved government at Stormont', which was their 'first priority'.[39]

Unionist concerns about Powell were unsurprising. During debates over Scottish and Welsh devolution, largely in the House of Commons, he left little room for doubt over his own position. Powell made it clear that his preference was to 'find perhaps the means whereby we can entrust perhaps a larger degree of control over administration and a larger jurisdiction to work within the law even than that enjoyed today by the GLC [Greater London Council] or the metropolitan county councils [the six councils, covering large urban areas, created in 1974]'.[40] Powell also emphasized two practical problems with federation: first, the large size of England, which meant that its representative institution would be a 'competitor' to the House of Commons; and, second, the powerful argument that became known as the 'West Lothian Question' after the constituency of the anti-devolutionist Labour MP Tam Dalyell—the fact that MPs from Scotland and Wales would be able to 'make law for the rest of the country upon the selfsame subjects over which legislative power is transferred to the new parliaments'.[41] Powell explicitly addressed the fact that, between 1920 and 1972, Northern Ireland 'had a regional parliament but was nevertheless represented, on a reduced scale, by a dozen Members of Parliament at Westminster no different from the rest' by arguing that this was 'a contradiction...on a small enough scale'— an argument he had made publicly as early as 1954.[42] Powell was, moreover, prepared to associate himself with the views of T. E. Utley, who had himself stood (unsuccessfully) as an Ulster Unionist parliamentary candidate in February 1974 and found the idea of integration, with proportional representation across the board, 'logically irresistible' if Northern Ireland was to remain in the United Kingdom.[43]

In 1977 Powell admitted frankly that: 'I regard the federal solution merely as a theoretical structure which solves the conundrum posed by the proposal for legislative devolution inside a unitary state. In practical terms, it is a *reductio ad absurdum*. Nothing that I have said shows that I think it is at all practical or desirable for the United Kingdom.'[44] His view remained that articulated by A. V. Dicey around the turn of the twentieth century: any form of devolution—called home rule at that point—would mean 'we have still destroyed the House and the Union'. Powell was adamant that the 'nature of the House of Commons is that its sovereignty reaches into every nook and cranny of the national life' and that there were 'no powers which it will concede within this realm to any other authority'.[45] In his biographical study of Joseph Chamberlain, the Liberal and then Liberal Unionist politician who opposed home rule in the late nineteenth century, Powell accepted that a federation—Chamberlain's preferred solution—was feasible at that point in time. But Powell still took the chance to repeat his view that it would have meant the 'absolute destruction of the historical constitution of the United Kingdom'.[46]

Powell's differences with a significant proportion of Unionist opinion were further exacerbated by his commitment to seeing Northern Ireland's economy operate under the same free-market principles as the rest of the United Kingdom. In 1972, at a time when he was drawing closer to the

Ulster Unionist MPs, Powell set himself at odds with them through his opposition to the Northern Ireland Finance Corporation, which had been created to help bolster the local economy amid continuing civil unrest. In line with his long-standing opposition to state and regional planning, which we have seen most starkly in respect to Scotland, he criticized the rationale of the body for mistakenly seeking to perform the kind of task best left to the private sector.[47] After being adopted as an OUP candidate, Powell offered a more conciliatory position. In an interview with Radio Éireann, he now defended British aid to industry in Northern Ireland given the 'assault' it was facing but sought to 'sharply distinguish' between this and what he saw as the prevailing trend in regional policy of 'sustaining industries which are not viable by an infusion of tax payers' money'.[48] Yet days before the general election, Powell's specific comments about subsidies to the Belfast shipbuilders Harland and Wolff put him more starkly at odds with the bulk of Unionist opinion that attached particular significance to the shipyard as a symbol of Ulster's industrial prowess and of its economic affinities with Britain. Pointedly, Powell stated that the 'most dangerous projects for Ulster are those selected on political and not economic grounds and propped up with subsidies because they cannot satisfy the test of fair and open competition'.[49] In March 1975, when the government announced it was taking over the shipbuilders, Powell duly criticized the move. To considerable Unionist affront, he told the Belfast Junior Chamber of Commerce that the nationalization was 'a deterrent to industry and enterprise' that sent damaging messages about the Northern Ireland economy akin to those projected by the nationalization of shipyards on the Clyde in Glasgow a few years earlier.[50]

At the same time, Powell emphasized those aspects of his economic policy that, while being in line with his advocacy of integration, were also more palatable to most Unionists. He made it clear that he objected to the 'absurdity' of attempting 'to construct a sort of balance of payments table between the different parts of a unitary nation like the United Kingdom'. In the widest sense, this indicated Powell's unhappiness with the imperfect financial integration deriving from the implementation of the 1920 Government of Ireland Act, whose complex fiscal arrangements had originally necessitated the collection of such data. In the immediate context, it provided a means for Powell to denounce those who, amid increasing net transfers to Northern Ireland, sought to use government statistics 'to show that Northern Ireland is an economic dead weight upon the United Kingdom' without fully acknowledging that it was 'living under continuous enemy attack'.[51]

Allegiance and the Union

As Powell became more deeply involved in Unionist politics, he found himself embroiled in a series of related disputes about the nature of Ulster's allegiance to Britain. This was arguably the most heavily contested element of Ulster Unionism in theory and practice, and became even more so as the Troubles unfolded. As early as 1972 Powell took issue with the notion of Ulster Loyalism. Addressing a rally at Banbridge, County Down, he provocatively asked:

> Loyalty to what? Union with what? There must be no doubt or division or prevarication about the answers to those questions. The answer is not loyalty to Ulster; no, nor loyalty to yourselves. The answer is not the union of these six counties; no, nor union among yourselves. The answer is loyalty to the United Kingdom of Great Britain and Northern Ireland.[52]

Despite this, Powell took an initially benevolent view of Loyalist paramilitaries. He did this in a broader context in which many Unionist politicians were more critical of Republican paramilitaries than Loyalist ones and in a specific setting in which, in 1972 and 1973, Craig rhetorically embraced the armed Loyalist cause. With the rise in particular of the Ulster Volunteer Force (UVF) since 1966, Powell criticized their strategy as 'misguided... self-defeating [and] disastrous to their own cause'. Yet on two separate occasions—in 1971 and again in 1972, just after the formation of the Ulster Defence Association (UDA)—he distinguished them from Republican paramilitaries on the basis that they sought to maintain their allegiance to the British nation, stating:

> There is a world of difference between a citizen who commits a crime, in the belief, however mistaken, that he is thereby helping to preserve the integrity of his country and his right to remain a subject of his sovereign, and a person, be he citizen or alien, who commits a crime with the intention of destroying that integrity and rendering impossible that allegiance. The former breaches the peace; the latter is executing an act of war... the one is a lawbreaker; the other is an enemy.[53]

Powell did not repeat these arguments as Loyalist political violence increased in the mid-1970s and he became increasingly concerned about the conditional allegiance exhibited widely in Unionist circles. He was aware of his own divergent position and so—when he planned to deliver a speech on the topic of allegiance at Kilkeel on 5 July 1975—he did not, in his customary manner, pre-distribute a copy of the speech through the OUP machinery.[54] Powell censured Loyalist paramilitaries for wanting to 'obey some laws but not others', such as holding firearms. He also argued that, in a more general sense, Unionists 'could not put conditions on their obedience to the Crown-in-Parliament'. As expected, this created a backlash. Craig and Martin Smyth, Grand Master of the Orange Order in Ireland, both emphasized the conditional and monarchical nature of Ulster loyalty. The speech also prompted a significant exchange with Paisley, who contended that there was a dangerous precedent in Powell's argument: 'If the Crown-in-Parliament decided to put Ulster into a united Ireland, according to Mr Powell, we would have to obey if we were loyal.' West made the same point, echoing a potent, and widely held, interpretation of Ulster defiance that had been made as it appeared that home rule would be given to all of Ireland before the First World War. This typically involved references to the signing of the Ulster Covenant in 1912, the formation of the Ulster Volunteers in 1912, and the arming of them as the Ulster Volunteer Force, the original UVF, in 1914.[55] West argued that 'if the people of Ulster had been at all times loyal to the British Parliament in the past they would not have a Northern Ireland today'.[56] In a subsequent interview, Powell recognized that, in such a scenario, 'the whole meaning of unionism would have been destroyed, and consequently, the meaning of loyalty', but he insisted that the prospect was frankly 'inconceivable'.[57]

Powell's awareness of the conditional nature of Ulster Unionist allegiance to Britain sat uneasily with the case he attempted to make that Ulster had a particular contribution to offer in offsetting the decline of the British nation. Amid the 'widespread loss of confidence in Britain itself' that Powell saw as underpinning the desire to join the European Community, he argued that 'Ulster asserts defiantly, in the face of all dissuasion and denigration, that it is part of a greater whole... the United Kingdom, the British nation'.[58] On another occasion, Powell stated: 'Ulster never forgets what a nation is or what it is to belong to a nation.'[59] By 1977, identifying a full-blown 'crisis of the nation's belief in its own existence', Powell argued more strongly than ever that Ulster Unionism offered a 'living protest against the prevalent self-abasement of the British nation'.[60]

As time went by, Powell gave increasing thought to explaining how unconditional allegiance to the Crown-in-Parliament secured the Union. In 1974 Powell had made this point in abstract terms: 'It simply is not within the range of political reality that a democratic nation state could sever off a part of itself where the majority of the inhabitants manifest repeatedly, under all manner of testing and despite all manner of pressure, their determination to remain part of the state.'[61] In the years that followed, Powell developed his position. He held that allegiance to the Crown-in-Parliament was demonstrated through the act of election by which 'the people gave in advance the pledge of their acceptance' of its sovereignty, constituting the 'consent of the nation'.[62] In 1981 he explicitly contended that electing MPs to Westminster guaranteed Northern Ireland's status as part of the United Kingdom because this made it 'impossible' for the House of Commons to 'reject a part of itself'.[63] This, of course, swiftly became a provocative argument as the Provisional IRA hunger striker, Bobby Sands, won a Westminster seat in April 1981 as part of a wider campaign for Republican inmates to be treated as political prisoners that, in turn, paved the way for the emergence of Sinn Féin as a political force, contesting, but not taking up, seats in the House of Commons. Powell's position also provoked a backlash from the devolutionist wing of the OUP. Edgar Graham, a rising figure in the party and a law lecturer at Queen's University Belfast, articulated the long-standing distrust of Westminster parties and politicians, arguing that if 'the union had to depend on the House of Commons for its defence, it would be a very fragile union indeed'.[64]

Powell's argument also contained some latent contradictions. It was seemingly underpinned by his belief in the overriding sovereignty of the Crown-in-Parliament to make or break any laws whatsoever. Accordingly, he distinguished it from the contention that Northern Ireland's constitutional position was secured as a result of any particular piece of legislation, including the 1973 Northern Ireland Act, which stated that it would remain part of the United Kingdom so long as this was the wish of a majority of its population.[65] Yet, at the same time, Powell attributed significant power to the people, going, in undefined ways, beyond that of election. Indeed, on one occasion he stated that it was 'the people of Northern Ireland themselves, and they alone, who have it in their power to destroy the Union with Great Britain'.[66] This mirrored arguments Powell had made about European Community membership when, as we have seen, amid parliamentary support for entry but before reluctantly endorsing a referendum on the issue, he had obliquely contended that the power to overturn the decision lay with the people.

Powell's acceptance of some degree of popular sovereignty had slowly become apparent in his discussion of the types of behaviour that put the

Union in jeopardy. In a widely circulated speech in 1976, Powell identified a particular danger from Loyalist paramilitary activity:

> [T]he nationalist, the rebel, the seceder – these are the people who can, and frequently do, obtain their aims by lawlessness and force. You can get out of an association or a society or a nation by breaking its laws and by turning your back upon it. What you cannot do is to maintain your membership of it by those methods...the aims of Unionism, because it is Unionism, can only be attained through and under the law of the Union, and therefore they can only be attained under and through Parliament.[67]

Powell also began to argue that Paisley's actions threatened to undermine the Union. He was critical of Paisley's involvement—alongside the UDA—in the May 1977 United Unionist Action Council strike, which sought the restoration of devolved government on the basis of Unionist majority rule together with tougher security measures against the Provisional IRA. Powell asserted that it was a case of 'direct action against Parliament and the Crown' that, if it had succeeded, would have led Parliament to conclude 'with justification, that Ulster had withdrawn its claim and cancelled its right to be part of the union'.[68] These comments were part of a developing feud between Powell and Paisley, which intensified after the UUUC broke down in 1977 and then involved speculation at each subsequent general election that the DUP would challenge Powell in South Down. Indeed, as animosities deepened further, Powell attacked Paisley's willingness to absent himself deliberately from the House of Commons, calling him an 'anti-Unionist' and dismissing the DUP as 'Protestant Sinn Féin', a jibe which was also aimed at its support for devolution.[69]

Conspiracy theories and the Thatcher government

There was no doubt that Powell was disappointed with the devolutionary direction of the Thatcher government's policy towards Northern Ireland. While the Conservatives were in opposition, Powell had been close to Airey Neave, the Conservative shadow Secretary for Northern Ireland who appeared willing to move along integrationist lines. Indeed, Powell had readily endorsed the regional council scheme—designed to strengthen local government—proposed by the Conservatives under Neave's guidance in 1978.[70] Neave was murdered by the Irish National Liberation Army (INLA), the military wing of the Irish Republican Socialist Party, on 30 March 1979, prompting Powell coldly to respond that: 'Airey Neave would have wished nothing better than to share the same end as so many of his innocent fellow citizens for whom the House of Commons is responsible.'[71] But, as the Conservatives entered government, Powell still had reason to be hopeful in policy terms. The Conservative manifesto had stated that in 'the absence of devolved government, we will seek to establish one or more elected regional councils with a wide range of powers over local services'.[72] Moreover, Ian Gow, appointed as Thatcher's Parliamentary Private Secretary, had, in the past, actively sought Powell's views on Northern Ireland.[73] Now, on Powell's prompting, Gow sought to establish relations between Powell and Thatcher. He told Thatcher: 'While I understand your concern at the wider implications of him being seen arriving at Downing Street at the present time, I believe that Enoch is wholly trustworthy in his personal (if not political) dealings.'[74] Thatcher and Powell duly met in late October 1979.[75]

Yet, the following month, with the regional council scheme abandoned and with Humphrey Atkins as Secretary of State for Northern Ireland seeking to establish a conference for the Northern Ireland political parties, Powell publicly argued that this represented a volte-face on the government's part, which now sought devolution. This was, of course, a continuation of the bipartisan British government approach, but Powell strikingly argued that Thatcher was pursuing it under pressure from Jack Lynch, the Republic of Ireland Taoiseach, who was himself acting, as Powell saw it, under malign US influence.[76] At this juncture, Powell was, as the Northern Ireland Office (NIO) noted, 'looking hard for conspiracies and hints of deception'.[77] This was a new departure, but it related to Powell's long-held suspicions of US foreign policy and the corresponding threat to the British nation. Earlier in 1979 Powell had argued that there was a particular American concern to put pressure on Britain to create an all-Ireland state.[78] He saw the reasoning as strategic: the entry of 'an all-Ireland state . . . into NATO . . . filling the gravest of all the gaps in the American strategy for Europe and the Atlantic'.[79] Powell had also suggested that parts of the British civil service were particularly susceptible to US pressure. He considered that the NIO was already dominated by the conviction that Ulster was 'England's "last colony"' and was accordingly 'dedicated to the task of removing that encumbrance from her shoulders as quickly as possible'.[80] In early 1980, at a point when he was critical of the Foreign Office embrace of the European Community as a means of increasing its own influence, Powell called it a 'nursery of traitors' and told an audience in Northern Ireland that it fixated 'above all on Washington DC, for whose favours and delectation this province is to be offered up a sacrifice'.[81]

Powell's arguments against devolution gained a limited amount of traction. Gow was favourable and sent Thatcher a recent memorandum by Utley, which argued in favour of 'full integration' and said that 'Humphrey Atkins has made a serious mistake in retreating from it'.[82] Powell also pushed for integration on the economic front. He asked John Biffen, Chief Secretary to the Treasury, to consider, in his drive for savings, whether 'wholly wasteful . . . duplication' could be identified among 'the functions which are performed for Ulster by the Government of Northern Ireland but not for Scotland by the Scottish office or for Wales by the Welsh Office'.[83] Despite his personal closeness to Powell, and his overall desire to reduce government intervention, Biffen was well aware that there was a 'major political difficulty in the nature of the suggestion itself and its timing'.[84] The view of the Treasury was even starker, considering that this was 'motivated as much by Mr Powell's desire to integrate Northern Ireland with Great Britain as by a desire for economy as such'.[85] The government was also confronted by Powell's claim, made to Kenneth Stowe, Permanent Under-Secretary of State for Northern Ireland, at the NIO, that the OUP had made a deal with Neave on 28 March 1979, agreeing that, in return for votes against the Labour government in the upcoming confidence motion, the Conservatives would, if elected, set up regional councils. Stowe reported that he was 'struck by the stark clarity and precise terms in which Mr Powell referred to his agreement with Mr Neave'.[86] Thatcher herself had been made aware of this by Molyneaux, now overall OUP leader, late the previous year.[87] Yet, in the end, the impact was minimal. Having consulted his colleagues on MISC 24, a subcommittee of the Cabinet, the Home Secretary Willie Whitelaw told Thatcher that: 'None of us had any knowledge of this alleged deal, and policy on Northern Ireland has therefore had to be developed without taking account of it.'[88]

Taking a different tack, Powell now sought to encourage inertia. At a meeting with Thatcher, he argued against the 'serious misapprehensions' that it was 'essential to do something about constitutional change in Northern Ireland now'. According to Gow's note, Powell suggested 'that if we were to do nothing, but simply to continue with Direct Rule, there would be no outcry in Ulster . . . and [it] would be something that would be wholly manageable'. Powell made clear his concerns about establishing an assembly in any form:

> If there was an Assembly, without an Executive, that Assembly would act irresponsibly, because it would have no responsibility. It would discuss any and all matters. It would be hostile and critical. Its criticism would be destructive. It would diminish the role of Ulster MPs at Westminster. An Assembly with an Executive could only be achieved as a result of power-sharing. Thus, the power

of the majority would be negated. Any Unionists who were to participate, would have their heads cuts off, as happened in the case of Faulkner. The I.R.A. would see a power-sharing Executive as a step in the direction in which they would like to go. The I.R.A. would be encouraged. They would argue that if they were to persevere, they would be able to force further constitutional change.[89]

Later in 1980, Powell's charges of collusion with the Republic of Ireland, at the bidding of the United States, increased. With talks taking place in Dublin on 8 December 1980 against the backdrop of the hunger strikes, Powell described it as a 'mini-Munich' on BBC Radio 4's 'The World at One', a reference to Prime Minister Neville Chamberlain's perceived capitulation to Hitler's territorial demands in 1938. With article 2 of the Republic of Ireland constitution stating that the 'national territory' comprised 'the whole island of Ireland', he argued that it was 'a visible humiliation of the United Kingdom to go and hob-nob...with a nation which claims sovereignty over part of its territory and to discuss with it the internal affairs of part of the United Kingdom, namely the management of Her Majesty's Prisons'.[90] Powell developed these themes further when he saw Thatcher in February 1981. He said that 'a reliable source' in the NIO had informed him that the preparations for the meeting in Dublin 'had been conducted with the knowledge of and agreed with the United States Government'. Powell suggested that there had been a clandestine arrangement whereby, in return for 'increased co-operation in defeating terrorism' from the Republic of Ireland, there was to be a 'recognition by us of the interests and aspirations of the Republic in Northern Ireland'. With the DUP more favourable to devolution, and thus more amenable to the government's plans than the OUP, Powell argued that it appeared as though 'the Conservative Party was countenancing the D.U.P. at the expense of the Official Unionists and that the Northern Ireland Office had its eye on Dr. Paisley as a possible future Prime Minister of Northern Ireland'.[91]

In June 1982, Powell went further. Speaking in the House of Commons, he cited notes taken by an academic researcher (later revealed to be Geoffrey Sloan, a PhD student at Keele University) of an interview with an NIO official—named as Clive Abbott without giving notice beforehand to the Secretary of State for Northern Ireland, Jim Prior. These purported to show that the NIO had informed the new Conservative government in 1979 that integration 'was just not on' because it would jeopardize cooperation over security as well as 'undertakings given to the Irish government over the constitutional future of Northern Ireland'.[92] There was a broader point here: in his memoirs Prior wrote frankly of his recognition that integration 'would have scuppered any hope of co-operation with Dublin'.[93] Yet, privately, Powell made an even more shocking suggestion, as Gow summarized for Thatcher:

> Enoch believes that, shortly before he was murdered, Airey had a meeting either with Roy Mason [Secretary of State for Northern Ireland, 1976-9], or with very senior civil servants in the Northern Ireland Office, or both; that he was informed that it would not be possible to implement our Party's policy towards Northern Ireland in the event of a change of Government because of undertakings or understandings reached with Dublin; that Airey asserted that the policy of a Conservative Government in regard to a part of the United Kingdom would be fashioned in London and not in Dublin...and that this response of Airey was communicated, directly or indirectly, to Dublin or to unfriendly sources in Belfast....Enoch believes Airey's determination to pursue a <u>Unionist</u> policy in regard to Northern Ireland was then communicated to the Irish National Liberation Army which then decided to eliminate the man whom it perceived to be the threat to the prospective unity of the Island of Ireland.[94]

Thatcher had herself been close to Neave, who had been the campaign manager in her party leadership bid, and Powell personally pressed her on the issue.[95] Meanwhile, an investigation into the claims that Powell had made in Parliament was set up under the overall direction of Robert Armstrong as Head of the Civil Service. Abbott, who was 'greatly incensed', was interviewed and denied Sloan's charges.[96] Powell obtained photocopies of the original notes from Sloan.[97] But these were 'very scrappy and disjointed', and it was also revealed that Sloan had undertaken some work for both Molyneaux and the Londonderry MP William Ross—casting doubt on his impartiality in Northern Irish politics.[98] In the end, Armstrong's judgement was he could see 'no way of resolving with certainty the conflict' between the accounts of Sloan and Abbott but that 'Sloan's notes could not be relied upon as an account of what Mr Abbott had said'.[99]

British political parties in Northern Ireland?

The early 1980s marked a significant change in Powell's articulation of integration. Until now, with wider debates about devolution still ongoing (Scottish and Welsh devolution was rejected by referenda in 1979), he had not only obscured some of his arguments under the cover of a superficial commitment to federalism but had also tended to suggest that parliamentary sovereignty—and hence the Union—were of intrinsic value. From this point on, he began to substantiate his case. In 1978 Powell had already stated that 'of all human contrivances, the parliamentary system of the United Kingdom affords the best available guarantee to those who live under it of justice and freedom'.[100] In the same year, he told a meeting of the pro-devolutionist Orange Order that: 'In no other framework and on no other plane [i.e., that of the UK Parliament] can the rights and liberties of all in Northern Ireland be assured.'[101] In 1980 Powell attempted to justify these claims, as the OUP stood aloof from the Atkins Conference of Northern Ireland's political parties. Countering the suggestion that a power-sharing local assembly was needed to protect the interests of the Nationalist minority in Northern Ireland, he contended that 'Parliament . . . is the natural protector of all minorities because it is itself made up of minorities.'[102] This was because 'both politically and geographically the consciousness that they are all minorities prevents them from coercing or trampling upon one another beyond a certain point'. Devolution in any form—the old Stormont regime as well as a power-sharing model—would only work to override the safeguards. Making a long-standing distinction between the political (Nationalist) and religious (Catholic) minorities that had recently gained renewed salience in Ulster Unionist circles, but also adapting the argument made in 1977 by Tam Dalyell that devolution would increase sectarian divisions in Scotland, he argued:

> [I]f Ulster is . . . endowed with the attributes of a separate state, all the proportions are changed: not only does the political minority that rejects the Union become relatively more significant, but its self-identification with the religious minority places that minority too in an altered situation. Power, and especially legislative power, which is the essential attribute of sovereignty, must then be exercised with a view above all to the maintenance of the state itself, and the differences which, diluted within the Union as a whole, were harmless and tolerated, become critically important . . . that everything which is done to guarantee and secure the rights of one minority will be a subtraction from the rights of other minorities and of the majority.[103]

As the OUP moved in a devolutionist direction, Powell was left in a 'very isolated position'.[104] He now entered new territory as he came very close to endorsing the integration of Northern Ireland into the British party system. Speaking in the House of Commons in 1982, he lamented the fact that 'the party political structure of Northern Ireland differs from the rest of the United Kingdom'. Powell argued that this had a 'profound effect on the relationship between subject and Government', leaving them 'exiled from the political system that is the United Kingdom as a whole' and constituting the 'biggest and most significant difference...between the Province and the rest of the kingdom'. Making it clear how this related to local political minorities, he argued, 'when, in the county of Durham, the Conservative minority contemplates the fact that it is unlikely to return a majority of Members to this House—or vice versa in Hampshire—it feels no estrangement as a result, because it identifies itself with the cause of the Labour Party, or the Conservative Party, as the case may be, throughout the nation'.[105] The centrality of party to Powell's arguments is striking, not only given his own uneasy relationship with first the Conservative Party and then the OUP, but also given his concern that, so far as Europe was concerned, the party system in Britain had failed.

Powell had not yet explained how he thought electoral integration should take place. Indeed, he faced some difficulties here that went beyond his own estrangement from the Conservative Party. Since the 1920s, the Ulster Unionist MPs had taken the Conservative whip at Westminster in return for administrative, electoral, and, very occasionally, financial help. But the relationship had weakened considerably by the 1960s and there had been Unionist dismay at the decision to suspend Stormont in 1972, with its MPs subsequently refusing to support Heath's attempts to form a government in the hung parliament after February 1974.[106] At the same time, there were tensions between Stormont and the Westminster Unionists by the early 1970s.[107] Some pro-Conservative sentiment remained among the Unionist grass roots but Powell—who had endorsed Labour in 1974 on account of its position on Europe—dismissed this as 'just stupid' on BBC Northern Ireland's 'Inside Politics' radio programme in 1977.[108] As time progressed, Powell's position became even more complicated. Having urged electors at the 1979 general election to vote for candidates—irrespective of party—who opposed European Community membership, by 1982 Powell was advising voters, once again, to choose Labour because of its professed desire to withdraw from the Community. Yet in 1983 it was the Conservative MP John Biggs-Davison, a supporter of electoral integration, who was told by Powell that 'it would be a sign and a seal of the permanence of the Union if the Parliamentary representation of the province were within the party structure of the rest of the kingdom; and I hope to be spared to live to see

this happen'.[109] Even so, it was not until November 1984 that Powell told a
Unionist political meeting, 'it is through the Conservative Party that those
Ulster electors who, in Great Britain, would be supporters and members of
the Conservative Party must find a way to participate in the ... political process of our nation'. Powell was still not supporting the Conservative Party
over Europe, but he made this statement amid his satisfaction, which he
voiced also to the OUP conference in the same week, that Thatcher had
emphatically rejected the proposals of the New Ireland Forum during a
press conference at Chequers. The Forum had sought to provide an agreed
constitutional nationalist approach to Northern Ireland and comprised representatives from the main political parties in the Republic of Ireland, Fianna
Fáil, Fine Gael, and the Irish Labour Party, as well as the SDLP. Significantly,
Powell interpreted Thatcher's rejection of each of its proposed solutions—a
unitary Ireland, a federal arrangement, or joint British–Irish authority—as
demonstrating that 'Ulster's constitutional status is now to be put beyond all
cavil and debate'.[110] Thatcher's desire to continue her day-to-day business
following the Provisional IRA bombing of the Grand Hotel in Brighton,
where the Conservative Party Conference was being held, may also have
influenced Powell, who was quick to praise her 'courage and insight'.[111]

The Anglo-Irish Agreement and its aftermath

Pessimism also ran alongside Powell's hopes. In August 1984, with specula-
tion mounting that a parliamentary tier would be created within the Anglo-
Irish Council established in 1981 to formalize relations between London and
Dublin, he argued that, if this happened, Parliament would be breaking the
Union and, in the process, relinquishing its claims on Ulster allegiance.
Adopting the familiar Unionist narrative—which West had deployed against
him in 1975—Powell stated:

> I say that the men of 1912 were right when they ... declared that the mother
> country would forfeit its right to their loyalty if it put them into a Dublin
> parliament. The methods ... have been refined and elaborated since 1912; but
> the substance and the end result intended are still the same. When a British
> government creates an Anglo-Irish body to comprise representatives and to
> deliberate on the affairs of this island, it will ... have renounced its claim upon
> the allegiance of the British people of this province.[112]

The signing of the Anglo-Irish Agreement on 15 November 1985, and its
subsequent passage through Parliament, thus placed Powell in an awkward

position. Having enjoyed direct contact with Thatcher, he had contributed
to the Unionist sense of betrayal by leading party colleagues to believe that
such an agreement would not take place, certainly not unless the Republic
of Ireland removed its constitutional claims to Northern Ireland.[113] That
said, following Gow's departure as Thatcher's Parliamentary Private Secretary
after the 1983 general election and his replacement by Michael Alison,
Powell had seen Thatcher much less frequently.[114] Taken as a whole, moreover,
the Unionists had been, according to Thatcher's official biographer, 'deliberately excluded' from the discussion process.[115] Yet the agreement had—
by the criteria Powell had set out—come close to breaking the Union. It
steered well clear of joint authority but, with the creation of the Anglo-Irish
Intergovernmental Conference, there was not only a shared commitment to
the longer-term promotion of devolved government between the constitutional parties but also an immediate aspiration that the Republic of Ireland
would be consulted, especially so far as the interests of Nationalists in
Northern Ireland were concerned. Speaking in the House of Commons,
Powell argued that it was 'an unprecedented arrangement whereby a formal
position is allocated to another country in respect of the conduct of affairs
in the United Kingdom'. Citing the 1979 referenda on Scottish and Welsh
devolution as precedent, Powell suggested that 'there is a counterpart to the
undoubted right of this Parliament to make law of the United Kingdom. It
is that, wherever it makes law differently for certain parts of the United
Kingdom, it can do so only in accordance with the wishes, and normally at
the petition, of the people of those parts of the United Kingdom.' Powell
stated that this left Ulster allegiance in an uncertain position: 'no one will
be able to say after the Division tonight that the people of Northern Ireland
are under an obligation to accept—whatever might be the meaning of the
term "accept" in that context—the Anglo-Irish agreement that has been
made between the two Prime Ministers. We are again straining beyond its
moral limit the authority of this House.'[116]

Yet in Northern Ireland, where Unionist anger at the agreement was
incandescent amid fears that it represented a movement in the direction of
a united Ireland, Powell did not pursue the implications of his argument.
After not appearing at the 'Ulster Says No' Unionist rally at Belfast City
Hall on 23 November, Powell argued that the 'Union is what Northern
Ireland has never had', since the existence of Stormont had ensured that it
was 'carefully kept at arm's length from the rest of the United Kingdom'.[117]
He made the same point after reluctantly joining other Unionist MPs, from
both the OUP and the DUP, in resigning his seat and fighting a by-election

on the issue of the agreement in late January 1986.[118] This was an exaggerated form of Powell's long-standing argument that Northern Ireland had never been fully integrated with the rest of the United Kingdom, but in the circumstances it was a clear attempt to avoid a judgement on what exactly had happened. At the same time, Powell counselled against those who argued that Britain had broken the Union, stating that their stance was what those opposed to the Union wanted to hear and seeking to quash any talk of Ulster independence, which had arisen in particular from the newly formed Ulster Clubs Movement.[119] Powell was decidedly uncomfortable with the defiant message projected by the Unionist 'Day of Action', effectively a general strike accompanied by considerable intimidation, which took place on 3 March 1986.[120] In the context of intensified violence from Loyalist paramilitaries against both the Royal Ulster Constabulary (RUC) and Catholics, he returned to an emphasis on popular sovereignty as a warning to Unionist opinion: 'nobody can take the Union forcibly from the people of Ulster so long as they maintain their claim of right intact. Only the Ulster people themselves can throw it away.'[121] Powell also revisited familiar terrain in blaming American pressure for the Anglo-Irish Agreement, contending that the 'strategic motive of purchasing American approval at whatever cost has risen to a point where it is no longer compatible with national self-respect'.[122]

As tensions in Northern Ireland over the agreement eased a little, Powell offered deeper reflection on the situation. Addressing the Queen's University Law Society in 1987, he identified it as an 'ethico-legal problem'. Stating explicitly that the 'general obligation of the citizen to obey the law depends on the law being duly made' and thus on its 'moral force', Powell repeated his argument that 'without the consent of the people of Northern Ireland' the agreement was 'monstrously inequitable'. Yet he placed this alongside his underlying conviction that 'to live is to live in society, and to live in society is to live under laws'. At this juncture, Powell did not fully pursue the implications of this analysis, reverting to describing his position in romantic terms by stating that 'this is our country, we have no other and can have no other, any more than a man can get himself another mother and father'.[123] The following year, after his general-election defeat in South Down by the SDLP's Eddie McGrady, Powell spoke in more depth about the 'insoluble contradiction which the Anglo-Irish Agreement...created for the people of Northern Ireland'. Grappling directly with the issue of allegiance, he accepted that there was 'a logical argument for treating the law of the United

Kingdom as no longer obligatory' but insisted that this still left the difficulty 'of claiming to belong to a state and not obeying its laws'. This was why Powell himself had decided that, even under strained circumstances, the 'law was still binding'.[124]

Meanwhile, however, the Anglo-Irish Agreement led Powell to withdraw his public endorsement of electoral integration. He did so as the agreement prompted Unionist politician Robert McCartney to form the Campaign for Equal Citizenship (CEC), in order urgently to demand British political-party organization.[125] Powell, however, considered that the agreement constituted a significant stumbling block to such an initiative. Accordingly, when the OUP conference in November 1986 debated McCartney's motion for the 'full integration of Northern Ireland into the political insti-tutions which apply to the rest of the United Kingdom', Powell played a part in its eventual rejection by introducing an amendment calling for the postponement of any policy statement until after the agreement had been overturned.[126] This led to a vitriolic backlash against Powell. The CEC's journal made a point of criticizing him for not following through on his advocacy of 'full integration'.[127] Others, such as Brendan Clifford from the British and Irish Communist Organisation that had also played a role in building the momentum for electoral integration, made similar comments in a stinging manner.[128] There were, it should be said, important differences between Powell and those involved in the CEC. Whereas they, embracing a civic interpretation of Unionism, emphasized the importance of the state, pitching their claims 'distinct from consideration of nationality', Powell viewed citizenship in terms of an attachment to the nation.[129] Moreover, Powell had not fundamentally changed his mind on British political-party organization in Northern Ireland. In private correspondence in summer 1986, he stated that: 'I think the true remedy is for us to be integrated not only into the administration but into the party system of the United Kingdom, and I look forward to this happening one day.'[130] In 1988, as both the Conservative and Labour parties discussed setting up constituency parties in Northern Ireland, Powell put forward a modified version of the same argu-ment. He told his former political secretary Peter Clarke that the candidates of both parties would be 'foredoomed to defeat by the commitment of their respective parties to the Anglo-Irish Agreement' but argued that, in the future, 'nothing can prevent politics in the province becoming aligned with those in the rest of the kingdom, though the alignment is more likely to take the form of the alliance between Ulster parties and mainland parties, like the present alliance of the SDLP and the Labour party and the former alliance of the Ulster Unionists with the Conservatives'.[131] Nonetheless, Powell's public resistance to electoral integration remained. In 1989, as the Conservative Party sought to form Conservative Associations and to put up candidates, Powell emphasized their difficult position as prospective candidates of the party that had made the agreement.[132]

As the peace process gathered momentum in the mid-1990s, Powell remained committed to integration as the 'only salvation for Northern Ireland'.[133] And, indeed, there was briefly a resurgence of interest in the idea from prominent journalists in *The Times*, the *Daily Telegraph*, the *Sunday Telegraph*, and *The Spectator*—sparked by concerns about the British commitment to Northern Ireland following the 1993 Downing Street Declaration, which argued for Irish self-determination but stipulated that both parts of the island had to agree to any new settlement, and heightened the following year as the Provisional IRA ceasefire made further negotiations possible.[134] We can safely assume that Powell, who died before its conclusion, would have disapproved of the 1998 Good Friday Agreement, under which a power-sharing assembly was set up and the people of Northern Ireland were able to hold British and/or Irish citizenship. Powell had frankly told Gow in 1982 that there was 'no serious prospect that politicians committed to oppose or to promote a united Ireland will ever co-operate in joint administration of the province'.[135] Furthermore, just weeks before his death in 1998 Powell accepted an invitation to remain as a Vice-President of the Queen's University Ulster Unionist Association, a position he had held since 1970, with an emphatic statement of his own position—'the struggle in Ireland is about the nation to which Ulster shall belong'—and significantly adding that there was 'no reason why it should depend upon . . . a single religion'.[136]

Conclusion

'The age of Brexit is the age of Powell'

The debates in which Powell participated have persisted to the present day, albeit in modified forms. In certain cases, this is because of recent developments in the Labour Party where, with Jeremy Corbyn as leader from 2015, arguments over opposition to the possession of nuclear weapons and in favour of the nationalization of certain industries have re-entered the foreground of British political discussion. Powell, as we have seen, eventually announced his commitment to unilateral disarmament in 1983, and he made a powerful public call for denationalization as early as 1968. Longer-term trends are also important.

Among Conservatives in the David Cameron-led Conservative–Liberal coalition government of 2010–15, the 'national interest'—on which Powell reflected at length from the early 1940s—played an important part in framing, and justifying, foreign policy. Yet, unlike Powell's narrow definition of the term, the coalition government's conception of the national interest was a broader one, linking Britain's interests to those of the international organizations of which the UK is part (the UN and NATO) and underpinning the Conservative case for humanitarian intervention. With Foreign Secretary William Hague talking of the 'enlightened national interest', this was the outlook that underpinned intervention in Libya in 2011.[1] Yet, two years later, as the House of Commons voted against a government motion for military action against Syrian President Bashar al-Assad's government to deter the use of chemical weapons, a more tightly defined national interest was reasserted. With thirty Conservative MPs voting against the government, one of them, Crispin Blunt, warned against the view that a 'country of our size can seek to be involved in every conceivable conflict that's going on'.[2] In economic affairs, following New Labour's embrace of the market,

the financial crisis of 2007–8 gave new life to critiques of it, now linked to
arguments against globalization. Yet it is perhaps fair to say that faith in the
market—which Powell did so much to encourage—has been shaken rather
than destroyed, with debates focusing on the best type of regulatory framework to adopt. The 2010 Conservative manifesto, for example, spoke of the
party's desire to 'bring law and order to our financial markets'.[3] Meanwhile,
two of Powell's great causes—opposition to immigration and to the
European Union (EU)—have been fused. This happened after the EU
enlargement of 2004 brought in the former Eastern bloc countries—the
Czech Republic, Estonia, Hungary, Latvia, Lithuania, Poland, Slovakia, and
Slovenia. With the government deciding not to restrict immigration from
these states in their first five years of membership, by 2013 EU citizens were
the single largest group of immigrants into the UK.[4] This was the context
in which the slogan of the Leave campaign in the 2016 referendum—to
'Take Back Control'—usually, in effect, referred to control of the UK's
borders.[5] The debate over devolution—in which Powell participated as the
MP for South Down—endures. The fragility of the Northern Ireland
Assembly, which is currently suspended after a breakdown of relations
between the two largest parties in the power-sharing government, the
Democratic Unionist Party (DUP) and Sinn Féin, leaves open the question
of the long-term future there. More widely, the issue Powell raised about
devolution in Scotland and Wales—where it leads—is one that is still live,
not least with the fiercely contested Scottish independence referendum in
2014, demanded by the Scottish National Party (SNP), which had made
significant gains in the 2011 Scottish parliamentary election.

Yet, strikingly, alongside the resilience of the debates, Powell himself is
marginalized and his public resonance revolves largely around immigration.
The only notable politicians who have explicitly identified with him are
Nick Griffin from the British National Party (BNP), most prominently in
2008, and UKIP's Nigel Farage who, in 2014, stated that he agreed with
the 'basic principle' of Powell's stance on immigration.[6] In early 2018 a
proposal (that was later abandoned) for the Civic and Historical Society of
Wolverhampton to put a blue plaque on Powell's former constituency home
generated opposition, including from the Bishop of Wolverhampton, Clive
Gregory, who argued that it would be 'widely interpreted as honouring
Enoch Powell's racist views'.[7] In the week before the fifty-year anniversary
of the 'Rivers of Blood' speech in April 2018, BBC Radio 4 broadcast a
documentary featuring a reading of the entire speech, performed by the

actor Ian McDiarmid, who had played Powell in a recent stage play, *What Shadows*, igniting controversy at the time by stating his view that Powell was 'no racist'.[8] With the programme advertised in advance, arguments erupted over whether it was right for the BBC to air it—with the Labour peer Lord Adonis writing to the communications regulator Ofcom to demand that the 'incendiary and racist' speech be dropped from the schedule—but there was near universal condemnation of Powell's speech itself.[9] Dissenting voices were few and far between but not, we should note, absent altogether.[10] Part of this sudden turn of the spotlight onto Powell is, of course, connected to the media interest in anniversaries—for which in-depth pieces can be prepared in advance. But it is also more widely representative of the fact that immigration, and the April 1968 speech in particular, is where Powell's impact was always greatest.

Nevertheless, there is a developing public sense that Powell has a significance beyond race and immigration—and it is against this backdrop that this book hopes to find a wide audience. In the build-up to the 2016 EU referendum, there were a few attempts to emphasize the importance of Powell to the longer-term debate.[11] In the aftermath of the 'Leave' result, this view has proliferated, and is linked to a desire to try to understand Powell as a populist politician.[12] An article in the *Financial Times* at the end of 2017 was probably exaggerating when it made the case that 'Powell is the politician who dominates our age as no other does', but it had a point, in one sense, when it went on to declare that: 'The age of Brexit is the age of Powell.'[13]

Assessing Powell

Powell's interpretation of international relations, underpinned by his call for Britain to view itself as a maritime power with an interest in the stability of the European continent, offered a potential way of adjusting to post-imperial realities. It was also—during the Cold War—a call for the United Kingdom to present itself in contrast to the ideological rhetoric adopted by both the United States and the Soviet Union (even if Powell thought that in practice they, like all states, pursued their own interests and operated within a balance of power). Yet Powell's analysis could appear cold, especially, for example, when justifying his preference for non-intervention in Rhodesia in the 1960s and the former Yugoslavia in the 1990s. Even so, his scepticism about the role of international organizations, especially the United Nations, was not that far out of line with wider public feeling.[14] Powell was also notable for demonstrating that opposition to nuclear weapons did not have to be either the preserve of the Left or tied to pacifist or religious arguments.

Powell was the foremost popularizer of neo-liberal ideas in British politics, working closely with the Institute of Economic Affairs (IEA). With a shrewd judge of strategy, in the mid-1960s Powell urged his party colleagues to present their political message as one of Conservative choice versus Labour control—a presentational twist that later found favour with Thatcher in her first party conference speech as leader in 1975.[15] What was equally striking, however, was Powell's willingness to depart from the IEA line over his commitment to the National Health Service (NHS)—which he considered the state had a responsibility to provide. Powell also held that the NHS was frankly popular with the people. Unlike many in the IEA, such as Arthur Seldon, he was unsurprised that expenditure on health rose in the 1980s under Thatcher.[16] Powell considered that there would be 'persistent pressure in favour of community-based rather than individual-based organisation' in the healthcare sector to which even a 'market-orientated, denationalising government' had to respond.[17]

In terms of predicted numbers on immigration, Powell was, as historian and policy analyst Nicholas Hillman has argued, 'in the right sort of range' with the forecasts he made in April 1968. Powell had argued that by 2000 the immigrant population would be 'in the region of 5–7 million, approximately one-tenth of the whole population'. The 2001 census showed that in England, non-white and mixed ethnic groups comprised 9.1 per cent of the population. For Great Britain as a whole, the figure was 8.1 per cent (4.63 million of 57.1 million).[18] On the other hand, Powell's prediction of widespread racial violence has proved unfounded. So too has his argument—which he only fully made in the 1980s and 1990s—that immigration, concentrated in certain areas, together with 'coloured MPs', would undermine democracy amid Indian-style communalism. Powell's old constituency, Wolverhampton South West, was represented by the Conservative Paul Uppal, of Sikh East African descent, between 2010 and 2015 and has been held since 2017 by Labour's Eleanor Smith, whose parents moved to Britain from the Caribbean in the 1950s. We should also appreciate that, in his desire for a homogeneous white society, Powell's choice of rhetoric was not only clearly highly provocative but also obscured his position. There was widespread confusion, for example, over whether he supported voluntary or compulsory repatriation. In the years immediately after 1968, debates over whether Powell was, or was not, racist and/or opportunist overshadowed much else. His call for a tight definition of UK citizenship, distinct from that of the Commonwealth, slipped from view as he made the wider populist argument that government and party elites were misleading ordinary people over the whole issue—a line he later took over Europe.

After initially supporting the bid to join the European Community, Powell became one of the most prominent voices arguing that membership would undermine parliamentary sovereignty. Yet, at a critical point during the 1975 referendum, this view appeared not to resonate. Political historian Robert Saunders has shown that in recent years opponents of EU membership have helped to augment a myth that sovereignty was not discussed in 1975. This has been an important part of their argument that the British people did not—at that stage—know what was at stake. The reality is that sovereignty was discussed but that it did not find an echo among the concerns of voters.[19] In the aftermath of the campaign Powell reflected on this and came to the conclusion that the presentation of the idea, where he had been so effective on the economy, was flawed. He wrote:

> [T]he word 'Sovereignty' has an old-fashioned, imperialistic sort of sound which for many people is repellent and to most is not conducive to clear thinking. It would probably be more enlightening if words such as 'independent' or 'self-governing' were used instead.[20]

In the 1970s and 1980s, Powell played a significant part in the debate about the future of Northern Ireland at a turbulent—and violent—time in its history. Yet, of course, his proposal for integration never looked likely to be adopted. And, in more recent years, Powell's argument has usually been dismissed (implicitly and explicitly) on the basis that the United Kingdom is not a unitary state. Instead, it has been suggested that it is better understood as a union state in which integration is less than perfect, partly due to its origins in two unions—the Scottish and Irish ones—rather than the simple extension of the sovereignty of the English Parliament.[21] It is, however, necessary to remember that this view only became the 'new orthodoxy' in the late 1990s, and that Powell was operating in a situation in which understandings of the United Kingdom constitution were more heavily contested.[22] At the same time, we should recognize that Powell's involvement in Northern Irish politics further exposed the tension in his thinking that had first been revealed in the debates over the staging of a referendum on European Community membership. Attempting to answer the question of who had the right to break the union, a central debate in twentieth-century Unionism, Powell stumbled between his emphasis on parliamentary sovereignty and the increasing claims of popular sovereignty. Powell was fully aware that his constituency in South Down was very different to Wolverhampton South West. Tom Nairn's quip—from a Scottish, pro-devolution, New Left perspective—that Powell deluded himself that Northern Ireland '*was* a bit of England' is wide of the mark.[23] Yet an examination of his involvement in Unionist politics does reveal the occasional use of the same tactical trait— his use of inflammatory rhetoric—that had generated such controversy in British politics from the late 1960s. In this respect, it is hard to avoid criticism of his decision to invoke the powerful legacy of resistance to home rule in 1912 amid increasing Loyalist unrest at Anglo-Irish negotiations in 1984, even if he swiftly backtracked from it.

Powell and decline

Powell's arguments can be understood as a whole by placing them in the context of a series of (sometimes overlapping) debates over decline. In international relations, Powell held that only a comprehension of the realities of power, as well as a keen sense of geography, could prevent Britain's international eclipse. Nuclear weapons—often considered essential to Britain's seat at the top international table—were, he suggested, unlikely to be used. In the economic sphere, Powell was at the forefront of the attack in the early 1960s on the left-wing cry for further state planning as a means of reversing what he saw as a mistaken diagnosis of British economic decline. Yet Powell could be equally critical of the Right and, in the 1980s, he blasted the Thatcher government for its misplaced attempt to link education policy and the promotion of economic growth. On Europe, Powell took a swipe at the party system as a whole, arguing that it was failing in its most important role of providing choice to the electorate. This was a distinctive approach to the larger debate on decline, but it was also, we should remember, a response to Powell's own detachment from the British party structure by the mid-1970s.

There is a need to treat Powell's engagement with decline cautiously. Above all, it was deployed for political purposes and was not always logically consistent within itself. Time and again, especially on Europe but also on immigration, Powell spoke of the threat to the very existence of the British nation. Yet the end never came—and Powell went on, warning of its demise in different forms. Powell also made specific arguments that he knew did not quite add up. He grudgingly accepted the conditional commitment to Britain and its institutions exhibited by many strands within Ulster Unionism but still liked to argue that, in its commitment to the British nation, Ulster Unionism stood to counteract the prevailing loss of national confidence. We should also recognize that, in recent years, the growing questioning of 'Britishness' in public life, sustained by academic foundations, has challenged the central premise of all Powell's arguments: the existence of the British nation. The emphasis instead has been placed on English, Scottish, Welsh, and Irish national dimensions, as well as on shared political and cultural values.[24]

Yet the British nation remained at the centre of Powell's position, as his response to one particular contribution to the decline debate, Martin Wiener's *English Culture and the Decline of the Industrial Spirit, 1850–1980* (1981), demonstrated.[25] The book by the US academic was soon celebrated in Thatcherite circles amid the call to embrace the free market and to foster a wider entrepreneurial culture, with Keith Joseph apparently giving a copy to every member of the Cabinet.[26] Powell took a different stance. Reviewing the book, he began favourably:

> I was waiting for this book to be written...He [Wiener] proves beyond peradventure that, at any rate since the middle of the nineteenth century, the British have not really put economic achievement at the head or anywhere near the head of their scale of national or social values. Throughout the political spectrum the British have been dubious or downright condemnatory of the consequences of the industrial revolution and the capitalist market system; their ideal Britain has not been the 'workshop of the world'; their values have been aristocratic, professional and above all rural.

But Powell then took issue with the manner in which 'Professor Wiener seems to conclude that, now a mirror has been held up to us in which we can read the causes of our alleged decline, we should "pull our socks up" and bustle about like everybody else'. When forced to choose between his competing commitments to neo-liberalism and to the British nation, Powell chose the nation. His frank view was that: 'Everything, even English values, has its price: the secret is, knowing the price, to pay it proudly and cheerfully.'[27]

Notes

INTRODUCTION

1. J. Enoch Powell, speech at Birmingham, 20 April 1968, Cambridge, Churchill Archives Centre, Enoch Powell papers, POLL 4/1/3 [hereinafter cited as Powell, speech at location, date, POLL reference].
2. Simon Heffer, '(john) Enoch Powell', *Oxford Dictionary of National Biography* (Oxford: Oxford University Press, 2008), http://www.oxforddnb.com.
3. David Frost, Interview with Margaret Thatcher, TV-am, broadcast 1 January 1989, Margaret Thatcher Foundation Website, 107022 [hereinafter MTFW, reference].
4. Iain Macleod, 'Enoch Powell', *The Spectator*, 16 July 1965, Powell papers, POLL 1/4/2 (hereinafter Powell papers simply cited as POLL).
5. T. E. Utley, *Enoch Powell: The Man and his Thinking* (London: Kimber, 1968), 27, 101–2, 138, 173. On Utley, see Julia Stapleton, 'T. E. Utley and the Renewal of Conservatism in Post-war Britain', *Journal of Political Ideologies*, 19/2 (2014), 207–26, 220; and Mark Garnett and Kevin Hickson, *Conservative Thinkers: The Key Contributors to the Political Thought of the Modern Conservative Party* (Manchester: Manchester University Press, 2009), 106–9. In the course of the 1960s the US term 'racism' gradually replaced 'racialism' in common usage: Brian Harrison, *Finding a Role? The United Kingdom, 1970–1990* (Oxford: Oxford University Press, 2010), 202.
6. Paul Foot, *The Rise of Enoch Powell: An Examination of Enoch Powell's Attitude to Race and Immigration* (London: Penguin, 1969), 7–8.
7. Powell, speech on 'Conservatism and Social Problems' at Swinton Conservative College, 28–30 June 1968, POLL 4/1/3.
8. Transcription of 'A Personal View', BBC Radio 3, 21 June (no year, but 1969—identified by the author on BBC Genome), POLL 1/2/1.
9. Centre for Contemporary Cultural Studies, *The Empire Strikes Back: Race and Racism in 1970s Britain* (London: Routledge, 1982), 9, 32; Zig Layton-Henry, *The Politics of Race in Britain* (London: HarperCollins, 1984), 70–80; Paul Gilroy, 'There ain't no Black in the Union Jack': The Cultural Politics of Race and Nation* (London: Hutchinson, 1987), 45–50, 104–9; Paul Rich, *Race and Empire in British Politics* (Cambridge: Cambridge University Press, 1990), 207–8.
10. Anna Marie Smith, *New Right Discourse on Race and Sexuality: Britain 1968–1990* (Cambridge: Cambridge University Press, 1994), 5, 7.

11. Noel O'Sullivan, 'The New Right: The Quest for a Civil Philosophy in Europe and America', in Roger Eatwell and Noel O'Sullivan (eds), *The Nature of the Right: American and European Politics and Political Thought since 1789* (London: Pinter, 1989), ch. 10. For a self-description of the New Right along these lines, see Maurice Cowling, 'The Sources of the New Right: Irony, Geniality and Malice', *Encounter*, November 1989, 3–13.

12. Powell to Samuel Carr (of the publisher Thomas Nelson & Sons Ltd), 28 January 1974, POLL 1/4/37.

13. K. W. Watkins to Powell, 20 February 1974; Powell to Watkins, 21 February 1974; both POLL 1/4/38.

14. A. R. 'Tony' Mills (Managing Editor, Thomas Nelson & Sons Ltd) to Powell, 6 June 1974; T. E. Utley to Powell, 12 July 1974, both POLL 1/4/38.

15. Utley to Powell, 12 July 1974; Michael Harrington to Mills, 11 July 1974; Robert Cross (Managing Director, Thomas Nelson & Sons Ltd) to Powell, 14 August 1974; Powell to Harrington, 26 August 1974; A. R. 'Tony' Mills to Powell, 9 April 1975; Powell to Mills, 11 April 1975; Mills to Harrington, 17 June 1975; all POLL 1/4/38.

16. K. W. Watkins to Powell, 9 May 1975, POLL 1/4/38.

17. Watkins to Michael Legat (Cassell & Co. Ltd), 5 February 1976, POLL 1/4/38.

18. Powell to Legat, 9 February 1976, POLL 1/4/38.

19. Roy Lewis to Powell, 14 February 1976; Legat to Powell, 10 March 1976; both POLL 1/4/38.

20. Powell to Legat, 16 March 1976; Powell to Simon Scott (Chief Editor, Cassell & Co. Ltd), 6 February 1979; Scott to Powell, 19 February 1979; all POLL 1/4/38.

21. Roy Lewis, *Enoch Powell: Principle in Politics* (London: Cassell & Co., 1979), esp. ix, 12–13, 48, 250–3.

22. Patrick Cosgrave, *The Lives of Enoch Powell* (London: Bodley Head, 1989), 476.

23. This episode is examined in Chapter 3.

24. Patrick Cosgrave, '...and Statistics', *The Spectator*, 10 January 1976, 5. See also Patrick Cosgrave, 'Powell: Betrayer or Betrayed?', *Books and Bookmen*, November 1978, POLL 1/4/37.

25. Patrick Cosgrave to Powell, 7 June 1982; Cosgrave to Powell, 21 July 1984; Cosgrave to Powell, 4 December 1984; Powell to Cosgrave, 11 December 1984; all POLL 3/2/4/19.

26. Cosgrave, *Lives*, 254.

27. Powell to D. Johns (Managing Director, Bodley Head), 9 January 1989; Cosgrave to Powell, 12 August 1988; both POLL 3/2/4/19.

28. Cosgrave, *Lives*, 475–6.

29. Robert Shepherd, *Enoch Powell: A Biography* (London: Hutchinson, 1996), esp. 185–6.

30. Tom Nairn, 'Enoch Powell: The New Right', *New Left Review*, I/61 (May–June 1970), 3–27. For a recent articulation of this view, see Julia Stapleton, *Political Intellectuals and Public Identities in Britain since 1850* (Manchester: Manchester University Press, 2001), 179–83.

31. Shepherd, *Powell*, 285, 351, 364–5.
32. Robert Shepherd to Powell, 7 February 1990, POLL 1/1/40.
33. Shepherd to Powell, 21 February 1995; Powell to Shepherd, 23 February 1995; both POLL 3/2/4/16.
34. Simon Heffer to Powell, 1 March 1985, POLL 1/3/32; Simon Heffer, 'The Story behind Enoch's Fight for the Embryo', *Medical News*, 14 March 1985, 9, 11, POLL 6/1/4.
35. Heffer to Powell, 13 August 1990, POLL 1/1/40; Heffer to Powell, 19 April 1989, POLL 3/2/4/14.
36. Simon Heffer, *Like the Roman: The Life of Enoch Powell* (London: Weidenfeld & Nicolson, 1998), xiii.
37. Heffer, *Like the Roman*, 334, 450, 958–9; Michael Kenny, *The Politics of English Nationhood* (Oxford: Oxford University Press, 2014), 192.
38. Bill Schwarz, *The White Man's World: Memories of Empire, Volume 1* (Oxford: Oxford University Press, 2011), esp. 9.
39. Camilla Schofield, *Enoch Powell and the Making of Postcolonial Britain* (Cambridge: Cambridge University Press, 2013).
40. Lord Howard of Riding (ed.), *Enoch at 100: A Re-evaluation of the Life, Politics and Philosophy of Enoch Powell* (London: Biteback, 2012). For the parliamentary focus, Iain Duncan-Smith, ibid., 'Foreword', xvii–xxiii, xxiii.
41. E. H. H. Green, *Ideologies of Conservatism: Conservative Political Ideas in the Twentieth Century* (Oxford: Oxford University Press, 2002), 2. He suggested that the same applied to their reception.
42. Colin Kidd, *Union and Unionisms: Political Thought in Scotland 1500–2000* (Cambridge: Cambridge University Press, 2008); Richard Bourke, *Peace in Ireland: The War of Ideas* (London: Pimlico, 2003); Alvin Jackson, *The Two Unions: Ireland, Scotland, and the Survival of the United Kingdom, 1707–2007* (Oxford: Oxford University Press, 2012). See also the individual case studies in Paul Ward, *Unionism in the United Kingdom, 1918–1974* (Basingstoke: Palgrave Macmillan, 2005).
43. Powell to Samuel Carr (chairman of B.T. Batsford Ltd), 20 June 1975; Powell to Carr, 29 October 1975; both POLL 1/4/37. On the important, but sometimes elusive, emphasis on the nation in Conservative thought, see W. H. Greenleaf, *The British Political Tradition. Volume 2: The Ideological Heritage* (London: Methuen, 1983), 195.
44. Typed copy of Powell to Angus Maude, 20 October 1952, London, London School of Economics and Political Science, Gilbert Longden papers, LONGDEN/4/1. See Arthur Aughey, 'Traditional Toryism', in Kevin Hickson (ed.), *The Political Thought of the Conservative Party since 1945* (Basingstoke: Palgrave Macmillan, 2005), ch. 1.
45. Green, *Ideologies of Conservatism*, 281, 286–7. See also Raymond Williams, *Keywords: A Vocabulary of Culture and Society* (London: Fontana/Croom Helm, 1976), 189–92; and Anthony Quinton, *The Politics of Imperfection* (London: Faber & Faber, 1978), 16.

46. Report of speech made by Enoch Powell to the Young Conservatives at Central Hall, School Street, 27 September 1949, Stafford, Staffordshire Record Office, Political Correspondence and Other Papers of J. Enoch Powell, D3123/223 [hereinafter, Powell Papers (Stafford), reference].

47. Angus Maude and J. Enoch Powell, *Biography of a Nation: A Short History of Britain* (London, 1955), 7.

48. C., 'Story of a Nation', *Express & Star*, 21 July 1955, POLL 1/4/11. Keith Feiling, *What is Conservatism?* (London: Faber, 1930), 8, identified the 'Tory interpretation' of history as a narrative of events revealing a 'continuing spirit', quoted in Green, *Ideologies of Conservatism*, 285.

49. A. J. P. Taylor, 'Without tears', *Manchester Guardian Weekly*, 4 August 1955, POLL 1/4/11.

50. Schofield, *Powell*, 93.

51. Powell, speech at St George's Day Banquet, 22 April 1961, POLL 4/1/1.

52. Robert Colls, *Identity of England* (Oxford: Oxford University Press, 2004), 51–3, 71–4.

53. J. Enoch Powell and Keith Wallis, *The House of Lords in the Middle Ages: A History of the English House of Lords to 1540* (London: Weidenfeld & Nicolson, 1968), ix.

54. Powell, speech at Manchester, 6 November 1965, POLL 4/1/2.

55. Powell, speech on 'Conservatism and Social Problems' at Swinton Conservative College, 28–30 June 1968, POLL 4/1/3.

56. Robert Eccleshall, 'The Doing of Conservatism', *Journal of Political Ideologies*, 5/3 (2000), 275–87; Peter Dorey, *British Conservatism: The Politics and Philosophy of Inequality* (London: I.B. Tauris, 2010). Ben Jackson, *Equality and the British Left: A Study in Progressive Political Thought 1900–64* (Manchester: Manchester University Press, 2007), examines what was meant by a commitment to 'equality' on the British Left.

57. Powell, speech on 'Conservatism and Social Problems' at Swinton Conservative College, 28–30 June 1968, POLL 4/1/3.

58. The debate over the 'post-war consensus' has produced a substantial literature. Paul Addison, *The Road to 1945: British Politics and the Second World War* (London: Jonathan Cape, 1975), is the classic account of its emergence. Ben Pimlott, 'The Myth of Consensus' in Lesley M. Smith (ed.), *The Making of Modern Britain: Echoes of Greatness* (Basingstoke: Palgrave Macmillan, 1988), 129–42, is the best-known critique of its existence.

59. Daniel Stedman Jones, *Masters of the Universe: Hayek, Friedman, and the Birth of Neoliberal Politics* (Princeton, New Jersey: Princeton University Press, 2012), 2, defines neo-liberalism as 'the free market ideology based on individual liberty and limited government that connected human freedom to the actions of the rational, self-interested actor in the competitive workplace'.

60. On the conflation, Bernard Crick, 'The English and the British', in Bernard Crick (ed.), *National Identities: The Constitution of the United Kingdom* (Oxford: Blackwell, 1991), 90–104.

61. Powell, speech at the Conservative Party Conference, 1965, POLL 4/1/1.

62. Powell, speech at Prestatyn, 27 September 1968, POLL 4/1/3.
63. Powell contended that 'Ulster is sufficiently appropriated to the six counties comprised in Northern Ireland to be a usable term': Letter from Powell, 4 January 1994, POLL 9/1/7.
64. Powell, speech at Salop, 27 August 1969, POLL 4/1/5.
65. Powell, speech at Derry/Londonderry, 15 January 1971, POLL 4/1/7.
66. Powell, speech at Mountpottinger, Belfast, 2 June 1972, POLL 4/1/8.
67. 'Westminster Rejects "Nonsense" of 1973 Act,' *The Irish Times*, 5 September 1974. Richard Bourke, 'Languages of Conflict and the Northern Ireland Troubles,' *Journal of Modern History*, 83/3 (2011), 544–78, 571–6.
68. Powell, speech at Banbridge, 25 September 1974, POLL 4/1/10.
69. Bourke, *Peace in Ireland*, 241–2, 266.
70. Philip Lynch, *The Politics of Nationhood: Sovereignty, Britishness and Conservative Politics* (Basingstoke: Palgrave Macmillan, 1999), esp. introduction, chs 1 and 2.
71. Powell, speech at Renfrew, 12 March 1976, POLL 4/1/11.
72. Powell, 'A Conservative Estimate', review of Maurice Cowling (ed.), *Conservative Essays* (London: Cassell, 1978), *Cambridge Review*, 17 November 1978, 52–4, 53, POLL 6/1/3. Noel O'Sullivan, *Conservatism* (London: Dent, 1976), 12, describes Conservatism as a 'philosophy of imperfection'.
73. Powell, 'The Church' (1951), 6pp., 1, POLL 3/2/1/1. One Nation minutes, 28 June 1951, Colchester, Albert Sloman Library, Essex University, Cuthbert Alport papers, box 37.
74. J. Enoch Powell, *No Easy Answers* (London: Sheldon, 1973), 4; Heffer, *Like the Roman*, 134–8; J. Enoch Powell, *The Evolution of the Gospel: A New Translation with Commentary and Introductory Essay* (New Haven: Yale University Press, 1994).
75. 'Frankly Speaking – The Rt. Hon. Enoch Powell, MBE, MP Questioned by John Bowen and A. P. Ryan', transmission on BBC Home Service, 28 February 1964, recorded 4 February 1964, POLL 4/1/27.
76. Maurice Cowling, *Religion and Public Doctrine in Modern England. Volume One* (Cambridge: Cambridge University Press, 1980), 431–40, argues that after April 1968, amid clerical criticism of his stance on immigration, Powell launched a 'full-scale assault on a whole phase of Anglican teaching about politics', asserting 'the autonomous nature of political judgment and the otherworldly nature of Christ and God'. For Powell's televised dispute with Trevor Huddleston, then Bishop of Stepney, over immigration in 1969, see Schofield, *Powell*, 257–9.
77. Letter from Powell, 21 December 1987, POLL 9/1/4.
78. 'Powell Boobs: Rules UUUC Chiefs out of Convention', *Belfast Telegraph*, 7 October 1974.
79. Powell to John Biggs-Davison, 10 March 1983, POLL 1/1/32.
80. Heffer, *Like the Roman*, 812.
81. Powell, speech at Newcastle, County Down, 8 December 1978, POLL 4/1/12.
82. 'DUP back Powell on Charles', *Belfast Telegraph*, 9 December 1978, Dublin, National Archives of Ireland, Department of Foreign Affairs, 2014/32/2031.

83. Powell, speech at East Grinstead, 5 December 1980, POLL 4/1/14.
84. http://enochpowell.info/. Powell had been invited to do so by the County Archivist in February, just as he left Wolverhampton: F. B. Stitt (Staffordshire County Archivist) to Powell, 8 February 1974; Powell to Stitt, 12 February 1974; both POLL 1/3/19. Material was deposited in 1976, 1977, 1979, 1980, and 1985. Powell also deposited constituency material at the Public Record Office of Northern Ireland (PRONI) in 1984, which is still closed to researchers. See POLL 1/3/19.
85. Philip Williamson, *Stanley Baldwin* (Cambridge: Cambridge University Press, 1999), 14–15, emphasis in original.
86. Lord Hailsham diary, 13 March 1978, MTFW, 111191; Heffer, *Like the Roman*, 558.
87. The major collections are: John Wood (ed.), *A Nation Not Afraid* (London: Hodder & Stoughton, 1965); John Wood (ed.), *Freedom and Reality* (London: Batsford, 1969); John Wood (ed.), *Still to Decide* (London: Elliot Right Way, 1972); Richard Ritchie (ed.), *A Nation or No Nation? Six Years in British Politics* (London: Batsford, 1978); Richard Ritchie (ed.), *Enoch Powell on 1992* (London: Anaya, 1989); Rex Collings (ed.), *Reflections of a Statesman: The Selected Writings and Speeches of Enoch Powell* (London: Bellew: 1991).
88. Powell, speech at the Dorchester Hotel, London, 29 April 1969, POLL 4/1/5.
89. Powell, speech at the Dorchester Hotel, London, 29 April 1969, POLL 4/1/5.
90. Ralph Harris to Powell, 28 October 1963, POLL 3/1/28.
91. Shepherd, *Powell*, 270, suggested that he did this from late January 1964. Powell was certainly doing so by the summer: Powell to George Hutchinson (Chief Public Relations Officer, Conservative Central Office), 27 July 1964, POLL 1/1/49.
92. Powell, speech at Trinity College Dublin, 13 November 1964, POLL 4/1/1.
93. Ralph Harris to Powell, 12 October 1965, POLL 1/1/49.
94. T. E. Utley, 'Powell the Political John the Baptist', *Daily Telegraph*, 20 April 1969, POLL 1/4/6. Williamson wrote about speeches that: 'Their function is not to satisfy academic tests or theory, but to attract and hold the support of diverse audiences possessing a range of conventional beliefs and present interests, as well as hopes for the future': Williamson, *Baldwin*, 15.
95. David Butler and Michael Pinto-Duschinsky, *The British General Election of 1970* (London: Macmillan, 1971), 231, 341, was dubious about the extent of Powell's influence, considering it 'hard to assess' beyond his success in bolstering the Conservative vote in Wolverhampton South West and neighbouring constituencies. David Butler and Dennis Kavanagh, *The British General Election of February 1974* (London: Macmillan, 1974), 105, 331, suggests that Powell had a very limited impact on persuading Conservatives to vote Labour but more success in convincing Labour supporters actually to vote Labour. In Wolverhampton South West, there was a 16 per cent swing to Labour, a trend that was replicated (on a less dramatic scale) across the Black Country. Douglas Schoen, *Enoch Powell and the Powellites* (London: Macmillan, 1977), 139, considered that it was 'certainly possible to argue that Powell may indeed have put Edward Heath into Downing

Street in 1970 and evicted him in 1974'. Iain McLean, *Rational Choice and British Politics:An Analysis of Rhetoric and Manipulation from Peel to Blair* (Oxford: Oxford University Press, 2001), 142, stated that 'Powell was responsible for the victory of the Conservatives in 1970 and of Labour in February 1974'.

96. Schoen, *Powell and the Powellites*, 269, 270, 273–7.
97. Andrew Gamble, *Britain in Decline* (London: Macmillan, 1981), 32; Richard English and Michael Kenny, 'Public Intellectuals and the Question of British Decline', *British Journal of Politics and International Relations*, 3/3 (2001), 259–83, 278 n. 9; Richard Vinen, *Thatcher's Britain:The Politics and Social Upheaval of the 1980s* (London: Simon & Schuster, 2009), 54.
98. Gilroy, *Ain't No Black*, 45–6. Hall spoke about Powell in this way as early as 1978: Stuart Hall, 'Racism and Reaction', in *Five Views of Multi-Racial Britain* (London: Commission for Racial Equality, 1978), 23–35, 30. See also Chris Waters, '"Dark Strangers" in our Midst: Discourses of Race and Nation in Britain 1947-1963', *Journal of British Studies*, 36/2 (1997), 207–38.
99. Amy Whipple, 'Revisiting the "Rivers of Blood" Controversy: Letters to Enoch Powell', *Journal of British* Studies, 48/3 (2009), 717–35, 720.
100. Nicholas Crafts, 'The Golden Age of Economic Growth in Western Europe, 1950–1973', *Economic History Review*, 48/3 (1995), 429–47.
101. Jim Tomlinson, 'Inventing "Decline": The Falling Behind of the British Economy in the Postwar Years', *Economic History Review*, 49/4 (1996), 731–57.
102. Stuart Ward (ed.), *British Culture and the End of Empire* (Manchester: Manchester University Press, 2001), 8–11; Jim Tomlinson, 'The Decline of the Empire and the Economic "Decline" of Britain', *Twentieth Century British History*, 14/3 (2003), 201–22, 203–4, 208.
103. David Cannadine, 'Apocalypse When? British Politicians and British "Decline" in the Twentieth Century', in Peter Clarke and Clive Trebilcock (eds), *Understanding Decline: Perceptions and Realities of British Economic Performance* (Cambridge: Cambridge University Press, 1997), ch. 12, esp. 275–81; Jim Tomlinson, 'Thrice Denied: "Declinism" as a Recurrent Theme in British History in the Long Twentieth Century', *Twentieth Century British History*, 20/2 (2009), 227–51, 235; Robert Saunders, 'Crisis? What Crisis? Thatcherism and the Seventies', in Ben Jackson and Robert Saunders (eds), *Making Thatcher's Britain* (Cambridge: Cambridge University Press, 2012), 25–42, at 25, 30.
104. The latter has been categorized as 'endism' in recent political science literature: Arthur Aughey, 'From Declinism to Endism: exploring the ideology of British break-up', *Journal of Political Ideologies*, 15/1 (2010), 11–30. Ian Hall, *Dilemmas of Decline: British Intellectuals and World Politics, 1945–1975* (Berkeley, CA: University of California Press, 2012).
105. Powell, speech at the Savoy Hotel, London, 27 January 1966, POLL 4/1/2.
106. Powell, speech at Bromsgrove, 6 July 1963, POLL 4/1/1.
107. Powell, speech at Trinity College Dublin, 13 November 1964, POLL 4/1/1.
108. Powell, speech at San Diego, California, 11 March 1974, POLL 4/1/10.
109. Powell, speech at Manchester, 6 November 1965, POLL 4/1/2.

110. Powell, 'Foreword', in Wood (ed.), *Nation not Afraid*, vii-viii, vii.
111. Powell, speech at Trinity College Dublin, 13 November 1964; Powell, speech at Bromsgrove, Worcestershire, 6 July 1963; both POLL 4/1/1.
112. Powell, speech at Birmingham, 20 April 1968, Powell papers, POLL 4/1/3.
113. Powell, speech at Armagh, 29 August 1974; Powell, speech at Banbridge, 25 September 1974; both POLL 4/1/10.

CHAPTER I

1. William C. Wohlforth, 'Realism', in Christian Reus-Smit and Duncan Snidel (eds), *The Oxford Handbook of International Relations* (Oxford: Oxford University Press, 2008), ch. 7.
2. Powell, 'If Korea goes Red', *Newcastle Journal*, 2 July (no year, but 1949), POLL 6/1/1.
3. Winston Churchill, speech at Westminster College, Fulton, Missouri, 5 March 1946, website of the International Churchill Society, https://winstonchurchill.org/resources/speeches/1946-1963-elder-statesman/the-sinews-of-peace/.
4. 'Victory', 11 October 1942, POLL 1/6/2.
5. '1943', 25 December 1942, POLL 1/6/2. The memorandum is unsigned, but Powell was the author. In 1966 he told Basil Liddell Hart that 'I looked up my own appreciation of Christmas 1942 and confirmed that I also was arguing for peace with a Germany which had given up its European conquests': Powell to Liddell Hart, 17 October 1966, London, Liddell Hart Centre for Military Archives, King's College, London, Sir Basil Liddell Hart papers, LH 1/580.
6. Memorandum, Powell, New Dehli, 16 December 1944, POLL 3/1/1.
7. John Ramsden, *The Making of Conservative Party Policy: The Conservative Research Department since 1929* (London: Longman, 1980), 121–2. The Parliamentary Secretariat merged with the Conservative Research Department in October 1948: Shepherd, *Powell*, 68.
8. Powell, 'Memorandum on Indian Policy', 16 May 1946, POLL 3/1/4.
9. Powell to R. A. Butler, 3 December 1946, POLL 3/1/4; Powell, Memorandum, 3 December 1946, POLL 3/1/4; Powell, 'India: Proposal for a Working Committee', 28 February 1947, POLL 3/1/5; 'India – 3rd June 1947', POLL 3/1/5.
10. Philip Murphy, *Party Politics and Decolonization: The Conservative Party and British Colonial Policy in Tropical Africa, 1951–1964* (Oxford: Clarendon Press, 1995), 30, 57.
11. Precis of Powell speech at St Philip's Parish Hall, Penn Fields, 16 February 1950, Powell papers (Stafford), D3123/223; Shepherd, *Powell*, 81.
12. Powell, 'Britain's Position in the World', enclosed with Powell to Charles Fenby (editor, *Birmingham Gazette*), 15 October 1951, Powell papers (Stafford), D3123/223; Schofield, *Powell*, 93.
13. Duncan Bell, *The Idea of Greater Britain: Empire and the Future of World Order, 1860–1900* (Princeton, NJ: Princeton University Press, 2007), 24–5, ch. 4.

14. Powell, 'Britain's Position in the World', enclosed with Powell to Charles Fenby (editor, *Birmingham Gazette*), 15 October 1951, Powell papers (Stafford), D3123/223.
15. Powell, 'The Revival of Britain' (no date, but 1951), 3 pp., POLL 3/2/1/1.
16. Powell, draft of 'Problems of Empire' for *Birmingham Post*, November 1952, POLL 6/1/1.
17. *Hansard*, HC, vol. 512, cols 240–8, 247 (3 March 1953).
18. *Hansard*, HC, vol. 520, cols 342–9, 348 (5 November 1953). John Ramsden, *The Age of Churchill and Eden, 1940–1957* (London: Longman, 1995), 264, on hostility to the United States in the group.
19. Powell, speech at the AGM of the Penn Ward Branch, South West Wolverhampton Conservative Association, Rose and Crown Inn, Penn Road, Wolverhampton, 6 November 1953, POLL 3/1/11; also in Powell papers (Stafford), D3123/223. See also Powell at the AGM of the South West Wolverhampton Conservative Association in the Churchill Hall, School Street, Wolverhampton, 20 November [no year, but 1953], Powell papers (Stafford), D3123/223.
20. Powell, speech at the AGM of the St Mark's and Merridale Ward Branch, South West Wolverhampton Conservative and Unionist Association, Central Hall, School Street, 4 December 1953, Powell papers (Stafford), D3123/223; Schofield, *Powell*, 105.
21. Schofield, *Powell*, 107. For the wider context on the British position on the Suez Canal, see Sean Greenwood, *Britain and the Cold War, 1945–1991* (Basingstoke: Macmillan, 2000), 112, 113, 115, 137.
22. Powell, 'The Empire of England', in *Tradition and Change. Nine Oxford Lectures* (London: Conservative Political Centre, 1954), 41–53, at 49, 50, 51, 53; Oxford, Bodleian Library, Conservative Party Archive, PUB 165/18. Schofield, *Powell*, 101.
23. Sue Onslow, *Backbench Debate within the Conservative Party and its Influence on British Foreign Policy, 1948–1957* (Basingstoke: Macmillan, 1997), 297.
24. Powell, speech at the AGM of the Penn Ward Branch of the Wolverhampton South West Conservative Association at the Rose and Crown Inn, Penn Road, Wolverhampton, 12 November 1954, Powell papers (Stafford), D3123/223; Schofield, *Powell*, 107.
25. Ruth Winstone (ed.), *Tony Benn: Years of Hope, Diaries, Papers and Letters, 1940–1962* (London: Cornerstone, 1994), 268 (entry for 8 March 1958).
26. Powell to Iain Macleod, 13 February 1957, POLL 3/2/1/2. See also Powell, 'An End to Charter Writing', *Crossbow*, spring 1958, POLL 6/1/1.
27. Powell, 'Britain's Position in the World', enclosed with Powell to Charles Fenby (editor, *Birmingham Gazette*), 15 October 1951, Powell papers (Stafford), D3123/223.
28. Onslow, *Backbench Debate*, 56.
29. Policy Study Group minutes, 15 February 1957, POLL 3/2/1/2.
30. Hedley Bull, 'What is the Commonwealth?', *World Politics*, 2/4 (1959), 582, cited in Hall, *Dilemmas of Decline*, 140.

31. *Hansard*, HC, vol. 610, col. 231 (27 July 1959).Violet Bonham Carter to Powell, 31 July 1959, POLL 3/1/18. Barbara Castle to Powell, 'Tuesday 2am', received 29 July 1959, POLL 3/1/18. Mark Bonham Carter to Powell, 28 July 1959, POLL 1/3/18. For discussion, see Schofield, *Powell*, 121–38.
32. Powell, speech at Bromsgrove,Worcestershire, 6 July 1963, POLL 4/1/1.
33. Powell at Bromley, 24 October 1963, POLL 4/1/1.
34. John Baylis, *Ambiguity and Deterrence: British Nuclear Strategy, 1945–1964* (Oxford: Clarendon Press, 1995), 1–2.
35. David French, *The British Way in Warfare 1688–2000* (London: Unwin Hyman, 1990), 219.
36. See the correspondence in POLL 1/6/8. Powell told Liddell Hart in 1966 that 'Years back, I wrote a large part of Kingston-McCloughry's *War in Three Dimensions*': Powell to Liddell Hart, 7 June 1966, Liddell Hart papers, LH 1/580.
37. Powell to Edgar Kingston-McCloughry, 29 December 1948, POLL 1/6/8.
38. Kingston-McCloughry to Powell, 8 August 1949, POLL 1/6/8.
39. Matthew Grant, *After the Bomb: Civil Defence and Nuclear War in Britain, 1945–68* (Basingstoke: Palgrave Macmillan, 2009), 6–7.
40. Powell, 'The Atom Bomb may not be used', *Newcastle Journal*, 30 July 1949, POLL 6/1/1.
41. Lawrence Freedman, *Britain and Nuclear Weapons* (London: Macmillan for the Royal Institute of International Affairs, 1980), 3–4.
42. BBC Light Programme', 8 October 1955, POLL 4/1/27.
43. International Commentary, 13 March 1960, POLL 4/1/27.
44. Freedman, *Nuclear Weapons*, 8, 10.
45. International Commentary, 13 March 1960, POLL 4/1/27.
46. On government policy towards the TA in the 1960s, David French, *Army, Empire, and Cold War: The British Army and Military Policy, 1945–71* (Oxford: Oxford University Press), 169–70, 291–3.
47. Powell, speech at Bromsgrove, 6 July 1963, POLL 4/1/1.
48. John W. Young, 'International Factors and the 1964 General Election', *Contemporary British History*, 21/3 (2007), 351–71, at 359, shows that during the 1964 general election it was the deliberate strategy of the Conservative leader Sir Alec Douglas-Home to contrast Conservative support for nuclear weapons with Labour's divisions.
49. Powell to Quintin Hogg, 23 August 1965, Cambridge, Churchill Archives Centre, Lord Hailsham (Quintin Hogg) papers, HLSM 2/14/19;'BBC Home Service, 10'O clock', 14 October 1965, POLL 4/1/27.
50. R. A. Brearley,W. M. Brown, and C. J. Hutchings, 'A New Reserve Army. The Alternative to Conscription.A Bow Group Memorandum', March 1965, London, London School of Economics and Political Science, George Wigg papers, WIGG/5/1.
51. Powell, speech at the Conservative Party Conference, 19 October 1967, POLL 4/1/3.
52. Brian Holden Reid,'The Legacy of Liddell Hart:The Contrasting Responses of Michael Howard and André Beaufre', *British Journal for Military History*, 1/1 (2014), 66–80, 69.

53. Powell to Basil Liddell Hart, 18 June 1966, Liddell Hart papers. LH 1/580.
54. Powell, 'Sir Solly Speaks', *The Spectator*, 24 July 1966, POLL 6/1/1.
55. Solly Zuckerman to Minister of Defence, 19 February 1960, TNA/DEFE/25/13, cited in Richard Maguire, '"Never a Credible Weapon": Nuclear Cultures in British Government during the Era of the H-bomb', *British Journal for the History of Science*, 45/4 (2012), 519–33, 528.
56. Maguire, 'Never a Credible Weapon', 527, 529.
57. Powell to Liddell Hart, 7 March 1967, Liddell Hart papers, LH 1/580.
58. *Hansard*, HC, vol. 742, cols 1191–202 (6 March 1967).
59. Liddell Hart to Powell, 8 March 1967, Liddell Hart papers, LH 1/580.
60. Denis Healey to Edward Heath, 7 March 1967, Wigg papers, WIGG/3/83.
61. Heath to Healey, 8 March 1967, Wigg papers, WIGG/3/83. Powell later told a correspondent that 'I have always regarded conscription as the least economic or efficient way of providing the land forces Britain needs in peace': letter from Powell, 11 June 1984, POLL 3/2/1/35.
62. Russell Lewis to Powell, 4 January 1967, POLL 1/1/15. Powell later published the article in the journal of the Royal United Services Institute (RUSI). Powell later told Colin Welch, deputy editor of the *Daily Telegraph,* that 'the article started life as a C.P.C pamphlet which was due to have been published in July 1967 but for certain reasons took this form': Powell to Colin Welch, 2 December 1971, POLL 1/1/16.
63. Powell, 'The Defence of Europe', *Royal United Services Institution Journal*, 113/649 (1968), 51–6, 51, 52, POLL 6/1/2.
64. Freedman, *Nuclear Weapons*, 10, 20. For British Army wariness of this US-led change, see French, *Army, Empire, and Cold War*, 212–14.
65. Powell, 'Defence of Europe', 52.
66. Alec Douglas-Home to Powell, 12 June 1967, POLL 1/1/15.
67. Michael Fraser to Powell, 21 July 1967, POLL 1/1/15.
68. Powell to Edward Heath, 29 August 1967, POLL 1/1/15.
69. Leader's Consultative Committee (LCC) minutes, 28 February 1968, POLL 3/2/1/8.
70. Powell, speech replying to the debate on National Defence at the Conservative Central Council, Theatre Royal, London, 15 March 1968, POLL 4/1/3.
71. Powell, lecture on 'Britain's military role in the 1970s' at the Royal United Services Institute, London, 18 September 1968, POLL 4/1/3.
72. 'South European Programme', 1 March 1965, POLL 4/1/27.
73. Shepherd, *Powell*, 301; John W. Young, *The Labour Governments: International Policy. Vol.* 2 (Manchester: Manchester University Press, 2003), 38.
74. Powell, speech at the Conservative Party Conference, 1965, POLL 4/1/1.
75. BBC Home Service, 'Conservative Party Conference', 22.55, 14 October 1965, POLL 4/1/27.
76. LCC minutes, 16 February 1966, Hailsham papers, HLSM 2/42/2/10.
77. LCC minutes, 25 July 1967, POLL 3/2/1/8.
78. Powell, speech at the Mansion House, London, 17 February 1966, POLL 4/1/2.
79. Powell, speech at Falkirk, 26 March 1966, POLL 4/1/2.
80. David Butler and Anthony King, *The British General Election of 1966* (London: Macmillan, 1966), 118.

81. Rhiannon Vickers, 'Harold Wilson, the British Labour Party and the War in Vietnam', *Journal of Cold War Studies*, 10/2 (2008), 41–70, esp. 47, 48, 50, 52, 58. Peter Busch, 'Supporting the War: Britain's Decision to send the Thompson Mission to Vietnam, 1960-1', *Cold War History*, 2/1 (2001), 69–94.

82. Powell, 'The Future of NATO', LCC (68) 78, 27 January 1966, Hailsham papers, HLSM 2/42/2/10.

83. Powell, speech at Falkirk, 26 March 1966, POLL 4/1/2.

84. Powell, speech at Wolverhampton, 17 December 1965, POLL 4/1/2.

85. Powell, speech at Painters' Hall, London, 7 December 1967, POLL 4/1/3. On the Monday Club, Murphy, *Party Politics*, 225; Schwarz, *White Man's World*, 428–34.

86. Powell, speech at Wolverhampton, 6 December 1968, POLL 4/1/3.

87. Powell, speech at Cleethorpes, 20 June 1969, POLL 4/1/5.

88. Powell, speech at Conservative Ladies' meeting in Wolverhampton, 24 September 1954, Powell papers (Stafford), D3123/223.

89. Powell, 'Defence of Europe'.

90. Powell, speech at Wadham College, Oxford, 21 July 1968, POLL 4/1/3.

91. Geraint Hughes, 'British Policy towards Eastern Europe and the Impact of the "Prague Spring", 1964-68', *Cold War History*, 4/2 (2004), 115–39, 118, 125–6.

92. Powell, speech at Cradley Heath, 9 September 1968, POLL 4/1/3.

93. Powell, speech at Conservative Ladies' meeting in Wolverhampton, 24 September 1954, Powell papers (Stafford), D3123/223.

94. Powell, speech at Farnham, 7 March 1969, POLL 4/1/5.

95. Brian White, *Britain, Détente and Changing East-West Relations* (London: Routledge, 1992), ch. 2; Robert D. Schulzinger, 'Détente in the Nixon-Ford Years', in Melvyn P. Leffler and Odd Arne Westad (eds.), *The Cambridge History of the Cold War, Vol. 2* (Cambridge: Cambridge University Press, 2009), 373–94.

96. E. H. H. Green, *Thatcher* (London: Hodder Arnold, 2006), 162.

97. Rhiannon Vickers, *The Labour Party and the World. Volume 2. Labour's foreign policy since 1951* (Manchester: Manchester University Press, 2011), 96–7.

98. Mike Bygrave, 'Penthouse Interviews: Enoch Powell', *Penthouse*, 12/3 (1977), 38–40, POLL 6/1/3.

99. Rosemary Foot, 'The Cold War and Human Rights', in Melvyn P. Leffler and Odd Arne Westad (eds.), *The Cambridge History of the Cold War, Vol. 3* (Cambridge: Cambridge University Press, 2009), 445–65. See also Mark Mazower, 'The Strange Triumph of Human Rights, 1933-50', *Historical Journal*, 47/2 (2004), 379–98.

100. Powell, speech at the dinner of the South West London Monday Club, Bressenden Place, 26 February 1977, POLL 4/1/12.

101. Powell, 'The World may shout as loud as it likes but Mother Russia will not be Moved', *The Times*, 21 June 1977.

102. Powell, speech at Doncaster, 20 January 1979, POLL 4/1/13.

103. James Cooper, 'The Foreign Politics of Opposition: Margaret Thatcher and the Transatlantic Relationship before Power', *Contemporary British History*, 24/1 (2010), 23–42.
104. Powell, speech at Lisburn, 14 January 1980, POLL 4/1/14.
105. On the wider debate here, Paul Corthorn, 'The Cold War and British Debates over the Boycott of the 1980 Moscow Olympics', *Cold War History*, 13/1 (2013) 43–66.
106. *Hansard*, HC, vol. 977, cols 975–7 (28 January 1980).
107. 10 Downing Street, Statement, 1100 hours, Thursday 6 May (no year, but 1982), POLL 3/2/1/95.
108. Powell, speech at Stoke-on-Trent, 7 May 1982, POLL 4/1/15.
109. Powell, 'UN: Time to Explode a Myth', *Daily Telegraph*, 19 October 1970, POLL 6/1/2.
110. Powell, speech at Birmingham, 21 May 1982, POLL 4/1/15.
111. Powell, speech at York, 17 January 1969, POLL 4/1/5. Powell published his speech from January 1969 in the *Daily Telegraph* on 20 April 1982, POLL 6/1/4.
112. Powell, speech at Stevenage, 9 September 1982, POLL 4/1/15.
113. Powell, speech at Newham, London, 12 November 1982, POLL 4/1/15.
114. Powell, speech at Epsom, 6 October 1982, POLL 4/1/15. Parts of the speech, including the last paragraph, reprinted as Powell, 'Questioning America's Vision of the World', *The Guardian*, 18 October 1982, POLL 6/1/4; and as Powell, 'Britain and the Alliance', *Salisbury Review*, Spring 1983, 28–9, POLL 6/1/4.
115. Mark Phythian, 'CND's Cold War', *Contemporary British History*, 15/3 (2001), 133–56, 149–52.
116. Powell, speech at Bristol, 29 October 1982, POLL 4/1/15. Powell privately accepted that 'there must be some slight residual possibility that a pre-emptive nuclear strike could be totally successful but this seems to me to be highly unrealistic as a basis for policy': letter from Powell, 13 December 1982, POLL 3/2/1/42.
117. Jodi Burkett, 'Re-defining British Morality: "Britishness" and the Campaign for Nuclear Disarmament, 1958–68', *Twentieth Century British History*, 21/2 (2010), 184–205.
118. Michael Hughes, *Conscience and Conflict: Methodism, Peace and War in the Twentieth Century* (Peterborough: Epworth, 2008), 145–6.
119. Rodney Barker, 'Powell the Unilateralist', *Marxism Today*, January 1983, 2–3, 3.
120. Powell, speech at Downpatrick, 31 May 1983, POLL 4/1/6. Charles Moore, *Margaret Thatcher: The Authorized Biography, Volume One: Not for Turning* (London: Allen Lane, 2013), 54.
121. *Hansard*, HC, vol. 44, cols 494–8, 496–7 (28 June 1983).
122. Powell, 'Nuclear Bluff Finally Called', *The Times*, 30 July 1987, POLL 6/1/5.
123. Powell, 'The Decline of America', *The Guardian*, 7 December 1988, POLL 6/1/6. This was Powell, speech at Chester, 6 December 1988, POLL 4/1/20.
124. Powell, 'Return to an Older Pattern of Europe', *The Guardian*, 7 December 1987, POLL 6/1/5. This was Powell, speech at Bloomsbury, 2 December 1987,

POLL 4/1/19. For the same argument, see Powell, 'We are Watching the World Change Shape', *Evening Standard*, 2 December 1987, POLL 6/1/5.

125. Powell, speech at Ballymoney, 6 January 1988, POLL 4/1/20.

126. White House Record of Conversation, Margaret Thatcher and Ronald Reagan, 13 October 1986, MTFW, 143809, cited in James Cooper, 'From Reykjavik to Fulton: Reagan, Thatcher and the Ending of the Cold War', *Journal of Transatlantic Studies*, 14/4 (2016), 383–400, 391. For wider context on the debates, see 388–91.

127. Powell, 'Sovereignty We Won't Surrender', *The Guardian*, 17 April 1989, POLL 6/1/7.

128. Powell to Douglas Hurd, 2 May 1989, POLL 3/2/5/7.

129. Powell, 'The Russian People's Search for Justice', *The Independent*, 27 June 1989, POLL 3/2/5/6; also in POLL 6/1/7. *Embracing the Bear* was shown on BBC1 on 3 July 1989.

130. Powell, 'Allied in a Common Interest', *Daily Telegraph*, 24 July 1989, POLL 6/1/7.

131. Powell, speech at Victoria, London, 15 November 1989, POLL 4/2/21.

132. Powell to editor, *Daily Telegraph*, 11 August 1990; Powell, 'Leave the Gulf to Settle its Own Fate', *Sunday Correspondent*, 21 October 1990; both POLL 6/1/8.

133. Powell, speech at Newham, London, 12 November 1982, POLL 4/1/15.

134. Powell, 'A Crusade Built on Sand', *Daily Telegraph*, 19 January 1991, POLL 6/1/9.

135. Powell, speech at Torquay, 8 March 1991, POLL 4/1/23.

136. Powell, speech at Birmingham, 26 September 1991, POLL 4/1/23.

137. Powell, speech at Ross-on-Wye, 26 March 1993, POLL 4/1/25.

138. Matt Beech and Timothy J. Oliver, 'Humanitarian Intervention and Foreign Policy in the Conservative-led Coalition', *Parliamentary Affairs*, 67/1 (2014), 102–18, 106–7.

139. Powell, speech at Daventry, 12 June 1992, POLL 4/1/24.

140. Powell, 'Nation Undermined by Supreme Act of Folly', *The Times*, 7 February 1994, POLL 6/1/12.

CHAPTER 2

1. Powell, speech at Ford Castle, Northumberland, 6 May 1988, POLL 4/1/20.

2. Adrian Williamson, *Conservative Economic Policymaking and the Birth of Thatcherism, 1964–1979* (Basingstoke: Palgrave Macmillan, 2015).

3. Stedman Jones, *Masters of the Universe*, 2.

4. Ben Jackson, 'Currents of Neo-Liberalism: British Political Ideologies and the New Right, c. 1955-1979', *English Historical Review*, 131/551 (2016), 823–50, 826, which shows how neo-liberalism has 'blended...into the ideologies of British Liberalism, Conservatism and even Labour Socialism'.

5. Milton Friedman to William Buckley, 2 December 1970, Milton Friedman papers, MF 22/13, cited in Ben Jackson, 'The Think-Tank Archipelago: Thatcherism and Neo-Liberalism', in Jackson and Saunders (eds), *Making Thatcher's Britain*, 43–61, 58.

6. On Labour planning, to which the party was committed after 1931, Richard Toye, *The Labour Party and the Planned Economy, 1931–1951* (Woodbridge: Boydell Press, 2003), esp. chs 8 and 9.

7. Report of Powell speech at Castleford, 3 February 1947, POLL 3/1/1.

8. Report of Powell speech at Featherstone, 4 February 1947, POLL 3/1/1.

9. For wider discussion, see Stuart Aveyard, Paul Corthorn, and Sean O'Connell, *The Politics of Consumer Credit in the UK, 1938–1992* (Oxford: Oxford University Press, 2018), ch. 2.

10. Report of Powell speech at Altofts Lee Brigg, 8 February 1947, POLL 3/1/1.

11. Report of Powell speech at Purston Jaglin, 6 February 1947, POLL 3/1/1.

12. Report of Powell speech at South Featherstone, 7 February 1947, POLL 3/1/1.

13. Richard Toye, 'Winston Churchill's "Crazy Broadcast": Party, Nation, and the 1945 Gestapo Speech', *Journal of British Studies*, 49/3 (2010), 655–80, at 655, 662–5. James Freeman, 'Reconsidering "Set the People Free": Neoliberalism and Freedom Rhetoric in Churchill's Conservative Party', *Twentieth Century British History*, 29/4 (2018), 522–46, argues for the distinctly Conservative interwar, and not Hayekian neo-liberal, origins of the rhetoric of freedom.

14. Jackson, 'Currents of Neo-Liberalism', 824–5.

15. Ben Jackson, 'At the Origins of Neo-Liberalism: The Free Economy and the Strong State, 1930–1947', *Historical Journal*, 53/1 (2010), 129–51, 131–2, 147.

16. Report of Powell speech at Altofts Lee Brigg, 8 February 1947, POLL 3/1/1; *Yorkshire Post*, 30 January 1947, POLL 3/1/2.

17. Report of Powell speech at Castleford, 3 February 1947, POLL 3/1/1.

18. Report of Powell speech at Whitwood, 5 February 1947, POLL 3/1/1.

19. Powell, 'Influences That Shape Party Programmes', *Birmingham Post*, 26 October 1950, POLL 6/1/1. For Powell's participation in its production, see Powell to Angus Maude, 10 August 1950, Cambridge, Churchill Archives Centre, Angus Maude papers, MAUD 2/1/1.

20. Robert Walsha, 'The One Nation Group: A Tory Approach to Backbench Politics and Organization', *Twentieth Century British History*, 11/2 (2000), 183–214, 194.

21. Iain Macleod and J. Enoch Powell, *The Social Services: Needs and Means* (London: Conservative Political Centre, 1952). Rodney Lowe, *The Welfare State in Britain since 1945* (London: Macmillan, 1993), 81–2. Green, *Ideologies*, 222. For press reception, see POLL 1/4/30.

22. One Nation minutes, 26 January 1956, Alport papers, box 37.

23. Powell to Iain Macleod, 13 February 1957, POLL 3/2/1/2.

24. Policy Study Group minutes, 15 February 1957, POLL 3/2/1/2.

25. Jackson, 'At the Origins', 146.

26. Powell, 'The National Insurance Scheme', 21 February 1957, Conservative Party Archive, Conservative Research Department, CRD 2/53/26; Shepherd, *Powell*, 157.

27. Precis of Powell speech at Grammar School, Compton Road, Wolverhampton, 20 February 1950, Powell papers (Stafford), D3123/223.

28. Powell, 'Can Britain remain a Great Power Economically?', (no date, but 1951), POLL 3/2/1/1.

29. J. Enoch Powell and Angus Maude (eds), *Change is Our Ally: A Tory Approach to Industrial Problems* (London: Conservative Political Centre, 1954), 96, quoted in Walsha, 'One Nation Group', 208. For Powell's prominence, see One Nation minutes, 26 March 1953 and 16 February 1954, Alport papers, box 37.
30. Policy Study Group minutes, 1 August 1957, POLL 3/2/1/2.
31. Green, *Ideologies*, 223–4.
32. Stedman Jones, *Masters of the Universe*, 190–2.
33. Powell, speech at Newcastle, 29 November 1957, POLL 4/1/1.
34. 'The Powell Interview', *New Agenda: Quarterly Journal of the Federation of Conservative Students* (no date, but 1986), POLL 6/1/4.
35. E. H. H. Green, 'The Treasury Resignations of 1958: A Reconsideration', *Twentieth Century British History*, 11/4 (2000), 409–30, 413–14, 420.
36. Powell to Sir Dennis Robertson, 4 June 1958, POLL 3/1/15; Powell to Robertson, 15 September 1958, Cambridge, Trinity College, Cambridge, Sir Dennis Robertson papers, C18/166; Robertson to Powell, 11 November 1958, Robertson papers, C18/166; Powell to Robertson, 17 November 1958, Robertson papers, C18/166.
37. Powell to Robertson, 4 August 1960, Robertson papers, C23/28.
38. Jackson, 'Currents of Neo-Liberalism', 833. See 'Chronology of the IEA', in Arthur Seldon (ed.), *The Emerging Consensus . . . ?: Essays on the Interplay between Ideas, Interests and Circumstances in the First 25 Years of the IEA* (London: Institute of Economic Affairs, 1981), 265–70.
39. Friedrich Hayek, 'Why I am Not a Conservative', postscript in Friedrich Hayek, *The Constitution of Liberty* (Chicago: University of Chicago Press, 1960).
40. Jackson, 'Currents of Neo-Liberalism', 826, 834.
41. Powell to Ralph Harris, 9 April 1959; Harris to Powell, 10 April 1959, both POLL 1/4/1. J. Enoch Powell, *Saving in a Free Society* (London: Hutchinson for the IEA, 1960), 8.
42. Harris to Powell, 20 May 1960, POLL 1/4/1.
43. Powell to Harris, 20 August 1960, POLL 1/4/1.
44. Jackson, 'Think-tank Archipelago', 44; Radhika Desai, 'Second-Hand Dealers in Ideas: Think-Tanks and Thatcherite Hegemony', *New Left Review*, I/203 (1994), 27–64, 31.
45. International Commentary, 3 January 1960, POLL 4/1/27.
46. Matthew Grant, 'Historians, the Penguin Specials and the "State-of-the-Nation" Literature, 1958-64', *Contemporary British History*, 17/3 (2003), 29–54.
47. Tomlinson, 'Inventing "Decline"', 735.
48. Powell, 'Introduction' in Jossleyn Hennessy, Vera Lutz, and Giuseppe Scimone, *Economic 'Miracles': Studies in the Resurgence of the French, German and Italian Economies since the Second World War* (London: A. Deutsch for the IEA, 1964), ix–xvii, xii, xv and xvii.
49. In 1967 it was revealed that *Encounter* had received covert subsidies from the US Central Intelligence Agency (CIA) for the first ten years of its existence after 1953: Hugh Wilford, '"Unwitting Assets?": British Intellectuals and the Congress for Cultural Freedom', *Twentieth Century British History*, 11/1 (2000), 42–60, 42.

50. Powell to Stephen Spender, 31 July 1963, Oxford, Bodleian Library, Stephen Spender papers, MS. Spender 60. Spender to Powell, 27 August 1963, POLL 1/1/49. Powell to Spender, 28 August 1963, Spender papers, MS. Spender 60.

51. Powell, 'Is it Politically Possible', in IEA, *Rebirth of Britain: A Symposium of Essays by Eighteen Writers* (London: Pan, 1964), 257–67, 257–8.

52. Tomlinson, 'Inventing "Decline"', 749–52. See Jim Tomlinson, *The Labour Governments 1964–70. Volume 3: Economic Policy* (Manchester: Manchester University Press, 2004), ch. 2, for Labour's renewed interest in planning, with Wilson talking the language of technological modernization. On the rise and fall of wholesale Labour planning, see Glen O'Hara, *From Dreams to Disillusionment: Economic and Social Planning in 1960s Britain* (Basingstoke: Palgrave Macmillan, 2006).

53. Powell, speech at Camborne, 12 May 1962, POLL 4/1/1.

54. Powell, speech at Louth, 8 March 1963, POLL 4/1/1.

55. Powell, speech at Narborough Hall, Norfolk, 15 June 1963, POLL 4/1/1.

56. Powell to Ralph Harris, 20 July 1960, Ralph Harris papers, cited in Heffer, *Like the Roman*, 266.

57. Jackson, 'Think-tank Archipelago', 58.

58. Powell, speech at Bromsgrove, 6 July 1963, POLL 4/1/1.

59. Powell, speech at Glasgow, 3 April 1964, POLL 4/1/1.

60. Powell, speech at Docking, Norfolk, 21 April 1964, POLL 4/1/1. Wary of Chartist calls for democracy, the Anti-Corn Law League linked increased consumerism, especially the freedom of exchange, with the extension of citizenship rights: Peter Gurney, *Wanting and Having: Popular Politics and Liberal Consumerism in England, 1830–70* (Manchester: Manchester University Press, 2015), xi, 17, 19, ch. 4, 313.

61. Tomlinson, 'Inventing "Decline"', 746–7.

62. Enid Russell-Smith, letters to her brother and sisters, 1 August 1963, Cambridge, Churchill Archives Centre, Dame Enid Russell-Smith papers, RUSM 1/23.

63. Powell, speech at Bromsgrove, 6 July 1963, POLL 4/1/1.

64. Powell, speech on 'The Consequences of the General Election' at Swinton Conservative College, 26–9 March 1965, POLL 4/1/1.

65. Powell, speech at the Savoy Hotel, London, 10 June 1965, POLL 4/1/1. See also Powell, speech at Aylesbury, 25 February 1965, POLL 4/1/1.

66. 'Any Questions?', BBC *Light Programme*, 28 May 1965, POLL 4/1/27.

67. Powell, speech at Wolverhampton, 13 December 1963, POLL 4/1/1.

68. Powell, speech at Manchester, 10 December 1964, POLL 4/1/1.

69. Jim Tomlinson, 'The Commonwealth, the Balance of Payments and the Politics of International Poverty: British Aid Policy, 1958-1971', *Contemporary European History*, 12/4 (2003), 413–29, 413, 418, 423–4, 428.

70. Powell, speech at Birmingham, 28 November 1964, POLL 4/1/1.

71. Powell, speech at Birmingham, 23 March 1962, POLL 4/1/1.

72. Powell, 'What Substitute for an Incomes Policy?', *The Times*, 18 December 1964.

73. Leader's Consultative Committee (LCC) minutes, 13 April 1965, Conservative Party Archive, LCC 1/2/2.

74. Powell, speech at Glasgow, 3 April 1964, POLL 4/1/1.

75. 'Text of a speech by the Rt Hon Quintin Hogg MP, Secretary of State for Education and Science, to a rally of Stirlingshire constituencies in the Albert Hall, Stirling, on Wednesday 22nd April 1964', POLL 3/1/30.

76. Ralph Harris to Powell, 17 November 1964, POLL 1/1/49.

77. Harris to Powell, 8 January 1965, POLL 1/1/49.

78. Antony Fisher (Managing Trustee, IEA) to Powell, 5 February 1964, POLL 3/1/29. Bruno Leoni, Professor Friedrich A. Lutz (President, Mont Pelerin Society), A. A. Shenfield (Economic Director, Mont Pelerin Society) to Powell, 30 September 1965, POLL 1/1/14; Powell to Leoni, 5 October 1965, POLL 1/1/14. Powell to Harris, 17 May 1980, POLL 1/1/30.

79. Noel Thompson, 'Hollowing out the State: Public Choice Theory and the Critique of Keynesian Social Democracy', *Contemporary British History*, 22/3 (2008), 355–82, esp. 360, 366–74.

80. Jackson, 'Currents of Neo-Liberalism', 834–5. On the IEA approach, see Ralph Harris and Arthur Seldon, *Not from Benevolence: Twenty Years of Economic Dissent* (London: IEA, 1977), 46–50.

81. Powell, speech at Llandudno, 27 October 1960, POLL 4/1/1. On the NHS not being exclusive, see also Powell at the Conservative Party conference (Conservative and Unionist Central Office press release), October 1960, POLL 4/1/1.

82. Enid Russell-Smith, letters to her brother and sisters, 21 November 1961, Russell-Smith papers, RUSM 1/21.

83. Sir George Godber to Powell, 15 May 1992, POLL 1/1/42.

84. Powell, speech at Bromsgrove, 6 July 1963, POLL 4/1/1.

85. J. Enoch Powell, *A New Look at Medicine and Politics* (London: Pitman Medical, 1966), p. 68.

86. Ralph Harris to Powell, 15 September 1966, POLL 1/1/49; also in POLL 1/4/31.

87. R.H., 'Observations on Conclusions of Medicine and Politics', September 1966, POLL 1/4/31.

88. Powell, *New Look*, 72.

89. Geoffrey Howe to Powell, 12 September 1966, POLL 1/4/31.

90. Powell, *New Look*, p. 73.

91. Arthur Seldon to Powell, 7 October 1966, POLL 1/4/31.

92. Powell to Seldon, 8 October 1966, POLL 1/4/31.

93. Arthur Seldon, 'False Freedoms of the Welfare State', *Sunday Telegraph*, 27 November 1966, POLL 1/4/31.

94. Richard Titmuss, 'A Rare Political Flair is Mixed with Cold Logic', *International Medical Tribune of Great Britain*, 8 December 1966, POLL 1/4/31.

95. Ralph Harris to Powell, 3 January 1967, POLL 1/4/31.

96. Butler and King, *General Election of 1966*, 20.

97. Powell, speech on 'Conservative Policies – at home' at Swinton Conservative College on 28–30 January 1966, POLL 4/1/2. A version of this was published as Powell, 'On Opposition', *Swinton College Journal*, summer 1966, 3–4, POLL 6/1/1. In 1959 Powell identified a 'categorical imperative' for the success of parties in opposition: they should concentrate on elaborating 'a great, simple,

central theme, branching into all fields and subjects of debate, but in itself easily grasped': J. Enoch Powell, '1951-59: Labour in Opposition', *Political Quarterly*, 30/4 (1959), 336–43, 340–1.

98. Powell, speech at Nottingham, 17 April 1967, POLL 4/1/2.

99. Powell, 'Advertising must Advertise', *The Spectator*, 6 March 1959, POLL 6/1/1. See the discussion of Ralph Harris and Arthur Seldon, *Advertising in the Free Society* (1959), in Peter Gurney, *The Making of Consumer Culture in Modern Britain* (London: Bloomsbury, 2017), 172. The New Left critique of advertising also attributed it a central place in what it attacked as the fundamentally unequal capitalist system.

100. Powell, speech at Barnstaple, 28 April 1967, POLL 4/1/2.

101. Powell, speech at Wembley, 9 May 1966, POLL 4/1/2.

102. Powell, speech at Wheatley, 11 March 1967. See also Powell, speech at Kidderminster, 31 March 1967; both POLL 4/1/2.

103. Report of Powell speech to the Young Conservative Organisation of the South-West Wolverhampton Conservative Association, 18 July 1949, Powell papers (Stafford), D3123/223.

104. Jim Tomlinson, 'Balanced Accounts? Constructing the Balance of Payments Problem in Post-war Britain', *English Historical Review*, 124/509 (2009), 863–84, 865, 877, 878, 882, 883.

105. Powell, speech at the Savoy Hotel, London, 30 November 1967, POLL 4/1/3.

106. Speaking copy, 28 January 1964, POLL 4/1/1. Powell, speech on 'International Money and the Investor', 30 November 1967, POLL 4/1/3; Powell, speech at Chippenham, 11 May 1968, POLL 4/1/3.

107. Robert Walsha, 'The One Nation Group and One Nation Conservatism, 1950-2002', *Contemporary British History*, 17/2 (2003), 69–120, 102. J. Enoch Powell, *Exchange Rates and Liquidity: An Essay on the Relationship of International Trade and Liquidity to Fixed Exchange Rates and the Price of Gold* (London: IEA, 1967). This was a 'paper read to Harry Schultz International Monetary Seminar in New York and Los Angeles in November 1967'.

108. Powell, speech at High Wycombe, 21 June 1968, POLL 4/1/3.

109. Powell, speech on 'The Fixed Exchange Rate and Dirigisme' at the Mont Pelerin Society Aviemore Conference, September 1968, POLL 4/1/3.

110. Powell, speech on 'Conservative Policies – at home' at Swinton Conservative College, 28–30 January 1966, POLL 4/1/2.

111. *Hansard*, HC, vol. 688, col. 82 (27 January 1964).

112. Peter Mandler, 'Educating the Nation: II. Universities', *Transactions of the Royal Historical Society*, 25 (2015), 1–26, 2.

113. Powell, speech at Stratford-on-Avon, 12 March 1967, POLL 4/1/2.

114. Powell, speech at Overseas House, London, 22 June 1968, POLL 4/1/3.

115. Powell, speech at Thetford, Norfolk, 13 December 1968, POLL 4/1/3.

116. Peter Mandler, 'The Two Cultures Revisited: The Humanities in British Universities Since 1945', *Twentieth Century British History*, 26/3 (2015), 400–23, 406–7, 409.

117. Powell, speech at Overseas House, London, 22 June 1968, POLL 4/1/3.

118. Powell, speech at Oxford, 20 January 1969, POLL 4/1/5.

119. Powell, speech at Keighley, 12 December 1969, POLL 4/1/5.

120. 1970 Conservative Party General Election Manifesto, http://www.conserva-tivemanifesto.com/1970/1970-conservative-manifesto.shtml

121. Green, *Ideologies*, 231–2.

122. Richard Cockett, *Thinking the Unthinkable: Think-tanks and the Economic Counter-revolution, 1931–1983* (London: HarperCollins, 1994), 200.

123. Powell, speech at Southport, 12 November 1970, POLL 4/1/6.

124. Powell, speech at Market Bosworth, 31 August 1968; Powell, speech at Watford, 12 September 1968; Powell, speech at Morecambe, 11 October 1968; all POLL 4/1/3.

125. Richard Stevens, 'The Evolution of Privatisation as an Electoral Strategy, c. 1970-90', *Contemporary British History*, 18/2 (2004), 47–75, 48–9. John Ramsden, *The Winds of Change: Macmillan to Heath, 1957–1975* (London: Longman, 1996), 237, on Ridley and Powell.

126. Powell, speech at Watford, 12 September 1968, POLL 4/1/3.

127. *Hansard*, HC, vol. 811, cols 80–3, 83 (8 February 1971).

128. Powell, speech at Dover, 20 February 1971, POLL 4/1/7.

129. Powell, speech at the London School of Economics, 16 June 1964, POLL 4/1/1; Powell, speech at Beaconsfield, 19 March 1965, POLL 4/1/1.

130. Powell, speech at Johnstone, 20 November 1970, POLL 4/1/6.

131. Milton Friedman to editor, *The Times*, 29 August 1973; Powell to Friedman, 2 September 1973, POLL 1/1/20.

132. Jackson, 'Currents of Neo-Liberalism', 838–40, on the debate in neo-liberal circles. On Powell's rejection of 'the causal position attributed by Hayek to labour monopoly', see 'Enoch Powell on Hayek', *Swinton Journal*, (autumn 1972), 57–8, 58, POLL 6/1/2.

133. Jim Tomlinson, 'British Government and Popular Understanding of Inflation in the mid-1970s', *Economic History Review* 67/3 (2014), 750–68, 766.

134. *Hansard*, HC, vol. 845, cols 631–2 (6 November 1972).

135. Powell, speech at Leamington Spa, 18 September 1972, POLL 4/1/8.

136. Powell, speech at Motherwell, 24 March 1973, POLL 4/1/9.

137. Powell, speech at Park Lane, London, 29 November 1973, POLL 4/1/9.

138. Ralph Harris to Powell, 25 September 1973, POLL 1/1/20.

139. Powell to Patrick Wall, 15 January 1974, Hull, Hull History Centre, Sir Patrick Wall papers, U DPW/1/208.

140. Powell to George Wilkes, 7 February 1974, POLL 1/1/22.

141. Milton Friedman to Powell, 11 February 1974, POLL 1/1/22.

142. Draft Memorial to JEP from some (candid) friends, August 1974, POLL 1/1/49. Other signatories included Graham Hutton, H. G. Johnson, Lord Rhyl, Arthur Shenfield, and Alan Walters.

143. Andrew Denham and Mark Garnett, *Keith Joseph* (Teddington: Acumen, 2001), 256–8.

144. Memorandum to J. Enoch Powell, November 1974, POLL 1/1/22.
145. Ralph Harris to Powell, 4 December 1974, POLL 1/1/22.
146. Powell, speech at the Reform Club, London, 31 January 1975, POLL 4/1/11.
147. Powell, speech at the Royal Lancaster Hotel, London, 5 September 1978, POLL 4/1/12.
148. Powell, speech at Eastbourne, 2 June 1978, POLL 4/1/12.
149. Moore, *Thatcher: Volume One*, 342, 523.
150. Frank Johnson, 'The Facts of Hayek', *Daily Telegraph Magazine*, 26 September 1975, POLL 1/1/23.
151. Friedrich Hayek to Powell, 6 October 1975, POLL 1/1/23.
152. Powell to Hayek, 10 October 1975, POLL 1/1/23.
153. Wyndham Davies to Powell, 20 November 1982, POLL 1/1/36.
154. Karl Popper to Powell, 22 July 1991, POLL 1/1/41.
155. Heffer, *Like the Roman*, 644.
156. Powell, speech at the Café Royal, London, 9 March 1977, POLL 4/1/12.
157. Jackson, 'Currents of Neo-Liberalism', 838.
158. Powell to Edwin. J. Feulner Jr (Treasurer, Mont Pelerin Society), 10 July 1980; Max Thurn (Secretary, Mont Pelerin Society) to Powell, 10 October 1980; both POLL 1/1/30.
159. Powell to Ralph Harris, 17 May 1980, POLL 1/1/30. Friedrich Hayek to editor, *The Times*, 11 July 1978.
160. Powell, speech at the University of Nottingham, 5 September 1980, POLL 4/1/14.
161. Powell, speech at Morecambe, 11 October 1968, POLL 4/1/3.
162. Jim Tomlinson, 'Mrs Thatcher's Macroeconomic Adventurism, 1979–1981, and its Political Consequences', *British Politics* 2/1 (2007), 3–19, 4–5.
163. Anthony Courtney to Powell, 14 October (no year, but 1981), POLL 1/1/29.
164. *Hansard*, HC, vol. 10, cols 886–90 (28 October 1981).
165. 'Archbishop Supports Efforts to Save Pits', *The Times*, 12 April 1984.
166. Powell, speech at Cambridge, 27 April 1984, POLL 4/1/16.
167. Powell, speech at Bury, 21 September 1984, POLL 4/1/16.
168. Powell, speech at the Annual Doctors' Dinner of the Merchant Taylors' Company of London, 20 December 1984, POLL 4/1/16.
169. *Hansard*, HC, vol. 79, cols 857, 861 (21 May 1985). *The Development of Higher Education into the 1990s*, Cmnd 9524 (1984–5).
170. Powell to Nicholas Barr, 16 March 1989, POLL 3/2/1/93. Under the White Paper proposals students were to borrow Treasury funds, with repayments being collected by banks. Barr was an LSE academic, who had co-authored a paper on an alternative loan structure—borrowing from banks and repaying through extra national-insurance contributions: Barr to Powell, 10 March 1989, POLL 3/2/1/93.
171. Powell, speech at the University of Newcastle, 16 December 1987, POLL 4/1/19. Powell opposed the announcement in 1991 that polytechnics could become universities: Powell, speech at Magdalene College, Cambridge, 12 June 1991, POLL 4/1/23.

CHAPTER 3

1. Influential accounts are Layton-Henry, *Politics of Race*, esp. 76, and Rich, *Race And Empire*, esp. 207–8. See also Richard Weight, *Patriots: National Identity in Britain, 1940–2000* (London: Macmillan, 2002), 431–3. Kathleen Paul, *Whitewashing Britain: Race and Citizenship in the Postwar Era* (Ithaca, NY: Cornell University Press, 1997), 178–9, offers the most circumspect judgement on the distinctiveness of Powell's contribution to the debate.

2. Daniele Albertazzi and Duncan McDonnell (eds), *Twenty-First Century Populism: The Spectre of Western European Democracy* (Basingstoke: Palgrave Macmillan, 2008), 3, defines populism as an outlook that 'pits a virtuous and homogeneous people against a set of elites...depriving (or attempting to deprive) the sovereign people of their rights, values, prosperity, identity and race'. See also Geoffrey K. Fry, 'Parliament and "Morality": Thatcher, Powell and Populism', *Contemporary British History*, 12/1 (1998), 139–47, 139.

3. Callum G. Brown and W. Hamish Fraser, *Britain Since 1707* (Harlow: Pearson, 2010), 585.

4. Report of Powell speech at Graiseley School Fellows Street, Wolverhampton, 14 December 1949, Powell papers (Stafford), D3123/223.

5. 'Bishops appeal to West Bromwich Bus Strikers', *Express & Star*, 24 February 1955, POLL 3/1/12.

6. Powell to Lord Bishop of Lichfield, 26 February 1955, POLL 1/1/11.

7. Heffer, *Like the Roman*, 196–7, quoted the document but not the part about democracy. Peter Brooke, 'India, Post-Imperialism and the Origins of Enoch Powell's "Rivers of Blood" Speech', *Historical Journal*, 50/3 (2007), 669–87, argues that Powell's link between homogeneity and democracy was established in, and just after his return from, India in 1946 amid the threat from communalism. This view was repeated on BBC Radio 4's '1968 Rivers of Blood: The Real Source' (produced by Robert Shepherd) on 3 March 2008. A couple of qualifications are needed. We have seen that Powell was committed to free movement within the Empire in 1949. The documents cited by Brooke in POLL 3/1/1 and POLL 3/1/4 were also written in a context where mass immigration was not anticipated and where Powell's proposals (discussed in Chapter 1) sought to maintain control of India until the last possible moment for strategic reasons. In pushing this argument above all others, Powell called for 'rapid economic development' to promote literacy and education so that votes could be 'exercised rationally'. Without it, he argued, 'the fact that the so-called Indian political parties are...fixed and unchanging communal bodies would render any system of self-government unworkable': Powell, 'Papers on Indian Policy', 3 December 1946, POLL 3/1/4. For a critique of Brooke, and his insistence that Powell's views were 'typical of liberal colonial governors' (671), see Schofield, *Powell*, 71–2.

8. Layton-Henry, *Politics of Race*, 31; Shepherd, *Powell*, 191. Powell was not present when the One Nation Group discussed Jamaican immigration: One Nation minutes, 15 February 1955, Alport papers, box 37. Commonwealth immigration

was discussed at the Policy Study Group but Powell was not minuted as taking a particular view: Policy Study Group minutes, 1 August 1957, POLL 3/2/1/2.

9. Stephen Brooke, 'The Conservative Party, Immigration and National Identity, 1948-68', in Martin Francis and Ina Zweiniger-Bargielowska, *The Conservatives and British Society 1880–990* (Cardiff: University of Wales Press, 1996), 147–70, 157.

10. Shepherd, *Powell*, 224–5.

11. 'A Conservative', 'Patriotism Based on Reality not on Dreams', *The Times*, 2 April 1964. Heffer, *Like the Roman*, 350.

12. Wendy Webster, *Englishness and Empire, 1939–1965* (Oxford: Oxford University Press, 2005), 149.

13. Elizabeth Buettner, '"This is Staffordshire not Alabama": Racial Geographies of Commonwealth Immigration in early 1960s Britain', *Journal of Imperial and Commonwealth History*, 42/2 (2014), 710–40.

14. *The Observer*, 4 October 1964, cited in Foot, *Rise of Enoch Powell*, 70.

15. A. W. Singham, 'Immigration and the Election', 360–8, in David Butler and Anthony King, *The British General Election of 1964* (London: Macmillan, 1965), 365.

16. Powell, 'How Money Works for Integration: *The Economics of the Colour Bar* by W. H. Hutt', *The Sunday Times*, 14 June 1964, POLL 6/1/1. Here Powell reflected on the potential for 'economic forces' in integration.

17. Powell, 'Integration is the Only Way – Over Many Years', *Express & Star*, 10 October 1964, POLL 6/1/1.

18. Home Affairs Committee minutes, 12 February 1965, TNA, HO 376/68, cited in Schofield, *Powell*, 217. The definition was repeated by Roy Jenkins in a speech to the National Committee for Commonwealth Immigration, 23 May 1966, in Roy Jenkins, *Essays and Speeches* (London: Collins, 1967), quoted in Harrison, *Finding a Role?*, 196.

19. David Butler to Powell, 4 November 1964, POLL 3/1/29.

20. Enoch Powell, 'Tories in the Wilderness', *The Sunday Telegraph*, 18 October 1964, POLL 6/1/1.

21. Powell to Paul Foot, 30 June 1969, POLL 1/2/2.

22. Steven Fielding, *The Labour Governments 1964–70. Volume 1. Labour and Cultural Change* (Manchester: Manchester University Press, 2003), ch. 6.

23. Powell to Alec Douglas-Home, 26 January 1965, POLL 3/2/1/6.

24. Douglas-Home to Powell, 28 January 1965, POLL 1/1/14. 'New Measures on Immigration Needed', *The Times*, 4 February 1965.

25. Leader's Consultative Committee (LCC) minutes, 1, 2 February 1965, Conservative Party Archive, LCC 1/2/1.

26. LCC minutes, 9 March 1965, Conservative Party Archive, LCC 1/2/2.

27. Layton-Henry, *Politics of Race*, 61–3.

28. Powell to Allan G. B. Fisher, 26 June 1964, POLL 3/1/29.

29. Powell, speech at Wolverhampton, 21 May 1965, POLL 4/1/1.

30. Powell, speech at Wolverhampton, 21 May 1965, POLL 4/1/1.

31. Powell, speech at Birmingham University, 20 November 1965, POLL 4/1/2.

32. Powell, speech at Camborne, 14 January 1966, POLL 4/1/2.

33. Powell, speech at Wolverhampton, 25 March 1966, POLL 4/1/2.

34. Powell, 'Can we afford to let our race problem explode?', *Sunday Express*, 9 July 1967, POLL 6/1/2. The figure was given in Parliament by Julian Snow, Parliamentary Secretary at the Ministry of Health, on 22 June 1967 in response to a written question from Cyril Osborne: Nicholas Hillman, 'A "Chorus of Execration"? Enoch Powell's "Rivers of Blood" Forty Years On', *Patterns of Prejudice*, 42/1 (2008), 83–104, 101.

35. Edward Heath to Powell, 28 July 1967, POLL 3/2/1/17.

36. Powell to Heath, 7 August 1967, POLL 3/2/1/17.

37. South European Service, 15 March 1965, POLL 4/1/27.

38. Powell, speech at Deal, 18 October 1967, POLL 4/1/3.

39. Randall Hansen, 'The Kenyan Asians, British Politics, and the Commonwealth Immigrants Act, 1968', *Historical Journal*, 42/3 (1999), 809–34, 813, 824.

40. Powell, 'Integration is the Only Way – Over Many Years', *Express & Star*, 10 October 1964, POLL 6/1/1.

41. Brooke, 'Origins of Enoch Powell's "Rivers of Blood" Speech', 679; Schofield, *Powell*, 213–14.

42. Powell, speech at Walsall, 9 February 1968, POLL 4/1/3.

43. Unless otherwise stated, all quotations in this section are from Powell, speech at Birmingham, 20 April 1968, POLL 4/1/3.

44. Richard Rose, 'Voters Show their Scepticism of Politicians', *The Times*, 9 April 1968, quoted in Schofield, *Powell*, p. 220.

45. Schwarz, *White Man's World*, 55–60.

46. Lord Hailsham, *A Sparrow's Flight: Memoirs* (London: Collins, 1990), 269.

47. LCC minutes, 10 April 1968, POLL 3/2/1/8; also in Conservative Party Archive, LCC 1/2/12.

48. Ian Trethowan, 'Tory Dilemmas over Race Bill', *The Times*, 18 April 1968, quoted in Schofield, *Powell*, 213.

49. Gilroy, *Ain't No Black*, 86.

50. *Gallup Political Index*, numbers 97–9, May 1968, 52, quoted in Hillman, 'Chorus', 83.

51. David Wood, 'Powell Out of Shadow Cabinet', *The Times*, 22 April 1968; 'Heath Gets Full Backing of His Shadow Cabinet', *The Times*, 23 April 1968; Edward Heath, *Course of My Life* (London: Hodder & Stoughton, 1998), 293; John Campbell, *Edward Heath: A Biography* (London: Pimlico, 1994), 239–41.

52. Powell to Edward Heath, 22 April 1968, POLL 1/1/26.

53. *Birmingham Post*, 5 May 1968, quoted in Shepherd, *Powell*, 364.

54. Leader, 'An Evil Speech', *The Times*, 22 April 1968; Powell to William Rees-Mogg (editor of *The Times*), 18 May 1968, POLL 1/3/26.

55. 'Mosley Speeches Recalled', *The Times*, 22 April 1968; Humphry Berkeley to Powell, 27 January 1977, POLL 1/1/27; Humphry Berkeley, *The Odyssey of Enoch: A Political Memoir* (London: Hamish Hamilton, 1977), 117–19, stressing Powell's commitment to Parliament in contrast to Mosley. 'Mosley Speeches Recalled', *The Times*, 22 April 1968, contains an early reference to the plural 'Rivers of

Blood', citing the Conservative MP Nicholas Scott. For other uses of the plural at this time, see 'Unions, MPs, and Dockers Line Up', *The Guardian*, 27 April 1968, citing the Conservative MP Geoffrey Rippon; and 'Some Tories "exploited" Immigration', *The Guardian*, 13 May 1968, citing Labour's David Ennals, the Undersecretary of State at the Home Office.

56. Schoen, *Powell and the Powellites*, 36–7.
57. Letter to Powell, 21 April 1968, POLL 1/1/26.
58. Schwarz, *White Man's World*, 50 for the range. See Fred Lindop, 'Racism and the Working Class: Strikes in Support of Enoch Powell in 1968', *Labour History Review*, 66/1 (2001), 79–100.
59. *Gallup Political Index*, numbers 97–9, May 1968, 52, quoted in Hillman, 'Chorus', 91.
60. Diana Spearman, 'Enoch Powell's Postbag', *New Society*, 9 May 1968, 667–9.
61. 'Heath Asks for Nation to be Calm, Fair, Responsible, Constructive', *The Times*, 27 April 1968, quoted in Schofield, *Powell*, 239.
62. Gilbert Longden, 'The Race Relations Bill and Mr Enoch Powell. Statement', 29 April 1968, London, London School of Economic and Political Science, Gilbert Longden papers, LONGDEN/18/5.
63. Schwarz, *White Man's World*, 432; Mark Pitchford, *The Conservative Party and the Extreme Right* (Manchester: Manchester University Press, 2011), 167. There were concerns in some quarters 'to avoid a headlong rush to Powellism': Adrian Fitzgerald to Julian Amery, 22 September 1968, Cambridge, Churchill Archives Centre, Julian Amery papers, AMEJ 2/1/55. For support from individual members of the Monday Club, see Patrick Wall to Powell, 30 April 1968; Julian Amery to Powell, 23 April 1968; and Harold Gurden to Powell, 1 May 1968; all POLL 4/1/4.
64. 'Draft Press Statement from the Law Officers' Department', 24 April 1968; Note for Prime Minister, 24 April 1968; Peter Le Cheminant (10 Downing Street) to T. C. Hetherington (Law Officers' Department), 25 April 1968; all London, The National Archives (TNA), PREM 13/2315.
65. Anthony Howard (ed.), *The Crossman Diaries: Selections from the Diaries of a Cabinet Minister 1964–1970* (London: Methuen, 1979), 24 April 1968, 484.
66. *Hansard*, HC, vol. 763, cols 67–81, 75 (23 April 1968). Geoffrey Lewis, *Lord Hailsham: A Life* (London: Jonathan Cape, 1997), 250.
67. 'Why I Abstained', *The Times*, 24 April 1968.
68. Editorial, *Express & Star*, 29 April 1968, quoted in Shepherd, *Powell*, 352.
69. Powell to J. Clement Jones, 5 May 1968; Jones to Powell, 18 May 1968, both POLL 1/3/26.
70. Jones to Powell, 20 May 1968, POLL 1/3/26.
71. Jasper More MP to constituents, 30 April 1968, POLL 4/1/4.
72. Powell to More, 5 May 1968, POLL 4/1/4.
73. Letter to Powell, 4 March 1968, Powell papers (Stafford), D4490/2. The letter has been marked 'Thanked 9/3'. The first reference to this letter appeared in Schofield, *Powell*, 233.

74. Letter from Powell, 8 May 1968; letter to Powell, 9 June 1968; letter from Powell, 27 June 1968; letter to Powell, 16 June 1970, marked 'THE correspondent'. E'; all Powell papers (Stafford), D4490/2.

75. Ann Dummett to editor, *The Times*, 24 April 1968. As a member of the Oxford Committee for Racial Integration, her perspective was clearly different to that of Powell. Her letter has been cited several times: Foot, *Rise of Enoch Powell*, 114; Shepherd, *Powell*, 363.

76. Shepherd, *Powell*, 363.

77. David Winnick to Powell, 29 April 1968, POLL 4/1/4.

78. Powell to Winnick, 5 May 1968, POLL 4/1/4.

79. According to Paul Foot, Powell stated in an interview with David Frost in January 1969 that he had 'not checked whether or not she existed': Foot, *Rise of Enoch Powell*, 116. Public interest has continued. On 22 January 2007 BBC Radio 4's 'Document' programme named her as Drucilla Cotterill.

80. John Biffen, *Semi-Detached* (London: Biteback, 2013), ch. 34; Shepherd, *Powell*, 359–60. Biffen had written to Powell in support after his speech in Birmingham: John Biffen to Powell, 'Tuesday', no date, but 23 April 1968, POLL 4/1/4. For contemporary coverage of the misquotation, see the article by the Labour MP Lena Jeger, 'A Classic Blunder,' *The Guardian*, 17 July 1968.

81. John Vincent, 'The People's Enoch', *The Listener*, 26 December 1968, 841–3, 842–3.

82. Powell to John Vincent, 27 December 1968, POLL 1/2/1. Powell said the same to Foot: Powell to Paul Foot, 30 June 1969, POLL 1/2/2.

83. *Evening Standard*, 18 February 1969, POLL 1/2/2.

84. Powell to Paul Foot, 20 February 1969; Foot to Powell, 8 March 1969; Powell to Foot, 13 March 1969; all POLL 1/2/2.

85. Paul Foot to Harold Gurden, 7 April 1969, POLL 1/2/2.

86. Gurden to Powell, 12 April 1969; Powell to Gurden, 16 April 1969; both POLL 1/2/2.

87. Foot, *Rise of Enoch Powell*, 9.

88. Powell to Ralph Harris, 8 March 1968, POLL 1/1/48.

89. Samuel Brittan, 'The Book of Enoch', *The Spectator*, 25 April 1969, POLL 1/4/6.

90. T. E. Utley, 'Powell the Political John the Baptist', *Daily Telegraph*, 20 April 1969, POLL 1/4/6.

91. Jim Callaghan to Quintin Hogg, no date, but late April 1968, Hailsham papers, HLSM 2/41/142.

92. Foot, *Rise of Enoch Powell*, 136.

93. Leon Brittan to Powell, 12 November 1968, POLL 1/2/2.

94. Utley, *Powell*, 23–4.

95. Tim Bale, *The Conservatives since 1945: The Drivers of Party Change* (Oxford: Oxford University Press, 2012), 144.

96. Ramsden, *Winds of Change*, 296; Layton-Henry, *Politics of Race*, 72.

97. Powell to Keith Joseph, 27 December 1968, Powell papers (Stafford), D4490/2.

98. Powell, speech at Eastbourne, 16 November 1968, http://www.enochpowell. net/fr-83.html. The speech is not in POLL 4/1/3. It was reprinted in Collings (ed.), *Reflections of a Statesman*, 382–93.

99. Transcript of London Weekend Television, 'Man in the News', 18 January 1969, POLL 3/2/1/17.

100. 'In the High Court of Justice Queen's Bench Division', 31 October 1969. The case was settled with *The Sunday Times* stating that 'the reference to "fantasies of racial purity" was never intended to suggest that Mr Powell had ever held or advanced doctrines of the type put forward by Nazi leaders before and during the Second World War'. Powell, in turn, accepted that 'the suggestion that he did not desire race relations to improve represents the sincere opinion of *The Sunday Times*': Draft of Statement in Open Court for Enoch Powell v. *The Sunday Times*; Sydney Morse solicitors to Powell, 8 April 1970, all POLL 8/1/7.

101. Transcript of Denis Frost, interview with Quintin Hogg, 10 June 1969, POLL 8/1/11.

102. Report of All Party Select Committee on Race Relations, 10 June 1969, POLL 8/1/11.

103. Powell to Cyril Northcote Parkinson, 19 September 1969, POLL 1/1/16.

104. Note by Sir Philip Allen, 2 November 1970, TNA, HO 376/173.

105. Powell speech at Scarborough, 17 January 1970, quoted in *The Times*, 19 January 1970. The speech is not in POLL 4/1/6.

106. Patrick Cosgrave, 'Mr Powell's Speech of 17th January 1970', 16 January 1970, Hailsham papers, HLSM 2/42/4/40.

107. 'Extract from *The World This Weekend*: Interview with Ted Heath/Opposition Meeting', Radio 4, 18 January 1970, POLL 3/2/1/17.

108. Powell to Edward Heath, 2 February 1970, POLL 3/2/1/17.

109. Political correspondent, *Sunday Telegraph*, 25 January 1970.

110. Powell to Peregrine Worsthorne, 25 January 1970, POLL 1/2/1.

111. Ralph Harris to Powell, 20 January 1970, POLL 8/1/12.

112. Schwarz, *White Man's World*, 4. The file is held among the Powell papers (Stafford) in D4490/49. Schwarz's argument is that Powell found it difficult to name the disorder because it was about the unspoken 'political-cultural effects of the end of empire "at home", in the domestic society itself'. See also Schofield, *Powell*, 272.

113. Powell, speech at York, 7 March 1970, POLL 4/1/6.

114. Powell, speech at Northfield, Birmingham, 13 June 1970, POLL 4/1/6. For the adoption of the title, see, for example, 'Conservative Anger with Powell over Rift on Immigrants', *The Times*, 15 June 1970; Heffer, *Like the Roman*, 559–61. The adopted title was repeated when the speech was reprinted in Collings (ed.), *Reflections of a Statesman*, 244–8.

115. Powell, speech at Southport, 1 May 1970, POLL 4/1/6.

116. Powell, speech at Wolverhampton, 11 June 1970, POLL 4/1/6.

117. 1970 Conservative Party General Election Manifesto; Layton-Henry, *Politics of Race*, 78.

118. Maurice Cowling, 'Mr Powell, Mr Heath and the Future', in John Wood (ed.), *Powell and the 1970 Election* (London: Elliot Right Way, 1970), ch. 1, 13.

119. Andrew Roth, *Enoch Powell: Tory Tribune* (London: Macdonald and Co., 1970), 1.

120. Office of Population Censuses and Surveys, 'Note on Speech by Mr Enoch Powell (1 May 1970)', 1 July 1970, TNA, HO 344/353.

121. Office of Population Censuses and Surveys, 'Statistics of the New Commonwealth Population: Comments on Charges by Mr Enoch Powell', 1 July 1970, TNA, HO 344/353.

122. Edward Heath to Home Secretary, 30 June 1970, TNA, HO 376/173; Home Secretary to Prime Minister, July 1970, TNA, HO 376/173 (received on the 6th in TNA, PREM 15/958); P. L. Gregson (10 Downing St.) to Mr Lloyd Jones (Cabinet Office), 7 July 1970, TNA, HO 376/173.

123. Reginald Maudling to Powell, 29 September 1970, POLL 8/2/2; Home Secretary to Prime Minister, 3 July 1972, TNA, PREM 15/958.

124. *The Spectator*, 6 March 1971, cited in Shepherd, *Powell*, 411.

125. *Hansard*, HC, vol. 813, cols 76–85 (8 March 1971).

126. Powell, speech at Huddersfield, 7 July 1971, POLL 4/1/7.

127. Powell, speech at Longford, 4 November 1971, POLL 4/1/7.

128. For this paragraph, Chibuike Uche, 'The British Government, Idi Amin and the Expulsion of British Asians from Uganda', *Interventions: International Journal of Postcolonial Studies*, 19/6 (2017), 818–36, esp. 819, 825–6, 829–35.

129. Powell, speech at Tettenhall, Wolverhampton, 16 August 1972, POLL 4/1/8.

130. Note for Attorney General, no date, but late August 1972, Cambridge, Churchill Archives Centre, Peter Rawlinson papers, RSWN 2/21.

131. Harrison, *Finding a Role?*, 202, for the poll.

132. Lord Hailsham to Peter Rawlinson, 15 September 1972, Rawlinson papers, RSWN 2/20.

133. Gilbert Longden to constituents, October 1972, Longden papers, LONGDEN/18/5.

134. Letter from the National Front (invitation to contest Wolverhampton South West), 12 February 1974, POLL 3/2/2/7; Graham Jones (press officer, Wolverhampton and South Staffordshire National Front) to Powell, 4 February 1977, POLL 3/2/1/10; Mike Scott (chairman, Preston branch of the National Front) to Powell, 6 August 1977, POLL 3/2/1/10.

135. Martin Webster to editor, *Daily Mirror*, 5 April 1977, POLL 3/2/1/10.

136. Hailsham diary, 2 November 1977, Hailsham papers, MTFW, 111189.

137. Schofield, *Powell*, 250, 290, 311.

138. Andrew G. Elliot to Powell, 22 April 1968, POLL 1/4/7.

139. Elliot to Powell, 1 July 1975, POLL 1/1/23.

140. Powell, speech at Croydon, 4 October 1976, POLL 4/1/11.

141. Solicitor General, 'Speech by Enoch Powell', 6 October 1976, TNA, LO 2/1171.

142. Note by Attorney General, 10 November 1976, TNA, LO 2/1171.

143. Heffer, *Like the Roman*, 527. Powell had also used the phrase in July 1969.

144. Letter from Attorney General, 16 November 1976, TNA, LO 2/1171. This was, for example, sent to Tom Litterick MP on 16 November 1976. Silkin informed

Powell of his position: Sam Silkin to Powell, 17 November 1976, TNA, LO 2/1171. The strengthened 1976 Race Relations Act had yet to come into force.

145. Moore, *Thatcher: Volume One*, 69, 178, 194–5.

146. Margaret Thatcher, speech to Finchley Conservative Association AGM, 6 March 1970, *Finchley Press*, 6 March 1970, MTFW, 101721.

147. Powell, speech at Swansea, 17 June 1977, POLL 4/1/12.

148. Matthew Parris (Private Office of the Leader of the Opposition) to Powell, 9 November 1977, POLL 8/2/8.

149. Moore, *Thatcher: Volume One*, 382.

150. *The Sunday Times*, 26 February 1978, cited in Layton-Henry, *Politics of Race*, 104.

151. Matthew Francis, 'Mrs Thatcher's Peacock Blue Sari: Ethnic Minorities, Electoral Politics and the Conservative Party, c. 1974–86', *Contemporary British History*, 31/2 (2017), 274–93, 274, 275, 279.

152. Powell, speech at Billericay, 10 June 1978, POLL 4/1/12.

153. Sir Patrick Donner to Powell, 2 February 1978, POLL 1/1/26.

154. Powell to Donner, 6 February 1978, POLL 1/1/26.

155. Powell, speech at Coventry, 18 February 1978, POLL 4/1/12.

156. *Hansard*, HC, vol. 982, col. 664 (3 April 1980).

157. Powell to William Waldegrave, 21 April 1980, POLL 1/1/30.

158. Waldegrave to Powell, 22 April 1980, POLL 1/1/30.

159. Powell to Andrew G. Elliot, 26 August 1981, POLL 1/1/29.

160. Elliot to Powell, 28 August 1981, POLL 1/1/29.

161. Powell, speech at Aberdeen, 20 March 1981, POLL 4/1/15.

162. Powell, speech at Central Hall, Westminster, 8 May 1982, POLL 4/1/15.

163. Powell, speech at Saltash, 16 October 1982, POLL 4/1/15.

164. Powell, speech at Brighton, 5 October 1982, POLL 4/1/15.

165. Powell, speech at Birkenhead, 20 September 1985, POLL 4/1/17. See also Powell, 'We Can Still Stop the Torch from Being Put to Britain's Funeral Pyre', *Sunday Express*, 15 September 1985, POLL 6/1/4.

166. Powell, speech at Denbigh, 28 September 1984, POLL 4/1/16.

167. The provocative title was 'Skin Colour is like a Uniform', translated interview with *Der Spiegel*. 'Powell…approved the original before publication', *New Statesman*, 13 October 1978, POLL 6/1/3, 460–1, 461. He had said: 'When a separate and strange population establishes numerical ascendancy in an area, then the very nature of its separateness and self-identification promotes the exploitation of the violent and criminal impulses which are common to humanity; and there is nothing strange in this. It is not Powell who says this. You can observe it anywhere. And of course, colour is part of this, because colour is the uniform.'

168. Roger Scruton, 'Where Blacks would be at Home', *The Times*, 5 March 1985.

169. Powell, speech at Gonville and Caius College, Cambridge, 9 March 1985, POLL 4/1/17. The following year Powell criticized equal-opportunities initiatives among civil servants as not being 'in search of "equal treatment" at all' but instead 'equal proportionate representation of various racial and ethnic groups

among the applicants and among the successful applicants': Powell, speech at Cottingham, 14 October 1986, POLL 4/1/18.

170. Powell, 'Britain's Ethnically Divided Peoples', *The Times*, 20 April 1993, POLL 6/1/11.

171. Harrison, *Finding a Role?*, 16, 196–9, 207. David Feldman, 'Why the English Like Turbans: A History of Multiculturalism in One Country', in David Feldman and Jon Lawrence (eds), *Structures and Transformations in Modern British History* (Cambridge: Cambridge University Press, 2011), 281–302, argues that a commitment to pluralism had not simply been prevalent on the Left but also took Conservative forms.

172. Powell, 'Britain's Ethnically Divided Peoples', *The Times*, 20 April 1993, POLL 6/1/11.

CHAPTER 4

1. Hugo Young, *This Blessed Spot: Britain and Europe from Churchill to Blair* (London: Macmillan, 1998); ch. 8 is entitled 'The Fissile Effect'.

2. There were, in fact, three European Communities that the UK joined in 1973—the European Coal and Steel Community (ECSC), the European Atomic Energy Community (Euratom), and the European Economic Community (EEC)—which were governed by common institutions after 1967. In everyday practice, the term 'European Community' was frequently used, as well as the EEC and the Common Market (with the latter adopted especially by opponents of membership). See Robert Saunders, *Yes to Europe! The 1975 Referendum and Seventies Britain* (Cambridge: Cambridge University Press, 2018), 24–5. For simplicity, except in quotations, this book uses 'European Community'.

3. Shepherd, *Powell*, 84–5.

4. The fullest account of the Conservative Party's overall trajectory, between 1945 and 2006, is Nicholas Crowson, *The Conservative Party and European Integration Since 1945: At the Heart of Europe?* (Abingdon: Routledge, 2007). This chapter draws extensively on it, especially chs 1 and 2, for wider context.

5. Report of Powell speech at the AGM of the Penn Ward Branch of the Wolverhampton South West Conservative Association at the Rose and Crown Inn, Penn Road, Wolverhampton, no date, but early 1950, Powell papers (Stafford), D3123/223.

6. Powell, speech at St Albans, 30 October 1962, POLL 4/1/1. Nicholas Crowson and James McKay, 'Britain in Europe? Conservative and Labour Attitudes to European Integration since World World II', in William Mulligan and Brendan Simms (eds), *The Primacy of Foreign Policy in British History, 1600–2000: How Strategic Concerns Shaped Modern Britain* (Basingstoke: Palgrave Macmillan, 2010), ch. 18, 306–7.

7. Powell, speech at Bromley, 24 October 1963, POLL 4/1/1.

8. South European Service, 5 April 1965, POLL 4/1/27.

9. Benjamin Grob-Fitzgibbon, *Continental Drift: Britain and Europe from the End of Empire to the Rise of Euroscepticism* (Cambridge: Cambridge University Press, 2016), 277.

10. Broad, *European Dilemmas*, 46.

11. Leader's Consultative Committee (LCC) minutes, 30 March 1965, Conservative Party Archive, LCC 1/2/2.

12. South European Service, 5 April 1965, POLL 4/1/27.

13. Powell, speech at Bloomsbury, London, 1 December 1965, POLL 4/1/2. See also BBC Light Programme, 'Any Questions?', 18 March 1966, POLL 4/1/27.

14. Powell, speech at the City of London, 31 May 1967, POLL 4/1/3.

15. Sir Evelyn Shuckburgh diary, undated briefing meeting before departure to Italy in November 1966, Birmingham, Cadbury Research Library, University of Birmingham, Sir Evelyn Shuckburgh papers, MS191/1/2/9.

16. Powell, 'The Defence of Europe', *Royal United Services Institution Journal*, 113/649 (1968), 51–6, 56, POLL 6/1/2.

17. Roger Broad, *Labour's European Dilemmas: From Bevin to Blair* (Basingstoke: Palgrave Macmillan, 2001), 75; Young, *Blessed Spot*, 266.

18. Powell, speech at Clacton, 21 March 1969, POLL 4/1/5.

19. Powell, speech at Smethwick, 5 September 1969, POLL 4/1/5.

20. Powell, speech at Clacton, 21 March 1969, POLL 4/1/5.

21. Powell, speech at Market Drayton, 6 June 1969, POLL 4/1/5.

22. Powell, speech at Smethwick, 5 September 1969, POLL 4/1/5.

23. Parliamentary Foreign Affairs Committee minutes, 18 February 1970, Conservative Party Archive, CRD 3/10/1/2.

24. Powell, speech at Tamworth, 15 June 1970, POLL 4/1/6.

25. Crowson, *Conservative Party*, 38.

26. *Hansard*, HC, vol. 809, col. 1404 (21 January 1971).

27. Powell, speech at Wolverhampton, 17 April 1971, POLL 4/1/7.

28. 'Extracts from a Speech by Mr Cranley Onslow, MP at Woking, 23 April 1971', enclosed in Cranley Onslow to Powell, 23 April 1971, POLL 1/1/17.

29. Edward Tomkins (British Ambassador to the Netherlands) to John S. N. Graham (Principal Private Secretary to the Foreign Secretary), 19 March 1971; Crispin Tickell (Private Secretary to the Chancellor of the Duchy of Lancaster) to Tomkins, 5 April 1971, both TNA, FCO 26/797.

30. Powell, speech at The Hague, 17 May 1971, POLL 4/1/7.

31. Powell, speech at Doncaster, 19 June 1971, POLL 4/1/7.

32. Powell, speech at the Conservative Party Conference, Brighton, 13 October 1971, POLL 4/1/7.

33. Powell, speech at Cardiff, 18 October 1971, POLL 4/1/7.

34. Powell, speech at East Cowes, Isle of Wight, 5 June 1971, POLL 4/1/7.

35. Powell, speech at Newport, 22 October 1971, POLL 4/1/7. Powell attributed Heath's comment to his speech to the British Chamber of Commerce in Paris on 5 May 1970 when he said: 'Nor would it be in the interests of the Community

that its enlargement should take place except with the full-hearted consent of Parliaments and peoples of the member countries': Powell to editor, *Daily Telegraph*, 26 February 1974.

36. Powell, speech at Newport, 22 October 1971, POLL 4/1/7.
37. Crowson, *Conservative Party*, 14.
38. Broad, *European Dilemmas*, 82, 94.
39. Andrew Thorpe, *A History of the British Labour Party* (Basingstoke: Macmillan, 1997), 183–4.
40. John Biffen to Powell, 1 November 1971, POLL 1/1/16.
41. Patrick Donner to Powell, 6 November 1971, POLL 1/1/16.
42. Powell to Bob Mellish, 8 February 1972, London, London School of Economics and Political Science, Peter Shore papers, SHORE/9/113; Powell to Peter Shore, 23 February 1972, Shore papers, SHORE/9/109; Foot to Powell, no date, but late June 1972, POLL 1/1/21; Powell to Foot, 27 June 1972, POLL1/1/21.
43. Powell, speech at Wolverhampton, 12 January 1972, POLL 4/1/8.
44. Powell, speech at Brussels, 24 January 1972, POLL 4/1/8. The assessment of the British Embassy in Brussels was that 'however polite his reception everyone has clearly shown that they do not agree with him and he has not been taken very seriously': Martin Bourke (British Embassy, Brussels) to Christopher Wilcock (Western European Department, Foreign and Commonwealth Office), 2 February 1972, TNA, FCO 26/1106.
45. Powell, speech at Chester-le-Street, 29 January 1972, POLL 4/1/8.
46. Powell, speech at Willenhall, 8 April 1972, POLL 4/1/8.
47. J. A. Robinson for Private Secretary at the Foreign and Commonwealth Office, 'The European Communities Bill and Mr Enoch Powell', 21 February 1972, TNA, FCO 26/1106.
48. Powell to Sir Martin Charteris (Private Secretary to Queen Elizabeth II), 12 May 1972, POLL 1/1/21.
49. Powell, speech at Rugeley, 2 December 1972, POLL 4/1/8.
50. Powell, speech at Chesterfield, 28 April 1973, POLL 4/1/9.
51. Powell, speech at Stockport, 8 June 1973, POLL 4/1/9, emphasis in original.
52. 'MPs Angry But Expulsion Unlikely', *The Times*, 11 June 1973.
53. Powell to Nicholas Kaldor, 15 June 1973, Cambridge, King's College, Cambridge, Nicholas Kaldor papers, NK/3/94/1.
54. Powell, speech at Alcester, 3 November 1973, POLL 4/1/9. Powell had voted against the Conservative leadership in 115 divisions in the House of Commons during the course of the Parliament: Philip Norton, *Conservative Dissidents: Dissent within the Parliamentary Conservative Party, 1970–74* (London: Temple Smith, 1978), 253.
55. George Wilkes (chairman, Wolverhampton South West Conservative Association) to Powell, 27 November 1973, POLL 1/1/22; Submission by Annual General Meeting of Tettenhall Wightwick ward branch, 3 December 1973, POLL 1/1/22.
56. Powell, speech at the AGM of the Wolverhampton South West Conservative Association, 14 December 1973, POLL 4/1/9.

57. Powell to Wilkes, 17 January 1974, POLL 1/1/22.
58. Powell to Wilkes, 7 February 1974, POLL 1/1/22.
59. On the proliferation of extra-parliamentary (and often cross-party) groups, especially after 1970, see Anthony Forster, *Euroscepticism in Contemporary British Politics: Opposition to Europe in the Conservative and Labour Parties since 1945* (London: Routledge, 2002), 35–8.
60. Powell to Sir Robin Williams (Anti-Common Market League), 19 February 1974; Williams to Powell, 13 February 1974, both POLL 3/2/2/8.
61. Ben Pimlott, *Harold Wilson* (London: HarperCollins, 1992), 611. Bernard Donoughue, *Downing Street Diary: With Harold Wilson in No. 10* (London: Pimlico, 2006), 30–1 (entry for 21 February 1974).
62. Powell, speech at Birmingham, 23 February 1974, POLL 4/1/9.
63. Powell, speech at Saltaire, Shipley, 25 February 1974, POLL 4/1/9.
64. George Wilkes to Powell, 18 March 1974, POLL 1/1/22.
65. Butler and Kavanagh, *General Election of February 1974*, 105.
66. John Biffen to Powell, 7 June 1973, POLL 1/1/47.
67. Biffen to Powell, 22 June 1974, POLL 1/1/47.
68. Nicholas Ridley to Pam Powell, 15 January (no year, but 1974), POLL 1/1/22. Ramsden, *Winds of Change*, 237.
69. Ridley to Powell, 16 June (no year, but 1974), POLL 1/1/22.
70. Kenneth O. Morgan, *Callaghan: A Life* (Oxford: Oxford University Press, 1997), 252.
71. James Callaghan to Powell, 1 July 1974; Powell to Callaghan, 4 July 1974, both POLL 1/1/22.
72. Powell to Michael G. Ionides, 2 August 1974, POLL 1/1/22.
73. Powell, speech at Manchester, 5 October 1974, POLL 4/1/10.
74. Powell, speech at Clifton, Bristol, 3 October 1974, POLL 4/1/10. See also Powell, speech at Norwich, 6 July 1974, POLL 4/1/10.
75. Powell, speech at the Hornsey Road, London, 22 February 1975, POLL 4/1/11.
76. National Referendum Campaign (NRC) meeting minutes, 7, 21, 28 April 1975, POLL 3/2/1/22.
77. Robert Saunders, 'A Tale of Two Referendums: 1975 and 2016', *Political Quarterly*, 87/3 (2016), 318–22, 319. Saunders, *Yes to Europe!*, ch. 8, for the background to the rest of this paragraph.
78. Transcript of 'The Great Debate', BBC Radio 3, recorded 2 May 1975, broadcast 4 May 1975, Shore papers, SHORE/10/59.
79. David Butler and Uwe Kitzinger, *The 1975 Referendum* (London: Macmillan, 1976), 109.
80. Powell, speech at Birmingham, 2 June 1975, POLL 4/1/11.
81. Powell, speech at Sidcup, 4 June 1975, POLL 4/1/11.
82. Jon Lawrence and Florence Sutcliffe-Braithwaite, 'Margaret Thatcher and the Decline of Class Politics', in Jackson and Saunders (eds), *Making Thatcher's Britain*, 132–47, 133.
83. Powell, speech at Bournemouth, 10 May 1975, POLL 4/1/11. Ben Clements, 'The Referendums of 1975 and 2016 Illustrate the Continuity and Change

in British Euroscepticism', http://blogs.lse.ac.uk/brexit/2017/07/31/the-referendums-of-1975-and-2016-illustrate-the-continuity-and-change-in-british-euroscepticism/

84. Powell, speech at Rickmansworth, 14 February 1976, POLL 4/1/11.

85. Powell, speech at Brighton, 24 October 1977, POLL 4/1/12.

86. Powell, speech at Bexhill, 25 November 1977, POLL 4/1/12.

87. Safeguard Britain Campaign (SBC) Committee agenda, 16 December 1975; SBC Committee minutes, 17 January 1978, both POLL 7/15. Saunders, *Yes to Europe!*, 373–4.

88. Harold Fieldman to Powell, 24 June 1976, POLL 7/15, emphasis in original.

89. Powell, speech at the Central Hall, Westminster, London, 3 June 1978, POLL 4/1/12.

90. *Hansard*, HC, vol. 953, col. 704 (6 July 1978).

91. *Sunday Express*, 8 February 1976, quoted in letter from Airey Neave (Head of Leader of the Opposition's Private Office) to correspondent, 5 April 1976, and enclosed with correspondent's letter to Powell, 15 May 1976, POLL 1/1/25.

92. Maurice Cowling to Powell, 16 January 1968, POLL 1/1/17.

93. Cowling to Powell, 18 February 1974, POLL 1/1/22.

94. *Daily Telegraph*, 11 June 1975, cited in Kevin Hickson, 'Lord Coleraine: The Neglected Prophet of the New Right', *Journal of Political Ideologies* 14/2 (2009), 173–87, 178–9.

95. Cowling to Powell, 3 March 1977, POLL 1/1/27.

96. Alfred Sherman Memorandum for Sir Keith Joseph, 'Britain and the EEC', 6 June 1978, Egham, Royal Holloway University of London, Alfred Sherman papers, box 3, MTFW, 111996. Saunders, *Yes to Europe!*, 247–8.

97. Alfred Sherman Memorandum for Sir Keith Joseph, 'Dinner with Enoch Powell', 7 June 1978, Sherman papers, box 3, MTFW, 111995.

98. Powell, speech at Birmingham, 28 April 1979, POLL 4/1/13.

99. Margaret Thatcher, General Election Press Conference, 2 May 1979, MTFW, 104069.

100. Powell, speech at Ballyroney, Banbridge, 1 June 1979, POLL 4/1/13. See also Powell, 'A Test of Nationhood that Britain must not Fail', *The Guardian*, 4 June 1979, POLL 6/1/3.

101. Cited in Broad, *European Dilemmas*, 135–7.

102. Powell, speech at Ballyroney, Banbridge, 1 June 1979, POLL 4/1/13.

103. SBC Committee minutes, 21 July 1981, POLL 7/15.

104. Corthorn, 'Cold War', 47–8.

105. Powell, speech at Penzance, 31 July 1981, POLL 4/1/15.

106. Powell, speech at Gloucester, 30 September 1981, POLL 4/1/15.

107. SBC Committee minutes, 21 July 1981, POLL 7/15. 'Declaration by the Safeguard Britain Campaign on the occasion of the meeting of the EEC Heads of Government in London on 26–27 November 1981', 19 November 1981, POLL 7/15. This drew on Powell, 'Draft: submitted to N. Spearing 17/10', POLL 7/15. Nigel Spearing to Powell, undated but October 1981, POLL 7/15.

108. Powell, speech at Gloucester, 30 September 1981, POLL 4/1/15. Powell had made this case earlier in the year: Enoch Powell, 'Market Ace may give Labour a Winning Hand', *The Guardian*, 2 February 1981, POLL 6/1/4.
109. Powell, speech at Grays, 30 October 1981, POLL 4/1/15.
110. Ivor Crewe and Anthony King, *SDP: The Birth, Life and Death of the Social Democratic Party* (Oxford: Oxford University Press, 1995), 106–8, 118–21.
111. Broad, *European Dilemmas*, 146–8.
112. Powell, speech at Central Hall, Westminster, London, 27 February 1982, POLL 4/1/15.
113. Powell, speech at Saltash, 16 October 1982, POLL 4/1/15.
114. Labour manifesto cited in Broad, *European Dilemmas*, 154. For Powell's endorsement of Labour, see David Butler and Dennis Kavanagh, *The British General Election of 1983* (London: Macmillan, 1984), 103.
115. Powell, speech at Eastbourne, 2 September 1983, POLL 4/1/16.
116. Powell to Betty Simmerson, 21 December 1987, POLL 1/1/48.
117. Margaret Thatcher, speech to the College of Europe, Bruges, 20 September 1988, MTFW, 107332.
118. Powell, speech at Trevelyan Hall, London, 15 April 1989, POLL 4/1/21. Powell, 'Preface', in Ritchie (ed.), *Powell on 1992*, ix–xiii, xi.
119. Powell, speech at Blackpool, 12 October 1989, POLL 4/1/21.
120. Margaret Thatcher, speech at the press conference after the Strasbourg European Council, 8 December 1989, MFTW, 107841; Powell to Mark Lennox-Boyd (Parliamentary Private Secretary to the Prime Minister), 9 December 1989, POLL 1/1/39; Margaret Thatcher to Powell, 13 December 1989, POLL 1/1/39.
121. Powell to Nicholas Budgen, 4 December 1989, POLL 1/1/39.
122. Patrick Robertson to Powell, 31 January 1989, POLL 7/16.
123. 'The Bruges Group', no date, but 1989, POLL 7/16.
124. Powell to Robertson, 10 February 1989, POLL 7/16.
125. Sir Robin Williams to Powell, 15 August 1989; Williams to Powell, 12 October 1989; both POLL 1/1/39.
126. Powell to Williams, 21 August 1989, POLL 1/1/39. For Powell's involvement, see Minutes of the Special General Meeting of the British Anti-Common Market Campaign, at the Trevelyan Hall, London, 9 December 1989, London, London School of Economics and Political Science, papers of the Campaign for an Independent Britain, CIB/3/6. For Powell's earlier withdrawal from the committee, Powell to Williams, 15 March 1985, POLL 7/13.
127. Derek James (CIB chairman) to Powell, 4 January 1990; Powell to James, 8 January 1990; both POLL 7/13.
128. Powell, speech at Skegness, 9 November 1990, POLL 4/1/22.
129. Powell to Norman Tebbit, 16 November 1990, POLL 1/1/40. The pledge was not part of Powell's prepared speech: Powell, speech at Ewell, 15 November 1990, POLL 4/1/22. Thatcher said she was 'delighted with this news': Peter Morrison (Parliamentary Private Secretary to Thatcher) to Powell, 23 November 1990, POLL 1/1/40.

130. Powell, speech at Ilkley, 26 May 1988, POLL 4/1/20. This led to discussions between Powell and Lawson: Nigel Lawson to Powell, 29 November 1988; Powell to Lawson, 1 December 1988; Lawson to Powell, 20 December 1988; Powell to Lawson, 10 January 1989; all POLL 1/1/39.

131. Powell, speech at the Economic Research Council dinner, 29 June 1988, POLL 4/1/20.

132. Powell, speech at the Intercontinental Hotel, London, 6 December 1990, POLL 4/1/22.

133. Powell, speech at Banbury, 25 October 1991, POLL 4/1/23.

134. Powell, speech at Sidney Sussex College, Cambridge, 31 January 1991, POLL 4/1/23.

135. Powell, speech at Earls Court, London, 15 March 1991, POLL 4/1/23.

136. Powell, speech at Blackpool, 8 October 1991, POLL 4/1/23.

137. Powell, speech at Newcastle-upon-Tyne, 22 February 1992, POLL 4/1/24.

138. 'The Anti-Federalist League', pamphlet/flyer, no date, but 1991 or 1992, POLL 3/2/2/22. For context on the creation and development of the AFL, see Robert Ford and Matthew Goodwin, *Revolt on the Right: Explaining Support for the Radical Right in Britain* (Abingdon: Routledge, 2014), 21–6.

139. Powell to Don Bennett (Chairman, United Anti-Common Marketeers), 15 March 1979. For the invitation, Bennett to Powell, 5 March 1979, both POLL 1/1/28.

140. Powell to Helen Szamuely (AFL), 26 March 1992, POLL 3/2/2/22; Powell to Stuart Millson (AFL), 2 April 1992, POLL 3/2/2/22. Powell had made the same point as discussion of federalism—the movement towards a single federal state with a central government, comprising partially self-governing federated states—emerged in late 1989 under the influence of Delors: Powell, speech at Derby, 27 October 1989, POLL 4/1/21.

141. Powell to Alan Sked, 16 March 1992, POLL 3/2/2/22. Powell also endorsed Sked at the Newbury by-election in 1993: 'Recording of Speech by JEP in support of Sked (candidate for Anti-Federalist League, Newbury by-election, Berkshire), 4 May 1993, POLL 5/52. See Powell's correspondence with two APL candidates (Mike Stoddart and Jan Clifford Lester) on 19 March 1992 in POLL 3/2/2/22.

142. Nigel Farage to Powell, 23 March 1994; Powell to Farage, 28 March 1994, both POLL 7/18.

143. Malcolm Floyd to Powell, 24 November 1994; Powell to Floyd, 25 November 1994, both POLL 7/18.

144. Powell, speech at the Central Hall, Westminster, London, 3 June 1978, POLL 4/1/12.

145. Alan Sked, email to author, 4 December 2017.

146. Alan Sked to Powell, 18 April 1994; Powell to Sked, 21 April 1994, both POLL 7/18.

147. Alexander Williams (chairman Nottingham University UKIP) to Powell, 7 November 1995; Powell to Williams, 13 November 1995, both POLL 7/18.

148. The term Eurosceptic was increasingly used from the mid-1980s. See its adoption, in the form 'Euro-sceptic', in *The Times*: Richard Owen, 'Tomatoes Throw Europe's Summit Progress', *The Times*, 11 November 1985.

149. Peter Lilley to Powell, 26 August 1990, POLL 1/1/40.

150. For context and background here, Tim Bale, *The Conservative Party: From Thatcher to Cameron* (Cambridge: Polity Press, 2010), 41–66.

151. Saunders, *Yes to Europe!*, 374–5.

152. Jonathan Aitken to Powell, 31 July 1994, POLL 1/1/44.

153. Redwood was clear that 'Mr Powell did not influence me at all on the EU', John Redwood, email to author, 4 December 2017.

154. Powell to John Redwood, 6 July 1995, POLL 1/1/45.

155. Powell to Teresa Gorman, 30 January 1995, POLL 7/9.

156. Powell to Bill Cash, 18 December 1995; Daniel Hannan to Powell, 2 February 1996; Powell to Hannan, 5 February 1996, all POLL 7/9.

157. Niall Ferguson, 'Yes, I agree with Enoch (except)', *The Independent*, 13 November 1995, POLL 3/2/5/11.

158. Powell to Nicholas Budgen, 17 April 1997, POLL 1/1/50. Powell had also endorsed him in 1992: Powell, speech at Wolverhampton, 3 April 1992, POLL 4/1/24.

159. Draft of Powell to Nicholas Budgen, no date, but mid-April 1997, POLL 1/1/50.

160. Pam Powell telephone note, 16 April 1997, POLL 1/1/50.

161. David Chambers to Pam Powell, 21 April 1997, POLL 1/1/50.

162. Letter from Powell, 23 June 1997, POLL 7/9.

163. Crowson, *Conservative Party*, 66, 165.

CHAPTER 5

1. On the 'bipartisan' nature of British government policy, see Michael Cunningham, *British Government Policy in Northern Ireland, 1969–2000* (Manchester: Manchester University Press, 2001).

2. Heffer, *Like the Roman*, 744–5, comments that 'Powell remained, in mind, a Conservative unable to take his eyes off the seismic events in his old party'.

3. The classic exposition of this distinction is Jennifer Todd, 'Two Traditions in Unionist Political Culture', *Irish Political Studies*, 2/1 (1987), 1–26. David Miller, *Queen's Rebels: Ulster Loyalism in Historical Perspective* (Dublin: Gill and Macmillan, 1978), characterized Ulster Unionism in terms of its conditional loyalty. More recently, Graham Walker, *A History of the Ulster Unionist Party: Protest, Pragmatism and Pessimism* (Manchester: Manchester University Press, 2004), 3–8, has emphasized the multiple and overlapping identities—Ulster, British, Protestant, monarchical—within Ulster Unionism.

4. Powell was thus more than just a primordial Unionist who held the Union to be of value in and of itself rather than because of any positive consequences. For this interpretation of Powell, see Iain McLean and Alistair McMillan, *State*

of the Union: Unionism and the Alternatives in the United Kingdom since 1707 (Oxford: Oxford University Press, 2005), 135, 173–7, 246.

5. Powell, speech at Prestatyn, 27 September 1968, POLL 4/1/3.

6. Graham Walker, 'Scotland, Northern Ireland and Devolution', *Journal of British Studies*, 49/1 (2010), 117–42, 118.

7. Powell, speech at Enniskillen, 7 February 1970, POLL 4/1/6.

8. 'Powell Urges Alien Status for Irish', *The Irish Times*, 9 February 1970. For the censure, '2 Governments turn a Blind Eye to Powell', *Belfast Telegraph*, 9 February 1970.

9. Powell, speech at Enniskillen, 7 February 1970, POLL 4/1/6.

10. Powell, speech at Omagh, 11 September 1971, POLL 4/1/7.

11. *Hansard*, HC, vol. 799, col. 291 (7 April 1970).

12. *This Week*, 21 January 1971, Belfast, Linen Hall Library, Northern Ireland Political Collection (NIPC). For coverage see 'Why Powell would Abolish Stormont', *Belfast Telegraph*, 15 January 1971.

13. Stuart Aveyard, *No Solution: The Labour Government and the Northern Ireland Conflict, 1974–9* (Manchester: Manchester University Press, 2016), 13. Powell, speech at Penzance, 13 November 1971, POLL 4/1/7.

14. Powell, speech at Newtownards, 6 May 1972, POLL 4/1/8.

15. *Hansard*, HC, vol. 857, col. 721 (24 May 1973).

16. Powell, speech at Warrenpoint, 27 January 1977, POLL 4/1/12.

17. Powell, speech at Portrush, 18 September 1973, POLL 4/1/9.

18. Powell, speech at Mountpottinger, Belfast, 2 June 1972; Powell, speech at Banbridge, 10 June 1972, both POLL 4/1/8. Ulster Vanguard Movement, *Ulster—A Nation* (Belfast: Ulster Vanguard, 1972).

19. Powell, speech at Inch, Downpatrick, 6 May 1978, POLL 4/1/12.

20. For example, in summer 1972 Molyneaux had told Powell that he was 'truly grateful for your advice and guidance at all times': Jim Molyneaux to Powell, 19 July 1972, POLL 1/1/21.

21. Note of Telephone Conversation with Jim Molyneaux, 22.45, 10 February 1974, POLL 1/1/22.

22. *Hansard*, HC, vol. 853, cols 1591–2 (29 March 1973); Powell, speech at Belfast, 18 April 1974, POLL 4/1/10.

23. 'New Loyalist Policy is UK Federation', *The Irish Times*, 27 April 1974.

24. Reil to Powell, 19 May 1974, POLL 1/1/22; Jim Molyneaux to Powell, 11 June 1974, POLL 1/1/22.

25. Note by Molyneaux, *c.* June–July 1974, POLL 1/1/22.

26. Powell to Molyneaux, 30 July 1974, POLL 1/1/22.

27. Molyneaux to Powell, 21 August 1974; Molyneaux to Powell, 22 August 1974; Harry West to Powell, 23 August 1974; Powell to S. Cowan (Assistant Secretary, South Down Imperial Unionist Association), 26 August 1974; all POLL 3/2/2/3.

28. Powell, speech at Armagh, 29 August 1974, POLL 4/1/10; 'Powell's View on UK Federation', *Belfast Telegraph*, 4 September 1974; Powell, 'Why I Want Your Vote', *Belfast Telegraph*, 8 October 1974. See also material issued on behalf of Powell in

South Down for the October 1974 general election—'The Policy I Stand For'—which stated that 'Ulster needs a regional legislature and administration', Belfast, Public Record Office of Northern Ireland (PRONI), D3268/4/9.

29. Powell, speech at Llwynypia, 9 May 1974, POLL 4/1/10.
30. James Mitchell, *Devolution in the UK* (Manchester: Manchester University Press, 2009), 4–5.
31. Vernon Bogdanor, *Devolution in the United Kingdom* (Oxford: Oxford University Press, 1999), 3.
32. Powell at Newcastle, County Down, 6 December 1974, POLL 4/1/10.
33. For the background, see Bogdanor, *Devolution*, 95–7, 99.
34. 'Tuesday 26th November 1974', POLL 1/6/28; H. W. [Harold Wilson], 'Record of a Conversation between the Prime Minister and the Rt. Hon. Enoch Powell MP at the House of Commons, 26 November 1974', TNA, CJ 4/971.
35. A. R. Williams, 'Call on the Prime Minister by Mr Enoch Powell MP', 30 October 1975, TNA, PREM 16/521.
36. Powell to Harry West, 3 April 1975; Powell to West, 8 April 1975; Jim Molyneaux to Powell, 14 April 1975; all POLL 9/1/8.
37. Powell to Harold Wilson, 6 January 1976, POLL 1/1/25; Wilson to Powell, 12 January 1976, POLL 1/1/25; Powell to Jim Callaghan, 29 April 1976, Cambridge, Churchill Archives Centre, Margaret Thatcher papers, THCR 2/6/1/102; Callaghan to Powell, 17 May 1976, Thatcher papers, THCR 2/6/1/102. Graham Walker and Gareth Mulvenna, 'Northern Ireland Representation at Westminster: Constitutional Conundrums and Political Manoeuvres', *Parliamentary History*, 34/2 (2015), 237–55.
38. Harry West to Powell, 7 May 1976, POLL 1/1/25.
39. E. H. Brush (President of South Down Imperial Unionist Association) to Jim Molyneaux, 24 July 1976, POLL 9/1/9. The file contains a mass of related correspondence.
40. *Hansard*, HC, vol. 922, cols 1818–19 (16 December 1976).
41. *Hansard*, HC, vol. 885, cols 1202–3 (4 February 1975).
42. Powell, speech at Houndsditch, London, 12 November 1975, POLL 4/1/11; Powell, 'Local Government Reform', *National and English Review*, 143/858 (August 1954), 150–6, 151, POLL 6/1/1.
43. T. E. Utley, *Lessons of Ulster* (London: Dent, 1975), 137–40, 143. Powell, 'Review of T. E. Utley, *Lessons of Ulster*', *Cambridge Review*, 27 February 1976, 114–16, POLL 6/1/3.
44. *Hansard*, HC, vol. 939, cols 505–6 (15 November 1977).
45. *Hansard*, HC, vol. 885, cols 1202–3 (4 February 1975).
46. J. Enoch Powell, *Joseph Chamberlain* (London: Thames & Hudson, 1977), 71–2, 74.
47. *Hansard*, HC, vol. 838, col. 185 (5 June 1972).
48. 'Powell Warns on Future of Shipyard', *The Irish Times*, 5 September 1974. On regional policy towards Northern Ireland, see R. I. D. Harris, *Regional Economic Policy in Northern Ireland* (Aldershot: Avebury, 1991).

49. Powell, speech at Newcastle, County Down, 7 October 1974, POLL 4/1/10. 'Powell and that Shipyard Attack', *Belfast Telegraph*, 8 October 1974.
50. Powell, speech at Belfast, 28 March 1975, POLL 4/1/11. For reaction, 'Enoch Slams Lame Duck Aid', *Belfast Telegraph*, 28 March 1975.
51. Powell at Newcastle, County Down, 7 October 1974, POLL 4/1/10; *Hansard*, HC, vol. 988, cols 1943–4 (18 July 1980). For the longer-term background, see Thomas Wilson, 'Devolution and Public Finance', in Thomas Wilson (ed.) *Ulster Under Home Rule: A Study of the Political and Economic Problems of Northern Ireland* (Oxford: Oxford University Press, 1955), 115–36.
52. Powell, speech at Banbridge, 10 June 1972, POLL 4/1/8.
53. Powell, speech at Beaconsfield, 19 March 1971, POLL 4/1/7; Powell, speech at Ballymena, 3 September 1972, POLL 4/1/8.
54. Heffer, *Like the Roman*, 758. Powell, speech at Kilkeel, County Down, 5 July 1975, POLL 4/1/11.
55. On subsequent Unionist interpretations of the period 1912–14, see Alvin Jackson, 'Unionist Myths 1912-1985', *Past and Present* 136/1 (1992), 164–85.
56. 'Row over Powell', *Newsletter*, 7 July 1975; 'Powell Talking Nonsense: Paisley', *Belfast Telegraph*, 7 July 1975; 'Loyalist Attack on Powell', *The Irish Times*, 7 July 1975.
57. *Belfast Telegraph*, 10 July 1975.
58. Powell, speech at Dromore, 25 January 1975, POLL 4/1/11.
59. Powell, speech at Newcastle, County Down, 10 December 1976, POLL 4/1/11.
60. Powell, speech at Belfast, 4 February 1977, POLL 4/1/12.
61. Powell, speech at Ballynahinch, 8 October 1974, POLL 4/1/10.
62. Powell, speech at Holywood, 5 May 1978, 4/1/12.
63. Powell, speech at Brookeborough Hall, Belfast, 8 January 1981, POLL 4/1/15.
64. Edgar Graham, *Devolution: Maintaining the Union* (Belfast: Unionist Devolution Group, 1982), 5–7.
65. Powell, speech at Brookeborough Hall, Belfast, 8 January 1981, POLL 4/1/15.
66. Powell, speech at Helen's Bay, 6 January 1982, POLL 4/1/15.
67. Powell, speech at Portadown, 28 May 1976, 4/1/11; reported in *Unionist Clarion*, June 1976, NIPC.
68. 'Statement: For Immediate Release', 27 April 1977, POLL 9/1/9; Powell, speech at Dromore, 3 January 1978, 4/1/12. Powell later made a tenuous distinction between this strike and the UUUC-backed 1974 Ulster Workers' Council strike, arguing that the latter 'was directed not against Parliament but against the misjudgement of the then Secretary of State in establishing an executive that he believed would command adequate public support': Powell, speech at Brookeborough Hall, Belfast, 8 January 1981, POLL 4/1/15. This ignored the fact that the 1973 Sunningdale Agreement, under which the Executive had been set up, had been greeted with approval in Parliament.
69. Powell, speech at Donaghadee, 26 January 1980, POLL 4/1/14; *Hansard*, HC, vol. 1000, col. 720 (9 March 1981); Powell, speech at Helen's Bay, 6 January 1982, POLL 4/1/15. As Northern Ireland Prime Minister, Terence O'Neill had used

the phrase 'Protestant Sinn Féin' in his 'Ulster at the Crossroads' speech in December 1968 to attack those within his own government, notably Bill Craig, who sought greater independence for Northern Ireland from Britain, loosely identifying with the Unilateral Declaration of Independence (UDI) made by Rhodesia: Marc Mulholland, *Northern Ireland at the Crossroads: Ulster Unionism in the O'Neill Years 1960-9* (Basingstoke: Palgrave Macmillan, 2000), 168-73. Colin Kidd, 'Protestant Sinn Féin: Ulster Unionism's Un-English Inflections', paper given at the conference on 'Ireland, Scotland and the Problem of English Nationalism: From Home Rule to Brexit', at the University of St Andrews, 1 June 2018, examined the arguments made by O'Neill and Powell.

70. Powell, speech at the Official Unionist Party Conference in Enniskillen, 21 October 1978, POLL 4/1/12.

71. *Daily Telegraph*, 31 March 1979, quoted in Shepherd, *Powell*, 479.

72. 1970 Conservative Party General Election Manifesto, http://conservativemanifesto.com/1979/1979-conservative-manifesto.shtml

73. Ian Gow to Powell, 1 September 1975, POLL 1/1/23.

74. Ian Gow, note for MT [Margaret Thatcher], 2 October 1979, Thatcher papers, THCR 2/6/2/129, MTFW, 118757.

75. MT [Margaret Thatcher] engagement diary, 23 October 1979, Thatcher papers, THCR 6/1/2/1, MTFW, 112947.

76. Powell, speech at Banbridge, 23 November 1979, POLL 4/1/13.

77. Roy Harrington (NIO) to Michael Alexander (Private Secretary for Foreign Affairs to the Prime Minister), 23 November 1979, TNA, PREM 19/83, MTFW, 117907. On conspiracy theories, including the claim of CIA involvement in the death of Lord Mountbatten in 1979, see Shepherd, *Powell*, 477-84.

78. Powell, speech at Kilkeel, 30 April 1979, POLL 4/1/13. See also *Hansard*, HC, vol. 969, cols. 1045-6 (2 July 1979).

79. Powell, speech at Coleraine, 5 December 1981, POLL 4/1/15.

80. Powell, speech at Donaghmore, 17 March 1979, POLL 4/1/13.

81. Powell, speech at Dundonald, 3 January 1980, POLL 4/1/14.

82. Ian Gow, 'Ulster', 27 November 1979, Thatcher papers, THCR 2/6/2/116; T. E. Utley, 'Thoughts on Ulster', November 1979, Thatcher papers, THCR 2/6/2/116. For Thatcher at this time, see Moore, *Thatcher: Volume 1*, ch. 21.

83. Powell to John Biffen, 6 December 1979, TNA, CJ 4/3465.

84. Biffen to Powell, 18 January 1980, TNA, CJ 4/3465.

85. J. Kelley (Treasury), 'The Chief Secretary and Mr Powell', 18 November 1980, TNA, CJ 4/3465.

86. Roy Harrington (NIO) to Michael Alexander (Private Secretary for Foreign Affairs to the Prime Minister), 18 April 1980, TNA, PREM 19/280, MTFW, 120427; Kenneth Stowe, 'Note. Meeting with Mr Powell', 15 April 1980, TNA, PREM 19/28, MTFW, 120427.

87. Ian Gow, 'Ulster', 27 November 1979, THCR 2/6/2/116.

88. Willie Whitelaw, 'Enoch Powell', 30 April 1980, TNA, PREM 19/280, MTFW, 120429.

89. Ian Gow, 'Note of a Meeting held at the House of Commons at 4.45pm on Thursday 1st May 1980', 2 May 1980, Thatcher papers, THCR 2/6/2/116, MTFW, 119447.
90. Text of 'Interview on the *World at One* with the Rt Hon Enoch Powell MP, Wednesday 10 December [1980]', TNA, PREM 19/507, MTFW 125322.
91. 'Note of a Meeting held at the House of Commons at 3.45pm on Tuesday 10th February 1981', Thatcher papers, THCR 1/12/10, MTFW, 121274.
92. *Hansard*, HC, vol. 26, cols 770–1 (29 June 1982).
93. Jim Prior, A *Balance of Power* (London: Hamilton, 1986), 194, cited in Marc Mulholland, '"Just Another Country"? The Irish Question in the Thatcher Years', in Jackson and Saunders (eds), *Making Thatcher's Britain*, 180–96, 186.
94. Ian Gow, 'Your meeting with JEP at 9.30 pm on Wednesday 14 July: Minute for PM', 13 July 1982, TNA, PREM 19/816, MTFW 137489, emphasis in original.
95. Moore, *Thatcher: Volume 1*, 285–6. Powell to Margaret Thatcher, 1 July 1982, TNA, PREM 19/816, MTFW, 137496.
96. Robert Armstrong to Clive Whitmore (Principal Private Secretary to the Prime Minister), 12 July 1982, TNA, PREM19/816, MTFW, 137492.
97. Powell to Robert Armstrong, 21 October 1982, POLL 3/2/1/108. Powell had told Sloan that: 'After careful collation with your transcripts of the interviews, I am satisfied there is no room for rational doubt about the authenticity of the statements and the crucial expressions attributed in them to Abbott': Powell to Geoffrey Sloan, 21 October 1982, POLL 3/2/1/108.
98. Robert Armstrong minute, 'Discussions between Mr Geoffrey Sloan and Mr Clive Abbott', 11 November 1982, TNA, PREM 19/816, MTFW 137455; 'Draft Note for the Record', no date, but November 1982, TNA, PREM 19/816, MTFW, 137455; *Belfast Telegraph*, 8 July 1982, POLL 3/2/1/108.
99. Robert Armstrong minute, 'Discussions between Mr Geoffrey Sloan and Mr Clive Abbott', 11 November 1982, TNA, PREM 19/816, MTFW 137455. This was conveyed to Powell in Armstrong to Powell, 6 December 1982, Thatcher papers, THCR 2/6/2/156, MTFW, 122833.
100. Powell, speech at Warrenpoint, 24 November 1978, POLL 4/1/12.
101. Powell, speech at Moira, 9 December 1978, POLL 4/1/12. For the order, see Henry Patterson and Eric Kaufmann, *Unionism and Orangeism in Northern Ireland Since 1945: The Decline of the Loyal Family* (Manchester: Manchester University Press, 2007), 204–6, 208.
102. Powell, speech at Eglinton, 25 April 1980, POLL 4/1/14.
103. Powell, speech at Antrim, 1 February 1980, POLL 4/1/14. For subsequent reiteration of the same overall argument, see Powell, speech at Brookeborough Hall, Belfast, 8 January 1981, POLL 4/1/15; Powell, speech at Belfast, 25 October 1985, POLL 4/1/17; and Powell, speech at Dundrum, 6 December 1985, POLL 4/1/17. Once he was no longer active in Ulster Unionist politics, Powell was more explicit that the old Stormont government had 'placed the political minority in Ulster in a position of permanent disadvantage from which no other minority in the UK suffers'. Powell, speech at Dromore, 20 January 1989,

POLL 4/1/21. Tam Dalyell, *Devolution: The End of Britain* (London: Jonathan Cape, 1977). I am grateful to Graham Walker for this insight and reference.

104. Jim Prior, Minute for MT [Margaret Thatcher], 21 December 1981, TNA, PREM19/814, MTFW, 137360.

105. *Hansard*, HC, vol. 22, cols 921–4 (28 April 1982). *Hansard*, HC, vol. 26, cols 1009–10 (30 June 1982).

106. Jeremy Smith, '"Ever Reliable Friends?": The Conservative Party and Ulster Unionism in the Twentieth Century', *English Historical Review*, 121/490 (2006) 70–103, 71, 74, 101.

107. Alvin Jackson, '"Tame Tory Hacks?": The Ulster Party at Westminster, 1922–72', *Historical Journal*, 54/2 (2011), 453–75, 464–5, 471–4.

108. *Inside Politics*, 21 April 1977, Belfast, Ulster Folk and Transport Museum, BBC Northern Ireland Archives, 701.

109. Powell to John Biggs-Davison, 10 March 1983; Biggs-Davison to Powell, 4 March 1983, both POLL 1/1/32.

110. *Belfast Telegraph*, 24 November 1984; Powell, speech at Warrenpoint, 30 November 1984, POLL 4/1/16.

111. Powell to Margaret Thatcher, 18 October 1984, Thatcher papers, THCR 1/3/14.

112. Powell, speech at Kilkeel, 4 August 1984, POLL 4/1/16.

113. Heffer, *Like the Roman*, 886; Feargal Cochrane, *Unionist Politics and the Politics of Unionism since the Anglo-Irish Agreement* (Cork: Cork University Press, 1997), 332.

114. Gow told Alison that: 'During the last Parliament, I used to see J.E.P. from time to time. Whenever he wished to see the Prime Minister, she saw him. J.E.P. never abused the direct access which the Prime Minister was always willing to accord to him. More frequently, he used to communicate to the Prime Minister through me. J.E.P. and I had a relationship of total trust, and I also saw J. M. [Jim Molyneaux] from time to time. The purpose of this note is simply to say that I think it would be helpful to the Prime Minister and to you if you were able to continue, in this Parliament, the happy relationship which I had with J.E.P. in the last': Ian Gow to Michael Alison, 12 July 1983, POLL 3/2/1/95. Yet by January 1984 Powell found it 'incredulous' that he had to wait until 16 February to see Thatcher, having raised the matter with Alison before Christmas: Note for Michael Alison, note for PM, no date, but late 1983; Michael Alison, note for PM, 9 January 1984; both Thatcher papers, THCR 6/2/3/11.

115. Charles Moore, *Margaret Thatcher: The Authorised Biography, Volume Two: Everything She Wants* (London: Allen Lane, 2015), 327.

116. *Hansard*, HC, vol. 87, cols 950–5 (27 November 1985).

117. Powell, speech at Dundrum, 6 December 1985, POLL 4/1/17.

118. Powell, speech at Ballynahinch, 18 January 1986, POLL 4/1/18.

119. Powell, speech at Newcastle, County Down, 6 January 1986, POLL 4/1/18.

120. Transcript of *Face the Press*, Channel 4, 2 March 1986, Powell papers, POLL 9/1/19.

121. Powell, speech at Spa, Ballynahinch, 31 May 1986, POLL 4/1/18.

122. Powell, speech at Queen's University Belfast, 7 March 1986, POLL 4/1/18.

123. Powell, speech at Queen's University Belfast, 6 February 1987, POLL 4/1/19.

124. *The History Makers*, recorded on 1 July 1988, BBC Northern Ireland archives, 2705.

125. Robert McCartney, *The Case for Integration* (Belfast: Ulster Unionist Party, 1986), 1, 2.

126. 'Party By-passes Integration', *Belfast Telegraph*, 10 November 1986; 'Unionists Reject Conference Integration Plea', *The Irish Times*, 10 November 1986; 'Deal "blocks hope for future"' and 'Molyneaux Demands Unity in Party Policy Battle', *Newsletter*, 10 November 1986.

127. *The Equal Citizen: Journal of the Campaign for Equal Citizenship*, January 1987, POLL 9/1/4. Arthur Aughey, *Under Siege: Ulster Unionism and the Anglo-Irish Agreement* (Belfast: Blackstaff, 1989), 137, 162, states that Powell advocated a 'minimalist' approach to integration which stopped short of calling for British political parties to organize in Northern Ireland.

128. Brendan Clifford, *The Road to Nowhere: A Review of Unionist Politics from O'Neill to Molyneaux and Powell* (Belfast: Athol, 1987), 7, 15. He remarked that it was 'not surprising that Powell, who came to South Down in flight from party politics, has not proved to be the statesman that the province needs'. For the background, see Colin Coulter, 'The Origins of the Northern Ireland Conservatives', *Irish Political Studies* 16/1 (2001), 29–48; Colin Coulter, 'Peering in from the Window Ledge of the Union: The Anglo-Irish Agreement and the Attempt to bring British Conservatism to Northern Ireland', *Irish Studies Review* 21/4 (2013), 406–24; Colin Coulter, '"British Rights for British Citizens": The Campaign for "Equal Citizenship" in Northern Ireland', *Contemporary British History* 29/4 (2015), 486–507; Colin Coulter, 'Not Quite as British as Finchley: The Failed Attempt to bring Conservatism to Northern Ireland', *Irish Political Studies* 23/4 (2015), 407–23.

129. Aughey, *Under Siege*, vii, 144; Julia Stapleton, 'Citizenship versus Patriotism in Twentieth-Century England', *Historical Journal*, 48/1 (2005), 151–78, 153, 173.

130. Letter from Powell, 5 August 1986, POLL 9/1/3.

131. Powell to Peter Clarke, 7 July 1988, POLL 9/1/5.

132. Powell, speech at Kilkeel, 27 April 1989, POLL 4/1/21.

133. Powell to editor, *The Times*, 22 June 1996, POLL 6/1/13.

134. Michael Cunningham, 'Conservative Dissidents and the Irish Question: The "Pro-integrationist" Lobby 1973-94', *Irish Political Studies* 10/1 (1995), 26–42, 38.

135. Powell to Ian Gow, 22 March 1982, TNA, PREM19/815, MTFW, 137114.

136. Letter from Powell, 26 January 1998, POLL 9/1/17. For Powell's initial election, see *Belfast Telegraph*, 1 May 1970.

CONCLUSION

1. Beech and Oliver, 'Humanitarian Intervention', 113–14.

2. 'Syria Crisis: Cameron loses Commons Vote on Syria Action', http://www.bbc.co.uk/news/uk-politics-23892783 (30 August 2013).

3. 2010 Conservative manifesto, http://www.conservatives.com/~/media/Files/Manifesto2010

4. Geoffrey Evans and Jonathan Mellon, 'How Immigration became a Eurosceptic Issue', http://blogs.lse.ac.uk/brexit/2016/01/05/how-immigration-became-a-eurosceptic-issue/

5. Saunders, 'Two Referendums', 320. On the importance of immigration as an issue, often linked to concerns about terrorism, see Harold D. Clarke, Matthew Goodwin, and Paul Whiteley, *Brexit: Why Britain Voted to Leave the European Union* (Cambridge: Cambridge University Press, 2017), ch. 7.

6. 'Enoch Powell's Speech Doctrine Failed, Says Race Boss', *Birmingham Post*, 21 April 2008; 'Nigel Farage Backs "Basic Principle" of Enoch Powell's Immigration Warning', *The Guardian*, 4 January 2014. After the terrorist attacks on London in July 2005, Griffin had contended that British rivers would soon 'foam with blood', cited in Matthew Goodwin, *New British Fascism: Rise of the British National Party* (Abingdon: Routledge, 2011), 158.

7. Harriet Sherwood, 'Bishop of Wolverhampton Backs Petition to Block Enoch Powell Plaque', *The Guardian*, 8 February 2018. Pete Madeley, 'Enoch Powell Blue Plaque Plans for Wolverhampton are Scrapped', *Express & Star*, 29 August 2018.

8. 'Fifty Years On: Rivers of Blood', *Archive on 4*, BBC Radio 4, 14 April 2018; Jonathan Walker, '"Enoch was no Racist", Says Actor Who Played Emperor in Star Wars', *Birmingham Post*, 5 September 2017.

9. Charlie Brinkhurst-Cuff, 'The BBC Must Withdraw its Dangerous Rivers of Blood Broadcast', *The Guardian*, 12 April 2018; 'Fury as BBC announces it will air Enoch Powell's "Rivers of Blood" Speech in Full', *The Independent*, 12 April 2018; Jemima Lewis, 'The BBC was Right to Broadcast Enoch Powell's "Rivers of Blood" Speech', *Daily Telegraph*, 19 April 2018.

10. The UKIP leader in Wales, Neil Hamilton, asserted that Powell 'wasn't a racist in the crude sense': 'Enoch Powell Right about Immigration, UKIP's Neil Hamilton Claims', http://www.bbc.co.uk/news/uk-wales-politics-43783172 (16 April 2018).

11. The pollster Peter Kellner made this point in 2015: 'EU Referendum: A Yes Won't Settle it—Look at Enoch Powell, *Prospect*, 11 June 2015. For an academic discussion, see David Shiels, 'How Enoch Powell Helped to Shape Modern Tory Euroscepticism', http://blogs.lse.ac.uk/brexit/2016/06/03/how-enoch-powell-helped-to-shape-modern-tory-euroscepticism/

12. Bagehot, 'The Shadow of Enoch Powell Looms Ever Larger over Britain', *The Economist*, 6 April 2017; James Beattie, 'Enoch Powell's Rivers of Blood Predictions Didn't Happen But is Brexit His Revenge 50 Years On?', *Daily Mirror*, 13 April 2018; John Lewis-Stempel, 'Enoch Powell: Forget "Rivers of Blood", Brexit is His Real Legacy', *Sunday Express*, 15 April 2018. For a thoughtful reflection, see Michael Kenny and Nick Pearce, 'Will Post-Brexit Britain Overcome or Fall Further upon Enoch Powell's Troubling Legacy?', *New Statesman*, 20 April 2018.

13. John McTernan, 'How British Politics Rediscovered Tony Benn and Enoch Powell', *Financial Times*, 29 December 2017.

14. Harrison, *Finding a Role?*, 6, states: 'the United Nations made surprisingly little headway with British opinion after 1970...becoming a mere arena within which national interests were protected'.

15. Margaret Thatcher, speech at the Conference Party Conference, 10 October 1975, MTFW, 102777.

16. Jackson, 'Currents of Neo-Liberalism', 837. For Seldon's initial hopes for welfare reform in the 1980s, see Arthur Seldon, *Wither the Welfare State* (London: IEA, 1981), 8.

17. Powell, 'In Defence of the Welfare State', *Sunday Telegraph*, 21 September 1986, POLL 6/1/4.

18. Hillman, 'Chorus', 103. This excludes Northern Ireland, where immigration has been much lower.

19. Saunders, 'Two Referendums', 319; Saunders, *Yes to Europe!*, 231–3.

20. Powell, 'The Nature of Sovereignty', in Douglas Evans and Richard Body (eds), *Freedom and Stability in the World Economy* (London: Croom Helm, 1976), 89, cited in Saunders, *Yes to Europe!*, 251.

21. Bogdanor, *Devolution*, 14–15; McLean and McMillan, *State of the Union*, ch. 1, 244–6.

22. Mitchell, *Devolution in the UK*, 1–15, esp. 4–6.

23. Tom Nairn, *The Break-Up of Britain: Crisis and Neo-Nationalism* (London: New Left Books, 1981), ch. 6, esp. 258, 280, emphasis in original.

24. For an overview of the diverse debates on Britishness, see Paul Ward, *Britishness Since 1870* (London: Routledge, 2004), 2–9. For a summary of the public and academic rejection of the concept of the British nation, see Christopher Bryant, *The Nations of Britain* (Oxford: Oxford University Press, 2005), 7–12. For a recent contribution to the debate, see Andrew Gamble and Tony Wright, *Britishness: Perspectives on the Britishness Question* (Oxford: Wiley-Blackwell, 2009).

25. Martin Wiener, *English Culture and the Decline of the Industrial Spirit 1850–980* (Cambridge: Cambridge University Press, 1981).

26. David Edgerton, *Warfare State: Britain, 1920–1970* (Cambridge: Cambridge University Press, 2006), 301; 'Empty Shelves', *The Economist*, 27 April 2010.

27. Powell, 'Paying the Price', *Book Choice*, June 1981, 7–8, POLL 6/1/4. Wiener, *English Culture*, 107–8, described Powell as a perpetuator of the 'rural myth' in the 1960s and did not mention his free-market credentials.

Bibliography

PRIMARY SOURCES

Archives

Bodleian Library, University of Oxford
    Conservative Party Archive
    Stephen Spender papers
Cadbury Research Library, University of Birmingham
    Sir Evelyn Shuckburgh papers
Churchill Archives Centre, Churchill College, Cambridge
    Papers of:
    Julian Amery
    Lord Hailsham (Quintin Hogg)
    Angus Maude
    J. Enoch Powell
    Peter Rawlinson
    Enid Russell–Smith
    Margaret Thatcher
Hull History Centre, Hull
    Sir Patrick Wall papers
International Churchill Society website
    http://www.winstonchurchill.org
King's College, Cambridge
    Nicholas Kaldor papers
Liddell Hart Centre for Military Archives, King's College London
    Sir Basil Liddell Hart papers
Linen Hall Library, Belfast
    Northern Ireland Political Collection (pamphlets and journals)
London School of Economics and Political Science
    Papers of:
    The Campaign for an Independent Britain
    Gilbert Longden
    Peter Shore
    George Wigg
The National Archives (TNA), Kew

CJ 4 Home Office and Northern Ireland Office: Registered Files (NI Series), 1930–1990
FCO 26 Foreign and Commonwealth Office and Predecessors: Information, News and Guidance Departments, 1967–1992
HO 344 Home Office: Commonwealth Immigration Files, 1949–1991
HO 376 Home Office: Racial Disadvantage Files, 1963–1985
LO 2 Law Officers' Department: Registered Files, 1885–1979
PREM 13 Prime Minister's Office: Correspondence and Papers, 1964–1970
PREM 15 Prime Minister's Office: Correspondence and Papers, 1970–1974
PREM 16 Prime Minister's Office: Correspondence and Papers, 1974–1979
National Archives of Ireland, Dublin
   Department of Foreign Affairs
Enoch Powell Speech Archive
   http://www.enochpowell.info
Public Record Office of Northern Ireland, Belfast
   South Down Constituency election literature
Albert Sloman Library, University of Essex
   Cuthbert Alport papers
Staffordshire Record Office
   J. Enoch Powell papers
Margaret Thatcher Foundation Website
   http://www.margaretthatcher.org
Trinity College, Cambridge
   Sir Dennis Robertson papers
Ulster Folk and Transport Museum, Cultra
   BBC Northern Ireland Archives

Official publications

The Development of Higher Education into the 1990s, Cmnd 9524 (1984–5)
Hansard, *The Official Report of Parliamentary Debates*

Newspapers and periodicals

BBC News website, http://www.bbc.co.uk/news
Belfast Telegraph
Birmingham Post
Daily Mirror
Daily Telegraph
The Economist
The Guardian
The Independent
The Irish Times
Marxism Today
Newsletter
Prospect

Sunday Express
The Times

Publications of J. Enoch Powell

Collings, Rex (ed.), Reflections of a Statesman: The Selected Writings and Speeches of Enoch Powell (London: Bellew, 1991).

Macleod, Iain and J. Enoch Powell, The Social Services: Needs and Means (London: Conservative Political Centre, 1952).

Maude, Angus and J. Enoch Powell, Biography of a Nation: A Short History of Britain (London, 1955).

Powell, J. Enoch, 'The Empire of England', in Tradition and Change. Nine Oxford Lectures (London: Conservative Political Centre, 1954).

Powell, J. Enoch, '1951–59: Labour in Opposition', Political Quarterly, 30/4 (1959), 336–43.

Powell, J. Enoch, Saving in a Free Society (London: Hutchinson for the IEA, 1960).

Powell, J. Enoch, 'Introduction', in Jossleyn Hennessy, Vera Lutz, and Giuseppe Scimone, Economic 'Miracles': Studies in the Resurgence of the French, German and Italian Economies since the Second World War (London: A. Deutsch for the IEA, 1964), ix–xvii.

Powell, J. Enoch, 'Is it Politically Possible?', in IEA, Rebirth of Britain: A Symposium of Essays by Eighteen Writers (London: Pan, 1964), 257–67.

Powell, J. Enoch, A New Look at Medicine and Politics (London: Pitman Medical, 1966).

Powell, J. Enoch, Exchange Rates and Liquidity: An essay on the Relationship of International Trade and Liquidity to Fixed Exchange Rates and the Price of Gold (London: IEA, 1967).

Powell, J. Enoch, Freedom and Reality (London: Batsford, 1969).

Powell, J. Enoch, Still to Decide (London: Elliot Right Way, 1972).

Powell, J. Enoch, No Easy Answers (London: Sheldon, 1973).

Powell, J. Enoch, Joseph Chamberlain (London: Thames & Hudson, 1977).

Powell, J. Enoch, The Evolution of the Gospel: A New Translation with Commentary and Introductory Essay (New Haven: Yale University Press, 1994).

Powell, J. Enoch and Keith Wallis, The House of Lords in the Middle Ages: A History of the English House of Lords to 1540 (London: Weidenfeld & Nicolson, 1968).

Ritchie, Richard (ed.), A Nation or No Nation? Six Years in British Politics (London: Batsford, 1978).

Ritchie, Richard (ed.), Enoch Powell on 1992 (London: Anaya, 1989).

Wood, John (ed.), A Nation Not Afraid (London: Hodder and Stoughton, 1965).

Other contemporary publications

Clifford, Brendan, The Road to Nowhere: A Review of Unionist Politics from O'Neill to Molyneaux and Powell (Belfast: Athol, 1987).

Commission for Racial Equality, Five Views of Multi-Racial Britain (London: Commission for Racial Equality, 1978).

Cowling, Maurice, 'Mr Powell, Mr Heath and the Future', in John Wood (ed.), Powell and the 1970 Election (London: Elliot Right Way, 1970), ch. 1.

Dalyell, Tam, Devolution: The End of Britain (London: Jonathan Cape, 1977).

Graham, Edgar, Devolution: Maintaining the Union (Belfast: Unionist Devolution Group, 1982).

Harris, Ralph and Arthur Seldon, Not from Benevolence: Twenty Years of Economic Dissent (London: IEA, 1977).

Hayek, Friedrich, 'Why I am Not a Conservative', postscript in Friedrich Hayek, The Constitution of Liberty (Chicago: University of Chicago Press, 1960).

McCartney, Robert, The Case for Integration (Belfast: Ulster Unionist Party, 1986).

Nairn, Tom, 'Enoch Powell: the New Right', New Left Review, I/61 (May–June 1970), 3–27.

Nairn, Tom, The Break Up of Britain: Crisis and Neo-nationalism (London: New Left Books, 1981).

Seldon, Arthur, Wither the Welfare State (London: IEA, 1981).

Spearman, Diana, 'Enoch Powell's Postbag', New Society, 9 May 1968, 6679.

Ulster Vanguard Movement, Ulster – A Nation (Belfast: Ulster Vanguard, 1972).

Utley, T. E., Lessons of Ulster (London: Dent, 1975).

Vincent, John, 'The People's Enoch', The Listener, 26 December 1968, 841–3.

Autobiographies, memoirs, and diaries

Biffen, John, Semi-Detached (London: Biteback, 2013).

Donoughue, Bernard, Downing Street Diary: With Harold Wilson in No. 10 (London: Pimlico, 2006).

Hailsham, Lord, A Sparrow's Flight: Memoirs (London: Collins, 1990).

Heath, Edward, Course of My Life (London: Hodder & Stoughton, 1998).

Howard, Anthony (ed.), The Crossman Diaries: Selections from the Diaries of a Cabinet Minister 1964–1970 (London: Methuen, 1979).

Winstone, Ruth (ed.), Tony Benn: Years of Hope, Diaries, Papers and Letters, 1940–1962 (London: Cornerstone, 1994).

Email correspondence

John Redwood, 4 December 2017.

Alan Sked, 4 December 2017.

SECONDARY SOURCES

Books

Addison, Paul, The Road to 1945: British Politics and the Second World War (London: Jonathan Cape, 1975).

Albertazzi, Daniele and Duncan McDonnell (eds), Twenty-First Century Populism: The Spectre of Western European Democracy (Basingstoke: Palgrave Macmillan, 2008).

Aughey, Arthur, Under Siege: Ulster Unionism and the Anglo-Irish Agreement (Belfast: Blackstaff, 1989).

Aveyard, Stuart, No Solution: The Labour Government and the Northern Ireland Conflict, 1974–79 (Manchester: Manchester University Press, 2016).

Aveyard, Stuart, Paul Corthorn, and Sean O'Connell, The Politics of Consumer Credit in the UK 1938–1992 (Oxford: Oxford University Press, 2018).

Bale, Tim, The Conservative Party: From Thatcher to Cameron (Cambridge: Polity Press, 2010).

Bale, Tim, The Conservatives since 1945: The Drivers of Party Change (Oxford: Oxford University Press, 2012).

Baylis, John, Ambiguity and Deterrence: British Nuclear Strategy, 1945–1964 (Oxford: Clarendon, 1995).

Bell, Duncan, The Idea of Greater Britain: Empire and the Future of World Order, 1860–1900 (Princeton, NJ: Princeton University Press, 2007).

Berkeley, Humphry, The Odyssey of Enoch: A Political Memoir (London: Hamish Hamilton, 1977).

Bogdanor, Vernon, Devolution in the United Kingdom (Oxford: Oxford University Press, 1999).

Bourke, Richard, Peace in Ireland: The War of Ideas (London: Pimlico, 2003).

Broad, Roger, Labour's European Dilemmas: From Bevin to Blair (Basingstoke: Palgrave Macmillan, 2001).

Brown, Callum G. and W. Hamish Fraser, Britain Since 1707 (Harlow: Pearson, 2010).

Bryant, Christopher, The Nations of Britain (Oxford: Oxford University Press, 2005).

Butler, David and Dennis Kavanagh, The British General Election of February 1974 (London: Macmillan, 1974).

Butler, David and Dennis Kavanagh, The British General Election of 1983 (London: Macmillan, 1984).

Butler, David and Anthony King, The British General Election of 1964 (London: Macmillan, 1965).

Butler, David and Anthony King, The British General Election of 1966 (London: Macmillan, 1966).

Butler, David and Uwe Kitzinger, The 1975 Referendum (London: Macmillan, 1976).

Butler, David and Michael Pinto-Duschinsky, The British General Election of 1970 (London: Macmillan, 1971).

Campbell, John, Edward Heath: A Biography (London: Pimlico, 1994).

Centre for Contemporary Cultural Studies, The Empire Strikes Back: Race and Racism in 1970s Britain (London: Routledge, 1982).

Clarke, Harold D., Matthew Goodwin, and Paul Whiteley, Brexit: Why Britain Voted to Leave the European Union (Cambridge: Cambridge University Press, 2017).

Cochrane, Feargal, Unionist Politics and the Politics of Unionism since the Anglo-Irish Agreement (Cork: Cork University Press, 1997).

Cockett, Richard, Thinking the Unthinkable: Think-tanks and the Economic Counter-revolution, 1931–1983 (London: HarperCollins, 1994).

Colls, Robert, Identity of England (Oxford: Oxford University Press, 2004).

Cosgrave, Patrick, The Lives of Enoch Powell (London: Bodley Head, 1989).

Cowling, Maurice, Religion and Public Doctrine in Modern England. Volume One (Cambridge: Cambridge University Press, 1980).

Crewe, Ivor and Anthony King, SDP: The Birth, Life and Death of the Social Democratic Party (Oxford: Oxford University Press, 1995).

Crowson, Nicholas, The Conservative Party and European Integration Since 1945: At the Heart of Europe? (Abingdon: Routledge, 2007).

Cunningham, Michael, British Government Policy in Northern Ireland, 1969–2000 (Manchester: Manchester University Press, 2001).

Denham, Andrew and Mark Garnett, Keith Joseph (Teddington: Acumen, 2001).

Dorey, Peter, British Conservatism: The Politics and Philosophy of Inequality (London: I.B. Tauris, 2010).

Edgerton, David, Warfare State: Britain, 1920–1970 (Cambridge: Cambridge University Press, 2006).

Fielding, Steven, The Labour Governments 1964–70. Volume 1. Labour and Cultural Change (Manchester: Manchester University Press, 2003).

Foot, Paul, The Rise of Enoch Powell: An Examination of Enoch Powell's Attitude to Race and Immigration (London: Penguin, 1969).

Ford, Robert and Matthew Goodwin, Revolt on the Right: Explaining Support for the Radical Right in Britain (Abingdon: Routledge, 2014).

Forster, Anthony, Euroscepticism in Contemporary British Politics: Opposition to Europe in the Conservative and Labour Parties since 1945 (London: Routledge, 2002).

Freedman, Lawrence, Britain and Nuclear Weapons (London: Macmillan for the Royal Institute of International Affairs, 1980).

French, David, The British Way in Warfare 1688–2000 (London: Unwin Hyman, 1990).

French, David, Army, Empire, and Cold War: The British Army and Military Policy, 1945–1971 (Oxford: Oxford University Press, 2012).

Gamble, Andrew, Britain in Decline (London: Macmillan, 1981).

Gamble, Andrew and Tony Wright, Britishness: Perspectives on the Britishness Question (Oxford: Wiley-Blackwell, 2009).

Garnett, Mark and Kevin Hickson, Conservative Thinkers: The Key Contributors to the Political Thought of the Modern Conservative Party (Manchester: Manchester University Press, 2009).

Gilroy, Paul, 'There ain't no Black in the Union Jack': The Cultural Politics of Race and Nation (London: Hutchinson, 1987).

Goodwin, Matthew, New British Fascism: Rise of the British National Party (Abingdon: Routledge, 2011).

Grant, Matthew, After the Bomb: Civil Defence and Nuclear War in Britain, 1945–68 (Basingstoke: Palgrave Macmillan, 2009).

Green, E. H. H., Ideologies of Conservatism: Conservative Political Ideas in the Twentieth Century (Oxford: Oxford University Press, 2002).

Green, E. H. H., Thatcher (London: Hodder Arnold, 2006).

Greenleaf, W. H., The British Political Tradition. Volume 2: The Ideological Heritage (London: Methuen, 1983).

Greenwood, Sean, Britain and the Cold War, 1945–1991 (Basingstoke: Macmillan, 2000).

Grob-Fitzgibbon, Benjamin, Continental Drift: Britain and Europe from the End of Empire to the Rise of Euroscepticism (Cambridge: Cambridge University Press, 2016).

Gurney, Peter, Wanting and Having: Popular Politics and Liberal Consumerism in England, 1830–70 (Manchester: Manchester University Press, 2015).

Gurney, Peter, The Making of Consumer Culture in Modern Britain (London: Bloomsbury, 2017).

Hall, Ian, Dilemmas of Decline: British Intellectuals and World Politics, 1945–1975 (Berkeley, CA: University of California Press, 2012).

Harris, R. I. D., Regional Economic Policy in Northern Ireland (Aldershot: Avebury, 1991).

Harrison, Brian, Finding a Role? The United Kingdom, 1970–1990 (Oxford: Oxford University Press, 2010).

Heffer, Simon, Like the Roman: The Life of Enoch Powell (London: Weidenfeld & Nicolson, 1998).

Lord Howard of Riding (ed.), Enoch at 100: A Re-evaluation of the Life, Politics and Philosophy of Enoch Powell (London: Biteback, 2012).

Hughes, Michael, Conscience and Conflict: Methodism, Peace and War in the Twentieth Century (Peterborough: Epworth, 2008).

Jackson, Alvin, The Two Unions: Ireland, Scotland, and the Survival of the United Kingdom, 1707–2007 (Oxford: Oxford University Press, 2012).

Jackson, Ben, Equality and the British Left: A Study in Progressive Political Thought 1900–64 (Manchester: Manchester University Press, 2007).

Kenny, Michael, The Politics of English Nationhood (Oxford: Oxford University Press, 2014).

Kidd, Colin, Union and Unionisms: Political Thought in Scotland 1500–2000 (Cambridge: Cambridge University Press, 2008).

Layton-Henry, Zig, The Politics of Race in Britain (London: HarperCollins, 1984).

Lewis, Geoffrey, Lord Hailsham: A Life (London: Jonathan Cape, 1997).

Lewis, Roy, Enoch Powell: Principle in Politics (London: Cassell, 1979).

Lowe, Rodney, The Welfare State in Britain since 1945 (London: Macmillan, 1993).

Lynch, Philip, The Politics of Nationhood: Sovereignty, Britishness and Conservative Politics (Basingstoke: Palgrave Macmillan, 1999).

McLean, Iain, Rational Choice and British Politics: An Analysis of Rhetoric and Manipulation from Peel to Blair (Oxford: Oxford University Press, 2001).

McLean, Iain and Alistair McMillan, State of the Union: Unionism and the Alternatives in the United Kingdom since 1707 (Oxford: Oxford University Press, 2005).

Miller, David, Queen's Rebels: Ulster Loyalism in Historical Perspective (Dublin: Gill and Macmillan, 1978).

Mitchell, James, Devolution in the UK (Manchester: Manchester University Press, 2009).

Moore, Charles, Margaret Thatcher: The Authorised Biography, Volume One: Not for Turning (London: Allen Lane, 2013).

Moore, Charles, Margaret Thatcher: The Authorised Biography, Volume Two: Everything She Wants (London: Allen Lane, 2015).

Morgan, Kenneth O., Callaghan: A Life (Oxford: Oxford University Press, 1997).

Mulholland, Marc, Northern Ireland at the Crossroads: Ulster Unionism in the O'Neill Years 1960–9 (Basingstoke: Palgrave Macmillan, 2000).

Murphy, Philip, Party Politics and Decolonization: The Conservative Party and British Colonial Policy in Tropical Africa, 1951–1964 (Oxford: Clarendon Press, 1995).

Norton, Philip, Conservative Dissidents: Dissent within the Parliamentary Conservative Party, 1970–74 (London: Temple Smith, 1978).

O'Hara, Glen, From Dreams to Disillusionment: Economic and Social Planning in 1960s Britain (Basingstoke: Palgrave Macmillan, 2006).

Onslow, Sue, Backbench Debate within the Conservative Party and its Influence on British Foreign Policy, 1948–1957 (Basingstoke: Macmillan, 1997).

O'Sullivan, Noel, Conservatism (London: Dent, 1976).

Patterson, Henry and Eric Kaufmann, Unionism and Orangeism in Northern Ireland since 1945: The Decline of the Loyal Family (Manchester: Manchester University Press, 2007).

Paul, Kathleen, Whitewashing Britain: Race and Citizenship in the Postwar Era (Ithaca, NY: Cornell University Press, 1997).

Pimlott, Ben, Harold Wilson (London: HarperCollins, 1992).

Pitchford, Mark, The Conservative Party and the Extreme Right (Manchester: Manchester University Press, 2011).

Quinton, Anthony, The Politics of Imperfection (London: Faber & Faber, 1978).

Ramsden, John, The Making of Conservative Party Policy: The Conservative Research Department since 1929 (London: Longman, 1980).

Ramsden, John, The Age of Churchill and Eden, 1940–1957 (London: Longman, 1995).

Ramsden, John, The Winds of Change: Macmillan to Heath, 1957–1975 (London: Longman, 1996).

Rich, Paul, Race and Empire in British Politics (Cambridge: Cambridge University Press, 1990).

Roth, Andrew, Enoch Powell: Tory Tribune (London: Macdonald and Co., 1970).

Saunders, Robert, Yes to Europe! The 1975 Referendum and Seventies Britain (Cambridge: Cambridge University Press, 2018).

Schoen, Douglas, Enoch Powell and the Powellites (London: Macmillan, 1977).

Schofield, Camilla, Enoch Powell and the Making of Postcolonial Britain (Cambridge: Cambridge University Press, 2013).

Schwarz, Bill, The White Man's World: Memories of Empire, Volume 1 (Oxford: Oxford University Press, 2011).

Shepherd, Robert, Enoch Powell: A Biography (London: Hutchinson, 1996).

Smith, Anna Marie, New Right Discourse on Race and Sexuality: Britain 1968–1990 (Cambridge: Cambridge University Press, 1994).

Stapleton, Julia, Political Intellectuals and Public Identities in Britain since 1850 (Manchester: Manchester University Press, 2001).

Stedman Jones, Daniel, Masters of the Universe: Hayek, Friedman, and the Birth of Neoliberal Politics (Princeton, NJ: Princeton University Press, 2012).

Thorpe, Andrew, A History of the British Labour Party (Basingstoke: Macmillan, 1997).

Tomlinson, Jim, The Labour Governments 1964–70. Volume 3: Economic Policy (Manchester: Manchester University Press, 2004).

Toye, Richard, The Labour Party and the Planned Economy, 1931–1951 (Woodbridge: Boydell Press, 2003).

Utley, T. E., Enoch Powell: The Man and his Thinking (London: Kimber, 1968).

Vickers, Rhiannon, The Labour Party and the World. Volume 2. Labour's Foreign Policy since 1951 (Manchester: Manchester University Press, 2011).

Vinen, Richard, Thatcher's Britain: The Politics and Social Upheaval of the 1980s (London: Simon & Schuster, 2009).

Walker, Graham, A History of the Ulster Unionist Party: Protest, Pragmatism and Pessimism (Manchester: Manchester University Press, 2004).

Ward, Paul, Britishness Since 1870 (London: Routledge, 2004).

Ward, Paul, Unionism in the United Kingdom, 1918–1974 (Basingstoke: Palgrave Macmillan, 2005).

Ward, Stuart (ed.), British Culture and the End of Empire (Manchester: Manchester University Press, 2001).

Webster, Wendy, Englishness and Empire, 1939–1965 (Oxford: Oxford University Press, 2005).

Weight, Richard, Patriots: National Identity in Britain, 1940–2000 (London: Macmillan, 2002).

White, Brian, Britain, Détente and Changing East-West Relations (London: Routledge, 1992).

Wiener, Martin, English Culture and the Decline of the Industrial Spirit 1850–1980 (Cambridge: Cambridge University Press, 1981).

Williams, Raymond, Keywords: A Vocabulary of Culture and Society (London: Fontana/Croom Helm, 1976).

Williamson, Adrian, Conservative Economic Policymaking and the Birth of Thatcherism, 1964–1979 (Basingstoke: Palgrave Macmillan, 2015).

Williamson, Philip, Stanley Baldwin (Cambridge: Cambridge University Press, 1999).

Young, Hugo, This Blessed Spot: Britain and Europe from Churchill to Blair (London: Macmillan, 1998).

Young, John W., The Labour Governments: International Policy. Volume 2 (Manchester: Manchester University Press, 2003).

Articles, chapters, and blogs

Aughey, Arthur, 'Traditional Toryism', in Kevin Hickson (ed.), *The Political Thought of the Conservative Party since 1945* (Basingstoke: Palgrave Macmillan, 2005), ch. 1.

Aughey, Arthur, 'From Declinism to Endism: exploring the ideology of British break-up', *Journal of Political Ideologies*, 15/1 (2010), 11–30.

Beech, Matt and Timothy J. Oliver, 'Humanitarian Intervention and Foreign Policy in the Conservative-led Coalition', *Parliamentary Affairs*, 67/1 (2014), 102–18.

Bourke, Richard, 'Languages of Conflict and the Northern Ireland Troubles,' *Journal of Modern History*, 83/3 (2011), 544–78.

Brooke, Peter, 'India, Post-Imperialism and the Origins of Enoch Powell's "Rivers of Blood" Speech', *Historical Journal*, 50/3 (2007), 669–87.

Brooke, Stephen, 'The Conservative Party, Immigration and National Identity, 1948–68', in Martin Francis and Ina Zweiniger-Bargielowska, *The Conservatives and British Society 1880–1990* (Cardiff: University of Wales Press, 1996), 147–70.

Buettner, Elizabeth, '"This is Staffordshire not Alabama": Racial Geographies of Commonwealth Immigration in early 1960s Britain', *Journal of Imperial and Commonwealth History*, 42/2 (2014), 710–40.

Burkett, Jodi, 'Re-defining British Morality: "Britishness" and the Campaign for Nuclear Disarmament, 1958–68', *Twentieth Century British History*, 21/2 (2010), 184–205.

Busch, Peter, 'Supporting the War: Britain's Decision to send the Thompson Mission to Vietnam, 1960–1', *Cold War History*, 2/1 (2001), 69–94.

Cannadine, David, 'Apocalypse When? British Politicians and British "Decline" in the Twentieth Century', in Peter Clarke and Clive Trebilcock (eds), *Understanding Decline: Perceptions and Realities of British Economic Performance* (Cambridge: Cambridge University Press, 1997), ch. 10.

Clements, Ben 'The Referendums of 1975 and 2016 Illustrate the Continuity and Change in British Euroscepticism', http://blogs.lse.ac.uk/brexit/2017/07/31/the-referendums-of-1975-and-2016-illustrate-the-continuity-and-change-in-british-euroscepticism/

Cooper, James, 'The Foreign Politics of Opposition: Margaret Thatcher and the Transatlantic Relationship before Power', *Contemporary British History*, 24/1 (2010), 23–42.

Cooper, James, 'From Reykjavik to Fulton: Reagan, Thatcher and the Ending of the Cold War', *Journal of Transatlantic Studies*, 14/4 (2016), 383–400.

Corthorn, Paul, 'The Cold War and British Debates over the Boycott of the 1980 Moscow Olympics', *Cold War History*, 13/1 (2013), 43–66.

Cosgrave, Patrick, '...and Statistics', *The Spectator*, 10 January 1976.

Coulter, Colin, 'The Origins of the Northern Ireland Conservatives', *Irish Political Studies* 16/1 (2001), 29–48.

Coulter, Colin, 'Peering in from the Window Ledge of the Union: The Anglo-Irish Agreement and the attempt to bring British Conservatism to Northern Ireland', *Irish Studies Review* 21/4 (2013), 406–24.

Coulter, Colin, '"British Rights for British Citizens": The Campaign for "Equal Citizenship" in Northern Ireland', *Contemporary British History* 29/4 (2015), 486–507.

Coulter, Colin, 'Not quite as British as Finchley: The Failed Attempt to bring Conservatism to Northern Ireland', *Irish Political Studies* 23/4 (2015), 407–23.

Cowling, Maurice, 'The Sources of the New Right: Irony, Geniality and Malice', *Encounter*, November 1989, 3–13.

Crafts, Nicholas, 'The Golden Age of Economic Growth in Western Europe, 1950–1973', *Economic History Review*, 48/3 (1995), 429–47.

Crick, Bernard, 'The English and the British', in Bernard Crick (ed.), *National Identities: The Constitution of the United Kingdom* (Oxford: Blackwell, 1991), 90–104.

Crowson, Nicholas and James McKay, 'Britain in Europe? Conservative and Labour Attitudes to European Integration since World World II', in William Mulligan and Brendan Simms (eds), *The Primacy of Foreign Policy in British History, 1600–2000: How Strategic Concerns Shaped Modern Britain* (Basingstoke: Palgrave Macmillan, 2010), ch. 18.

Cunningham, Michael, 'Conservative Dissidents and the Irish Question: The "Pro-integrationist" Lobby 1973–94', *Irish Political Studies* 10/1 (1995), 26–42.

Desai, Radhika, 'Second-Hand Dealers in Ideas: Think-Tanks and Thatcherite Hegemony', *New Left Review*, I/203 (1994), 27–64.

Eccleshall, Robert, 'The Doing of Conservatism', *Journal of Political Ideologies*, 5/3 (2000), 275–87.

English, Richard and Michael Kenny, 'Public Intellectuals and the Question of British Decline', *British Journal of Politics and International Relations*, 3/3 (2001), 259–83.

Evans, Geoffrey and Jonathan Mellon, 'How Immigration became a Eurosceptic Issue', http://blogs.lse.ac.uk/brexit/2016/01/05/how-immigration-became-a-eurosceptic-issue/.

Feldman, David, 'Why the English Like Turbans: A History of Multiculturalism in One Country', in David Feldman and Jon Lawrence (eds), *Structures and Transformations in Modern British History* (Cambridge: Cambridge University Press, 2011), 281–302.

Foot, Rosemary, 'The Cold War and Human Rights' in Melvyn P. Leffler and Odd Arne Westad (eds.), *The Cambridge History of the Cold War, volume 3* (Cambridge: Cambridge University Press, 2009), 445–65.

Francis, Matthew, 'Mrs Thatcher's Peacock Blue Sari: Ethnic Minorities, Electoral Politics and the Conservative Party, c. 1974–86', *Contemporary British History*, 31/2 (2017), 274–93.

Freeman, James, 'Reconsidering "Set the People Free": Neoliberalism and Freedom Rhetoric in Churchill's Conservative Party', *Twentieth Century British History*, 29/4 (2018), 522–46.

Fry, Geoffrey K., 'Parliament and "Morality": Thatcher, Powell and Populism', *Contemporary British History*, 12/1 (1998), 139–47.

Grant, Matthew, 'Historians, the Penguin Specials and the "State-of-the-Nation" Literature', 1958–64', *Contemporary British History*, 17/3 (2003), 29–54.

Green, E. H. H., 'The Treasury Resignations of 1958: A Reconsideration', *Twentieth Century British History*, 11/4 (2000), 409–30. (Also in Green, E. H. H., *Ideologies of Conservatism*.)

Hansen, Randall, 'The Kenyan Asians, British Politics, and the Commonwealth Immigrants Act, 1968', *Historical Journal*, 42/3 (1999), 809–34.

Heffer, Simon, '(john) Enoch Powell', *Oxford Dictionary of National Biography* (Oxford: Oxford University Press, 2008), http://www.oxforddnb.com.

Hickson, Kevin, 'Lord Coleraine: The Neglected Prophet of the New Right', *Journal of Political Ideologies* 14/2 (2009), 173–87.

Hillman, Nicholas, 'A "Chorus of Execration"? Enoch Powell's "Rivers of Blood" Forty Years On', *Patterns of Prejudice*, 42/1 (2008), 83–104.

Holden Reid, Brian, 'The Legacy of Liddell Hart: The Contrasting Responses of Michael Howard and André Beaufre', *British Journal for Military History*, 1/1 (2014), 66–80.

Hughes, Geraint, 'British Policy towards Eastern Europe and the impact of the "Prague Spring", 1964–68', *Cold War History*, 4/2 (2004), 115–39.

Jackson, Alvin, 'Unionist Myths 1912–1985', *Past and Present* 136/1 (1992), 164–85.

Jackson, Alvin, '"Tame Tory Hacks?": The Ulster Party at Westminster, 1922–72', *Historical Journal*, 54/2 (2011), 453–75.

Jackson, Ben, 'At the Origins of Neo-Liberalism: the free economy and the strong state, 1930–1947', *Historical Journal*, 53/1 (2010), 129–51.

Jackson, Ben, 'The Think-Tank Archipelago: Thatcherism and Neo-Liberalism', in Ben Jackson and Robert Saunders (eds), *Making Thatcher's Britain* (Cambridge, 2012), 43–61.

Jackson, Ben, 'Currents of Neo-Liberalism: British Political Ideologies and the New Right, c. 1955–1979,' *English Historical Review*, 131/551 (2016), 823–50.

Lawrence, Jon and Florence Sutcliffe-Braithwaite, 'Margaret Thatcher and the Decline of Class Politics', in Jackson and Saunders (eds), *Making Thatcher's Britain*, 132–47.

Lindop, Fred, 'Racism and the Working Class: Strikes in Support of Enoch Powell in 1968', *Labour History Review*, 66/1 (2001), 79–100.

Maguire, Richard, '"Never a Credible Weapon': Nuclear Cultures in British Government during the Era of the H-bomb', *British Journal for the History of Science*, 45/4 (2012), 519–33.

Mandler, Peter, 'Educating the Nation: II. Universities', *Transactions of the Royal Historical Society*, 25 (2015), 1–26.

Mandler, Peter, 'The Two Cultures Revisited: The Humanities in British Universities since 1945', *Twentieth Century British History*, 26/3 (2015), 400–23.

Mazower, Mark, 'The Strange Triumph of Human Rights, 1933–50', *Historical Journal* 47/2 (2004), 379–98.

Mulholland, Marc, '"Just Another Country"? The Irish Question in the Thatcher Years', in Ben Jackson and Robert Saunders (eds), *Making Thatcher's Britain* (Cambridge, 2012), 180–96, ch. 10.

O'Sullivan, Noel, 'The New Right: The Quest for a Civil Philosophy in Europe and America', in Roger Eatwell and Noel O'Sullivan (eds), *The Nature of the Right: American and European Politics and Political Thought since 1789* (London: Pinter, 1989), ch. 10.

Phythian, Mark, 'CND's Cold War', *Contemporary British History*, 15/3 (2001), 133–56.

Pimlott, Ben, 'The Myth of Consensus', in Lesley M. Smith (ed.), *The Making of Modern Britain: Echoes of Greatness* (Basingstoke: Palgrave Macmillan, 1988), 129–42.

Saunders, Robert, 'Crisis? What Crisis? Thatcherism and the Seventies', in Jackson and Saunders (eds), *Making Thatcher's Britain*, 25–42.

Saunders, Robert, 'A Tale of Two Referendums: 1975 and 2016', *Political Quarterly*, 87/3 (2016), 318–22.

Schulzinger, Robert D., 'Détente in the Nixon-Ford Years', in Melvyn P. Leffler and Odd Arne Westad (eds.), *The Cambridge History of the Cold War, Volume 2* (Cambridge: Cambridge University Press, 2009), 373–94.

Shiels, David, 'How Enoch Powell Helped to Shape Modern Tory Euroscepticism', http://blogs.lse.ac.uk/brexit/2016/06/03/how-enoch-powell-helped-to-shape-modern-tory-euroscepticism/.

Smith, Jeremy, '"Ever Reliable Friends?": The Conservative Party and Ulster Unionism in the Twentieth Century', *English Historical Review*, 121/490 (2006) 70–103.

Stapleton, Julia, 'Citizenship versus Patriotism in Twentieth-Century England', *Historical Journal*, 48/1 (2005), 151–78.

Stapleton, Julia, 'T. E. Utley and the Renewal of Conservatism in Post-war Britain', *Journal of Political Ideologies*, 19/2 (2014), 207–26.

Stevens, Richard, 'The Evolution of Privatisation as an Electoral Strategy, c. 1970–90', *Contemporary British History*, 18/2 (2004), 47–75.

Thompson, Noel, 'Hollowing out the State: Public Choice Theory and the Critique of Keynesian Social Democracy', *Contemporary British History*, 22/3 (2008), 355–82.

Todd, Jennifer, 'Two Traditions in Unionist Political Culture', *Irish Political Studies* 2/1 (1987), 1–26.

Tomlinson, Jim, 'Inventing "Decline": The Falling Behind of the British Economy in the Postwar years', *Economic History Review* 49/4 (1996), 731–57.

Tomlinson, Jim, 'The Commonwealth, the Balance of Payments and the Politics of International Poverty: British Aid Policy, 1958–1971', *Contemporary European History*, 12/4 (2003), 413–29.

Tomlinson, Jim, 'The Decline of the Empire and the Economic "Decline" of Britain', *Twentieth Century British History*, 14/3 (2003), 201–22.

Tomlinson, Jim, 'Mrs Thatcher's Macroeconomic Adventurism, 1979–1981, and its Political Consequences', *British Politics* 2/1 (2007), 3–19.

Tomlinson, Jim, 'Balanced Accounts? Constructing the Balance of Payments Problem in Post-war Britain', *English Historical Review*, 124/509 (2009), 863–84.

Tomlinson, Jim, 'Thrice Denied: "Declinism" as a Recurrent Theme in British History in the Long Twentieth Century', *Twentieth Century British History*, 20/2 (2009), 227–51.

Tomlinson, Jim, 'British Government and Popular Understanding of inflation in the mid-1970s', *Economic History Review* 67/3 (2014), 750–68.

Toye, Richard, 'Winston Churchill's "Crazy Broadcast": Party, Nation, and the 1945 Gestapo Speech', *Journal of British Studies*, 49/3 (2010), 655–80.

Uche, Chibuike, 'The British Government, Idi Amin and the Expulsion of British Asians from Uganda', *Interventions: International Journal of Postcolonial Studies*, 19/6 (2017), 818–36.

Vickers, Rhiannon, 'Harold Wilson, the British Labour Party and the War in Vietnam', *Journal of Cold War Studies*, 10/2 (2008), 41–70.

Walker, Graham, 'Scotland, Northern Ireland and Devolution', *Journal of British Studies*, 49/1 (2010), 117–42.

Walker, Graham and Gareth Mulvenna, 'Northern Ireland Representation at Westminster: Constitutional Conundrums and Political Manoeuvres', *Parliamentary History*, 34/2 (2015), 237–55.

Walsha, Robert, 'The One Nation Group: A Tory Approach to Backbench Politics and Organization', *Twentieth Century British History*, 11/2 (2000), 183–214.

Walsha, Robert, 'The One Nation Group and One Nation Conservatism, 1950–2002', *Contemporary British History*, 17/2 (2003), 69–120.

Waters, Chris, ' "Dark Strangers" in our Midst: Discourses of Race and Nation in Britain 1947–1963', *Journal of British Studies*, 36/2 (1997), 207–38.

Whipple, Amy, 'Revisiting the "Rivers of Blood" Controversy: Letters to Enoch Powell', *Journal of British Studies*, 48/3 (2009), 717–35, 720.

Wilford, Hugh, ' "Unwitting Assets?": British Intellectuals and the Congress for Cultural Freedom', *Twentieth Century British History*, 11/1 (2000), 42–60.

Wilson, Thomas, 'Devolution and Public Finance', in Thomas Wilson (ed.), *Ulster Under Home Rule: A Study of the Political and Economic Problems of Northern Ireland* (Oxford: Oxford University Press, 1955), 115–36.

Wohlforth, William C., 'Realism', in Christian Reus-Smit and Duncan Snidel (eds), *The Oxford Handbook of International Relations* (Oxford: Oxford University Press, 2008), ch. 7.

Young, John W. 'International Factors and the 1964 General Election', *Contemporary British History*, 21/3 (2007), 351–71.

Picture Acknowledgements

1. Haywood Magee/Picture Post/Hulton Archive/Getty Images
2. Reproduced with permission of the Churchill College in the University of Cambridge
3. ZUMAPRESS.com / age fotostock
4. Daily Express/Hulton Archive/Getty Images
5. ZUMAPRESS.com / age fotostock
6. George Wilkes Archive/Hulton Archive/Getty Images
7. Popperfoto/Getty Images
8. ZUMAPRESS.com / Keystone Pictures USA / age fotostock
9. STR/AFP/Getty Images
10. Courtesy of the Deputy Keeper of the Records, the Public Record Office of Northern Ireland and the Ulster Unionist Council. PRONI Reference D3268/4/9.

Index

Abbott, Clive 150–1
Adonis, Lord 160–1
Afghanistan 41, 123–4
Aitken, Jonathan 130–1
Alexander, Andrew 117
Alison, Michael 154–5
Alliance Party 137–8
Anglo-Irish Agreement (1985) 154–8
Anti-Common Market League 117
Anti-Federalist League 104–5, 129
Armstrong, Robert 151
Atkins, Humphrey 148–9

Baker, Kenneth 74
Benn, Tony 27, 108, 123
Berkeley, Humphry 86
Bevan, Aneurin 49
Bevin, Ernest 21
Biffen, John 90, 114, 117–19, 149
Biggs-Davison, John 153–4
Birch, Nigel 53
Birmingham Post 97–8
Blair, Tony 131–2
Blunt, Crispin 159–60
Bow Group 30–1
British Anti-Common Market
    Campaign 125–7
British Army of the Rhine
    (BAOR) 107–8
British National Party (BNP) 160–1
Brittan, Leon 91
Brittan, Samuel 90–1
Brooke, Peter 77
Bruges Group 126–7, 129
Budgen, Nicholas 125–6, 131
Bull, Hedley 27
Burke, Edmund 13
Butler, David 78–9
Butler, R. A. 'Rab' 27

Callaghan, James 'Jim' 91, 117–19, 141
Campaign for an English Parliament
    7–8
Campaign for an Independent
    Britain 126–7
Campaign for Equal Citizenship 157–8
Campaign for Nuclear Disarmament
    (CND) 42–3
Carrington, Peter 123–4
Carter, Jimmy 39–41
Carthew, Bee 97–8
Cash, Bill 131
Castle, Barbara 119–20
Centre for Contemporary Cultural
    Studies (University of
    Birmingham) 5
Centre for Policy Studies 70, 122–3
Chamberlain, Joseph 142
Chamberlain, Neville 150
Chichester-Clark, James 135–7
China 24, 34–5, 40–1, 100–1
Church of England 13–15
Churchill, Winston 21, 49–50
Clark, Alan 33
Clarke, Peter 157–8
Clifford, Brendan 157–8
Cold War 1–2, 13, 20–47, 161–2
Coleraine, Lord (Richard Law) 69
Consensus 11
Conservatism 8–14, 23, 50
Corbyn, Jeremy 159
Cormack, Patrick 47
Cosgrave, Patrick 6–7, 92–3
Courtney, Anthony 72
Cowling, Maurice 122–3
Craig, William 'Bill' 137–8, 144–5
Crewe, Ivor 124
Crosland, Anthony 65–6
Crossman, Richard 87–9

Daily Express 87
Daily Mail 7–8
Daily Mirror 97–8
Daily Telegraph 4, 7–8, 17, 44, 54, 71, 158
Dalyell, Tam 141–2, 151–2
Davies, Wyndham 71
Day, Robin 119–20
Deedes, Bill 54
de Gaulle, Charles 105–9
Delors, Jacques 125–7
Democratic Unionist Party (DUP) 14–15,
    136–8, 147, 150, 155–6, 159–60
Détente 38–9
Devolution 1–2, 13, 133–60, 163–4
Dicey A.V. 13, 142
Donner, Patrick 99–100, 114
Douglas-Home, Alec 2, 32–3, 79–80, 87

East of Suez 34–5, 107–8
Economist, The 5–6
Eden, Anthony 27, 49
Elizabeth II, Queen 114–15
Elliot, Andrew G. 97–8, 100–1
Empire/Commonwealth 10, 19, 21–8,
    52–3, 57, 76, 105, 107
  Hola Camp Debate (1959) 27–8
  India 22–3, 76, 82–3, 162–3
Encounter 54
Europe 1–2, 5–8, 19, 104–32, 135,
    139–41, 145–6, 148, 159–60,
    163–4
  Brexit 1–2, 104, 159–61
  Exchange Rate Mechanism 127–8
  Maastricht Treaty (1992) 127–9
  Referendum (1975) 2, 104–5, 109–10,
    112–23, 146, 163–4, *See also* National
    Referendum Campaign
European Foundation 131
European Research Group 131
Exchange Rates 63–4, 127–8
Express & Star (Wolverhampton) 76,
    78, 87–9

Falklands War 41–2, 73
Farage, Nigel 129, 160–1
Faulkner, Brian 136–9
Ferguson, Niall 131
Fisher, Allan G. B. 80
Fisher, Antony 53–6, 69
Financial Times, The 90–1, 161

Floyd, Malcolm 129
Foot, Michael 42–3, 106, 114, 117–20, 124
Foot, Paul 4, 78–9, 90
Foreign Office 110–11, 123–4, 148
France 33–6, 46, 54, 105–9, 114–15
Fraser, Michael 32–3
French, David 28
Friedman, Milton 48–9, 67–9, 71–2, 90–1

Gaitskell, Hugh 105–6
Germany 21–2, 34–5, 37–8, 43–4, 54,
    105, 107–8
Get Britain Out 117
Gilroy, Paul 5
Godber, George 59
Good Friday Agreement (1998) 158
Gorbachev, Mikhail 43–4, 125–6
Gordon Walker, Patrick 78–9
Gorman, Teresa 131
Gow, Ian 147–51, 154–5, 158
Graham, Edgar 145–6
Gray, John 126–7
Green, E. H. H. 8–9
Gregory, Clive 160–1
Griffin, Nick 160–1
Griffiths, Peter 78–9
Grimond, Jo 91–2
Gulf War (1990-1) 44–7
Gulf War (2003) 20
Gurden, Harold 90

Hague, William 131–2, 159–60
Hailsham, Quintin Hogg, Baron Hailsham
    of St Marylebone 57–8, 83–4, 86–9,
    91–2, 97–8, 119–20, 134–5
Hall, Stuart 5
Hannan, Daniel 131
Hansen, Randall 81–2
Harrington, Michael 5–6
Harris, Ralph 16–17, 53–6, 59–61, 69–72,
    90–1, 126–7
Hayek, Friedrich 11, 49–56, 67–9, 71–2
Healey, Denis 31–2, 35–6
Heffer, Simon 7–8, 75–6
Heath, Edward 20–1, 31–3, 66–9, 80–1,
    86, 91–6, 108, 110–14, 136–7, 153–4
Heseltine, Michael 42–3, 127
Higher Education 64–6, 74
Hillman, Nicholas 162–3
Hobbes, Thomas 20–1

Hogg, Quintin *see* Hailsham
Hong Kong 100–1
Howard, Michael 131
Howe, Geoffrey 61, 127–8
Human Rights 39–40
Hurd, Douglas 47

Immigration 1–2, 19, 75–105, 112, 131,
    159–65
  'Rivers of Blood' speech 1–2, 5, 7, 19,
    83–94, 160–1
Institute of Economic Affairs (IEA)
    16–17, 48–9, 53–6, 58–67, 69, 162
Irish Free State 134–5
Irish National Liberation Army 147–8
Italy 54, 105

Jackson, Ben 48–9
Jay, Douglas 62, 106, 117–20
Jenkins, Roy 78, 80–1, 124
Jewkes, John 69
John Paul II, Pope 14–15
Jones, J. Clement 87–9
Joseph, Keith 70, 74, 122–3, 165

Kaldor, Nicholas 115
Kent, Bruce 42–3
King, Anthony 124
Kingston-McCloughry, Edgar 28–9
Kinnock, Neil 125
Kissinger, Henry 38–9
Koestler, Arthur 54
Korean War 27

Lawson, Nigel 127–8
Layton-Henry, Zig 5
Lewis, Roy 5–6
Lewis, Russell 32–3
Libya 159–60
Liddell Hart, Sir Basil 30–2
Lilley, Peter 130
Lippman, Walter 50
Longden, Gilbert 87, 97
Lynch, Jack 148

Machiavelli, Niccolò 20–1
Mackintosh, John P. 134
Macleod, Iain 4, 51, 81–2, 86
Macmillan, Harold 27, 108
Major, John 127–9

Mandler, Peter 64–5
Marten, Neil 114–15, 119–21
Mason, Roy 151
Maude, Angus 8–10
Maudling, Reginald 95–6
McCartney, Robert 157–8
McDiarmid, Ian 160–1
McGrady, Eddie 156–7
Mellish, Bob 114
Minford, Patrick 126–7
Minogue, Kenneth 126–7
Molyneaux, Jim 137–8, 141, 149
Monday Club 36–7, 87, 98–9, 127
Monetarism 53, 70, 72
Montagu, Victor 105–6
Mont Pelerin Society 50, 58, 64, 71
More, Jasper 87–9
Morgenthau, Hans 20–2
Moscow Olympics (1980) 41
Mosley, Sir Oswald 86

Nairn, Tom 163–4
National Front 97–8, 121
National Health Service (NHS) 48–9,
    51, 58–61, 162
National Referendum Campaign 119–21
Neave, Airey 147, 151
Neo-liberalism 11, 48–74, 162, 165
News of the World 87
New Labour 7–8, 131–2, 159–60
New Left 5, 18
New Right 5
Nietzsche, Friedrich 13–14
Nixon, Richard 38–9
North Atlantic Treaty Organisation
    (NATO) 21, 29–30, 35–8, 107–8,
    122–3, 148, 159–60
Northern Ireland 1–2, 12–15, 133–58,
    159–60, 163–5
Northern Ireland Office 148–51
Nuclear weapons 1–2, 28–33, 42–3, 159,
    161–2, 164
  Nuclear civil defence 29 *See also*
    Campaign for Nuclear
    Disarmament

O'Neill, Terence 135
One Nation Group 13–14, 24, 51–3, 63–4
Orange Order 14–15, 151–2
Orr, Lawrence 'Willy' 138

Osborne, Cyril 77–8
Owen, David 124

Paisley, Ian 14–15, 135–8, 144–5, 147, 150
Parkinson, Cyril Northcote 92–3
Poland 44, 160–1
Popper, Karl 71
Populism 42–3, 75–6, 104–5, 112, 161
Portillo, Michael 131
Powell, J. Enoch
    Background and career 2
    Interpretations of 4–8
Powell, Pam 2, 131
Prague Spring (1968) 37–8
Prices and incomes policies 57, 67–9
Prior, Jim 150–1
Privatization 48, 67
Provisional Irish Republican
    Army (IRA) 12–13, 136–7, 145–7,
    149–50, 153–4, 158

Racism/racialism 4–8, 75, 86–94, 98–9,
    160–1
Radcliffe, Lord 98–9
Rawlinson, Sir Peter 97
Reagan, Ronald 43–4
Realism (international relations) 20
Redwood, John 131
Regional policy 57–8
Republic of Ireland 61, 133, 135–6, 150,
    153–8
Reeve, A. Stretton 76
Rex, John 5
Rhodesia 36–7, 161–2
Ridley, Nicholas 67, 117–19
Rioting (1980–1) 100–1
Rippon, Geoffrey 110–11
Robertson, Sir Dennis 53
Rodgers, Bill 124
Royal Ulster Constabulary (RUC) 12–13,
    155–6
Rose, Richard 83
Ross, William 151
Roth, Andrew 95
Russell-Smith, Enid 56, 59

Safeguard Britain Campaign 121, 123–5
Salisbury, Lord 36–7
Salisbury Group 5, 122–3
Sands, Bobby 145–6

Saunders, Robert 163
Scarman Report (1981) 100–1
Schoen, Douglas 17–18
Schofield, Camilla 8, 27–8
Schwarz, Bill 8, 83, 94
Scruton, Roger 101–2, 126–7
Seldon, Arthur 34–5, 53–6, 61,
    67–9, 162
Selsdon Group 70
Shanks, Michael 54, 106–7
Shepherd, Robert 7, 75–6
Sherman, Alfred 122–3
Shonfield, Andrew 54, 106–7
Shore, Peter 106, 114, 119–20
Shuckburgh, Sir Evelyn 107–8
Silkin, Sam 98–9
Sinn Féin 12–13, 145–6, 159–60
Sked, Alan 129–30
Sloan, Geoffrey 150–1
Smith, Eleanor 162–3
Smith, Ian 36–7
Smyth, Martin 144–5
Snow, C. P. 65–6
Social and Democratic Labour Party
    (SDLP) 137–8, 153–4, 157–8
Social Democratic Party (SDP) 124
South Down (constituency) 2, 13–15,
    138–9, 141, 147, 156–7, 159–60, 163–4
Sovereignty 1–2, 8–14, 19, 23–4, 39–40,
    44, 104–58, 163–4
Soviet Union 1–2, 20, 125–6, 161–2
Spearman, Diana 87
Spender, Stephen 54
Spectator, The 4, 96, 158
Sunday Express 80–1
Sunday Telegraph 93–4, 158
Sunday Times, The 91–2
Stone, Norman 126–7
Stowe, Kenneth 149
Suez Crisis (1956) 20–1, 27
Suez Group 25, 27
Syria 159–60

Taylor, A. J. P. 10
Tebbit, Norman 127
Territorial Army 29–31
Thatcher, Margaret 1–3, 6–7, 18, 20–48,
    70–4, 99–100, 122–9, 147–51,
    153–5, 162
Thorneycroft, Peter 53, 72, 79–80

Thucydides 20–1
Titmuss, Richard 61
Times, The 5–6, 57, 67–9, 72, 78, 83, 86, 89, 101–2, 158
Tomlinson, Jim 18, 72–3
Toye, Richard 49–50
Trade Unions 67–9, 73
Transport and General Workers' Union (TGWU) 76

Ulster Clubs 155–6
Ulster Defence Association 144, 147
Ulster Volunteer Force 144–5
Unionism 8–14, 57–8, 133–58
United Kingdom Independence Party (UKIP) 104–5, 129–30, 160–1
United Nations (UN) 27, 41–2, 44–6, 159–62
United States 1–2, 20, 56–7, 64, 82, 105, 107–8, 125–6, 148, 150, 155–6, 161–2
Uppal, Paul 162–3
Utley, T. E. 'Peter' 4, 17, 90–1, 141–2, 149

Vanguard Movement 137–8
Vietnam War 33–6
Vincent, John 90

Waldegrave, William 100–1
Walker-Smith, Derek 106
Wall, Patrick 36–7, 69
Walsha, Robert 51
Watkins, K. W. 5–6
West, Harry 137–8, 141, 144–5, 154
Whipple, Amy 18
Whitelaw, Willie 149
Wiener, Martin 165
Wilkes, George 69, 116–19
Williams, Sir Robin 126–7
Williams, Shirley 124
Williamson, Philip 15–16
Wilson, Harold 54, 107–8, 117, 119–20, 135–6, 139–41
Wilson, J. Leonard 76
Winnick, David 89
Wolverhampton South West (constituency) 2, 5–6, 15–16, 23, 52, 69, 76, 78, 90–1, 95, 116–19, 122–3, 125–6, 131, 162–4
Wood, John 58, 67–9
Worsthorne, Peregrine 93–4

Yugoslav Wars 47, 161–2
Young, Hugo 104

Zuckerman, Sir Solly 30–1